Yishar Koach:

FORWARD WITH STRENGTH

THE STORY OF
SHOAH SURVIVOR
FERDINAND FRAGNER

BY

SUSAN LYNN SLOAN

Interior photographs, unless otherwise noted, © 2016 Susan Lynn Sloan.

Cover images © 2016, courtesy of the Fred Fragner estate.

Cover and book design: Vladimir Verano.

Copy editor: Chas Hoppe.

ISBN: 978-0-9976586-0-6
LCCN: 2016908990

Published by Susan Lynn Sloan
contact: yisharkoach@gmail.com

Printed by VILLAGE BOOKS in Bellingham, WA
villagebooks.com/book/9780997658606

For my brave and loving son,
Joseph Byron Sloan
(1985 - 2014)

TABLE OF CONTENTS

ACKNOWLEDGMENTS

At the time I undertook the writing of this biography of the life of Fred Fragner, I had no idea the enormity of the act of documenting someone's story. Being an evaluator by profession, I occasionally longed to write a book about someone's life rather than an evaluation of someone's program. However, it wasn't until I came across the amazing life of Fred Fragner that I found a story that cried out to be told and remembered. It became my passion to make sure it happened.

Thank you, Fred, for the person you were and the life you lived so well under such exacting circumstances. Your life reflected strength, generosity of spirit, humor, and caring for others. I hope that these pages evoke these qualities and encourage their emulation.

The largesse of Fred's family and many friends provided great encouragement in the writing of this book. I persevered in large part because of their enthusiasm to see his story told.

I thank all of the individuals who populate these chapters. Some I have had the pleasure of knowing, and some I have known only through the words and writings of Fred or others. They are all very special to me in every sense.

I would also like to offer my heartfelt thanks to a number of other individuals for making this book what it is. First and foremost, I would like to thank my dear mother, Trudy Sloan, who taught me the joys of reading at a very young age. Although she died when I was eight, her influence on my life was profound. Enduring great loss as a child set my life course. Our love and her death have really made me who I am as both a person and a writer. My father, Cal Sloan, on the other hand, made me who I am through his love and caring for people of all races, cultures, and creeds. He was a gentle soul who had the sometimes annoying, but more often endearing, quality of never calling any person a stranger.

What we like doesn't always reflect our own skills and aptitudes, but these preferences do provide a "wish list" of what we would like to emulate. In this regard, I would like to thank several contemporary writers whose work has ever so subtly contributed to my perspectives and aspirations as a writer. Thanks to Alan Brennert, the author of *Moloka'i** and *Honolulu*.** To me, his style of combining fact and fiction is perfect in every way. My attraction has always been to the amazingness of people's real-life adventures, but there is something so wonderful about mixing the real with how we imagine things should or could be. It is an irresistible combination. Thanks to Stephen King for his book *On Writing*.† I think it was this book that gave me the courage to imagine myself as a writer and create that future. Thanks to Melissa Green for showing me the true beauty of language in her exquisite 1996 memoir, *Color Is the Suffering of Light*.‡ My desire would be to have even half of her abilities to describe sensory experience through language. Thanks also to the master of the fractured fairy tale, Gregory Maguire, and my favorite history writer extraordinaire, David McCullough. And finally, a big shout-out to Michael Perry, my favorite laugh-out-loud writer and master of vocabulary, and the author of *Population: 485*¶ and other wonderful works.

A special thanks to The Red Wheelbarrow Writers of Bellingham, Washington for their support but especially for the encouragement and expertise that writer Cami Ostman provided throughout my journey. You are amazing.

To my dear husband Tom, who endured this journey, including countless hours of my absence. You're my forever friend and love.

NOTES

*   Alan Brennert, *Moloka'i* (New York: St. Martin's Griffin, 2003).

**   Alan Brennert, *Honolulu* (New York: St. Martin's Griffin, 2010).

†   Stephen King, *On Writing* (New York: Scribner, 2000).

‡   Melissa Green, *Color is the Suffering of Light* (New York: Simon & Schuster, 1996).

¶   Michael Perry, *Population: 485* (New York: Harper Collins, 2002).

PREFACE

Sylvia Fragner is standing in the doorway of Margarette's office at the health department. She is sixty, pretty and petite, and wearing an attractive plaid coat of many colors. She's taken to wearing a stylish wig of late, and she looks at least ten years younger than she had before Fred's death. I remark, "Sylvia, you look so beautiful, and what an attractive coat."

She talks a bit about how Fred bought her this coat. "He had such good taste," she says in response to my compliment.

I say, "You must miss him so much."

"Yes," she says. "I miss him—every day."

I had first heard about Fred in about 2005, when I first went to work for Whatcom County Health Department. At the time, Sylvia was a program supervisor in our Community Health Division. I knew that Fred was many years Sylvia's senior and that he was in declining health. I had also heard that he was a Holocaust survivor and had spent five years in Buchenwald Concentration Camp.

I only met him twice. Once, he had dropped in during a health department potluck, and the following time, I was formally introduced to him at the Daisy Café in downtown Bellingham, Washington, when it was still Café Toulouse. Fred and Sylvia were sitting at a corner table to the left of the door, and Sylvia introduced me ever so briefly. But I vividly remember that moment.

It was the encounter with Sylvia in Margarette's office in 2010 that first piqued my interest in writing about Fred. In the days following, the idea was deeply planted in my soul and began to grow. Soon, I found myself becoming ever more passionate and committed to telling his story.

To be a Holocaust survivor is both a blessing and a curse. Survivorship means the continuation of life, distinguishing the survivor for the remainder of life as someone who persevered through tremendous hardship and who is fortunate to be alive. However, the curse is the inevitable and enduring wounds that result from having known cruelty and death too intimately. Like a gyroscope[†] that stubbornly maintained its orientation, Fred bore his wounds and moved forward with the inner conviction that he had survived for a purpose, and this purpose was intrinsically "other-centered."

This is the story of Ferdinand Fragner, those he loved, those he lost, those who loved him, and those who love him still. As much as it is a love story, it is also a cautionary tale of how very bad things can go when we fail to respect and love one another, and when we mindlessly follow those with magnetism—but ill intent.

Much of the source material came from interviews with and lectures by Fred during the latter years of his life. Additional materials came from interviews I conducted with family and friends. All interviews have been transcribed verbatim from audio and video files. Some chapters are largely composed of Fred's notes, such as "Fred's Speech on the Jewish Annual Day of Remembrance" and "Kind Caretaker," where Fred's scrapbook notes on his experiences at Aglasterhausen are provided.

The book is organized more by the roles Fred played in his life than in any strict chronological order. Each of us plays many roles in life—some chosen and some foisted upon us, some essential and some minor, some taken up for a season and others for a lifetime. What we bring to each persona marks the quality of our character. In his character and moral fiber, Fred shone brightly like the morning sun and brought both truth and light to each part he played.

NOTES

† "A gyroscope is a spinning wheel or disk in which the axis is free to assume any orientation. When rotating, the orientation of this axis is unaffected by tilting or rotation of the mounting, according to the conservation of angular momentum. Because of this, gyroscopes are useful for measuring or maintaining orientation." *Wikipedia*, s.v. "Gyroscope," last modified June 27, 2015, http://en.wikipedia.org/wiki/Gyroscope.

YISHAR KOACH:

FORWARD WITH STRENGTH

Sylvia took this picture of Fred late in his life. It is posted on the Western Washington University site under Woodring School of Education, Northwest Center for Holocaust, Genocide and Ethnocide Education:
https://wce.wwu.edu/nwchgee/fred-fragner
As of August 2016, the center became The Ray Wolpow Institute for the Study of the Holocaust, Genocide and Crimes Against Humanity.

MORTAL

When you were born, you cried and the world rejoiced. Live your life
so that when you die, the world cries and you rejoice.

~ Cherokee Expression

ON THE AFTERNOON OF SHABBAT ZACHOR, 5769 (March 7, 2009), in the comfort and company of loving family and friends, Fred Fragner passed on to whatever new life awaited him. Although he wasn't a proponent of life after death, if anyone was ever a candidate for making it into the afterlife, it certainly was this survivor.

It was a Saturday, the sixty-sixth day of the year 2009 in the Gregorian calendar. Also on that day, NASA had launched the Kepler space observatory "to survey a portion of the Milky Way galaxy and discover dozens of Earth-size planets in or near the habitable zone and determine how many of the billions of stars in our galaxy have such planets."[1]

That same week, an abbreviated version of the following obituary ran in the local newspaper, *The Bellingham Herald*:[2]

FRED FRAGNER, *beloved husband, father, grandfather, and friend,* passed away peacefully at home on March 7, 2009, surrounded by his loving family and cherished friends. Fred was born on April 22, 1915, in Nový Jičín, Czechoslovakia, to Maurice and Rosalie

Fragner. He lost his parents at a very young age and his two older sisters, Lola and Helen, perished in the death camps during the Holocaust. Following the death of his parents, Fred supported himself by working in coal yards, attending school during the day, and sleeping in cemeteries or walking the streets at night. Despite the hardships that he faced, Fred finished school and enrolled in the Charles University in Prague where he studied for his PhD in Psychology. In 1938, when Czechoslovakia was occupied by Germany, Fred joined with members of the partisan fighters Underground, attacking Nazis, their collaborators, and their installations. His decision to do so was based on his never wavering stance that every man and woman must stand up for what they believe. It was during his period of service in the Underground that Fred learned that his entire family along with his entire Jewish community had been deported by the Nazis to extermination camps. Then, three years after joining the Underground, during a raid on a prison to free his comrades, Fred was shot, captured, interrogated, and tortured by the Gestapo. He was deported to the concentration camp at Buchenwald, spending the next five years there and in several other concentration camps and enduring conditions and treatment beyond comprehension; beyond descriptive words known to humanity. While in Bergen Belsen concentration camp, Fred met his former wife Kay, now deceased, and the two were secretly married by a rabbi. Fred was liberated from the concentration camps on May 5, 1945. He and Kay went to work for the United Nations Relief and Rehabilitation Association (UNRRA) at a 150-bed Children's Center for war orphans in Aglasterhausen, Germany, where Fred served as school principal and teacher for children of numerous nationalities, religions, and cultural backgrounds. He always asserted that "working with these children saved my life; together we created an atmosphere of kindness and understanding, of love, freedom, democracy and brotherhood, of cooperation, trust, and most important, of unforgettable healing relationships." In May 1946, Fred and Kay brought sixty of these children to the United States under the auspices of the US Committee for the Care of European Children. Adoptive families were awaiting their arrival in New York City and Fred has maintained contact with several of the children to this day. From New York, Fred and Kay went to Chicago, where Fred enrolled in the University of Chicago, studying and learning English at the same time. He was awarded his Master's Degree in Social Work from the University of Chicago in 1951. Following receipt of his degree, Fred's experiences ranged from working in the National Jewish Hospital, a TB hospital in Denver, Colorado; to serving as director of a Jewish Child Welfare Agency and Jewish Children's Home in St. Louis, Missouri; to Chief of Probation for the Juvenile Court services in Cincinnati, Ohio. He established a Child Guidance Clinic in Richmond, Indiana and has taught at several American universities, nursing, and medical schools. In 1965, Fred moved to Newark, Delaware, where he met his present wife, Sylvia. From 1965 until his retirement in 1982, he developed a statewide outpatient mental health system in Delaware and provided oversight for outpatient drug and alcohol treatment programs. When he retired, he was serving in the position of Assistant Director of the state Mental Health Division. Following Fred's retirement, he and Sylvia moved to Federal Way, Washington, where Fred continued his tradition of service to others in many volunteer positions. A plaque given to honor Fred, by students at the Spanaway Alternative High School, reads, "After 40 years of liberation, you are still liberating us. We love you, Fred." After moving to Whatcom County, Fred volunteered at the mental health center, was an ombudsman for a local nursing home, served on several boards including the board of the Regional Support Network, and was very active with the National Alliance for the Mentally Ill and the Health Support Center. He also was honored to serve in an advisory capacity to the Rainbow Center. He was an enthralling speaker with countless speaking engagements throughout his life. He was a man of strong faith and was an active member of the Beth Israel Synagogue. Although Fred lived through many horrors in his life, he always had hope and always looked for the goodness in life. He believed in living one's dreams and in living life to the fullest. He and Sylvia enjoyed life together and both loved to travel and explore new places. He was an expert skier in his younger years, was an avid tennis player, and was a member of the Bellingham Tennis Club for many years. Fred Fragner's spirit will always be with those who know and love him and with those who will come to know him by the wisdom and knowledge that he continues to share. He believed in, celebrated, and had a deep and abiding respect for individual differences; he offered unconditional love; and he had a tremendous passion for life as well as a wonderful sense of humor. He was kind and gentle, fiery, and stubborn and epitomized the ideals of great strength, character, and integrity. Fred did not just talk the talk; he truly walked the walk. Fred is survived by his wife, Sylvia Fragner, his daughter, Anita Ware, and his grandson, Ryan Cornell. A private service will be held for Fred and at his request a community-wide celebration of his life will occur at a later date with notification going to the many groups of people that Fred felt so honored to know. In lieu of flowers, Fred has requested memorial contributions to the Rainbow Center, Hadassah, or Beth Israel Synagogue. Please sign the Book of Memories, light a candle and leave your condolences for the family. Arrangements have been entrusted to Jerns Funeral Chapel in Bellingham, WA.

The community memorial service for Fred was held in the Squalicum Boathouse building at Zuanich Point Park in Bellingham, Washington. The building is in a lovely location with awe-inspiring views of Bellingham Bay and Lummi Island. It was a worthy place for a last farewell to Fred.

One of Fred's dearest friends, Buz Peoples, delivered the following eulogy to approximately one hundred guests:

Fred's dear friend Buz Peoples

There are few people in my life to whom I refer as a true friend. Fred was even more.

I met him in 1968 in Wilmington, Delaware. I was working as a child placement worker at the Division of Social Services, and he was an administrator at Delaware State Hospital. I took his evening psychology seminar, offered to DSS employees. His reputation preceded him for offering interesting, stimulating, provocative instruction. After class, over coffee, we would come to forge a friendship that would last over forty years.

He never failed to heed my concerns. Always the consummate listener, he, in return, shared his thoughts and feelings with me. He was the rock against which I continued to lean throughout my life. He was my teacher and confidant, argumentative yet supportive, guiding and shepherding me through rough times and celebrating my joys. Through failed relationships, the early loss of my father and later my mother, to the final discovery of who I was capable of becoming, he was probably the most instrumental person to share my life. His steadfast concern and love was his gift to me. In every sense of the words, he created balance, stability, support, and love.

He built me up, taught me to use my strengths and not dwell on perceived weaknesses, never wanting me to allow anyone to make me feel less than the person I knew myself to be.

I honor him, with pride, for how his life touched and nourished my own.

I loved the sparkle in his eyes, the sound of his voice, his determination, resolve, and accomplishments. When deep in thought, while considering our conversations, there was a certain sound he made, which was his alone.

Unlike some friends, who wait too long to let one another know how much they mean to one another, Fred knew how much he meant to me and, likewise, I knew how much I meant to him. I thank God for that small comfort.

I would never really know the depth of the horrors he suffered during WWII. He shared them, bits and pieces, as well as the years after, when he worked with the children from the camps. Those years of suffering shaped who he became. They were reflected throughout his life by his passion for justice and his own continued personal renewal.

In the early 1970s, he met Sylvia. I must admit a certain envy when he told me about her. She brought him a love, devotion, and an acceptance for the man he truly was. I had never seen him so happy or content. I followed their moves across the United States to their final home at "The Woods." I loved the banter and interactions between them. She was truly the light of his life.

Though I never met Anita, I know how proud Fred was of his daughter and how much he loved her and her son.

It was a new relationship, between him and Yari, Fred and Sylvia's Wheaten Terrier, that tickled me, as Fred had never been particularly fond of dogs. After Yari came Gigi. Photos I have reflect his love for them.

Fred and I shared a common appreciation of the Oregon Coast, around Cannon Beach, plus a continuing love of travel and exploration of new places. I find it interesting that we met on the East Coast yet, over the decades, managed to move westward separately to eventually spend our final years in the Pacific Northwest, where we reunited at Mount St. Helens, Federal Way, San Juan Island, and Bellingham.

There is an empty spot in my life now. I shall miss the kind resonance of his voice, saying, "Hello, Buz," the welcoming hug of our greetings.

He was my surrogate father, my trusted friend, and the cherished enduring presence throughout my life. I miss him.

His legacy, to me, will be his soul mate, Sylvia.

Go in peace, dear friend.

There are places I will see you again—laughing, smiling, waving me onward.

NOTES

1   *Wikipedia*, s.v. "Kepler (Spacecraft)," last modified May 23, 2015, accessed April 13, 2013, http://en.wikipedia.org/wiki/Kepler_(spacecraft).

2   Anita Fragner, Fred Fragner, and Sylvia Fragner, "Fred Fragner Obituary," Obits for Life.com, accessed February 14, 2015, http://obitsforlife.com/obituary/135391/Fragner-Fred.php.

Fred and Gigi, who loved Fred dearly. She adopted him from the
moment she met him. She ran in the Fragners' front door for the first
time, ran down the stairs, flew into his lap, licked his face, turned
around and sat down on his lap, as if to say "I'm home!"

FRED'S SPEECH ON THE JEWISH ANNUAL DAY OF REMEMBRANCE

If you find a path with no obstacles, it probably doesn't lead anywhere.

~ Frank A. Clark

As some of you know, I have spent several years in a concentration camp. I am one of the dying-out group of survivors, the remaining witnesses of the horrors of the Holocaust, and like many other survivors, I have a responsibility to talk with you about it.

Today, while we memorialize the Holocaust and pay respect to the six million Jews who have perished, including my whole family, we need to take a few moments out of our busy schedules and think about all the stories you may have heard and/or read, the movies and documentaries you have seen about the Holocaust, and familiarize yourself with the history of Hitler's rise to power and how the most cultured nation changed to a bloodthirsty monster. Some of you may not know that the Nazis lost the elections, and only after German president Hindenburg, an old, senile man, appointed Hitler to be the chancellor, did the Nazis using brute power become the masters of Germany. Using this knowledge you may try to project yourself into today's world with all its hatred, prejudice, and terrorism. Because if the Holocaust is to us just another moment in history and we have learned nothing from it, then we may be inviting another holocaust.

A couple years ago, after addressing the congregation of St. Paul's in Bellingham, some members of the congregation expressed disappointment that I haven't shared with them more of my personal experiences from the concentration camp. I have regretted to disappoint them, but to me the Holocaust is more than a horror story to be told once a year on Yom HaShoa, it is a very painful experience, which left deep scars in my psyche. So, while I am willing to share some highlights of my life in the concentration camp, I am more interested in talking about the lessons we need to learn from it and how it relates to the present. Let's talk about the destructive forces of hatred, of Nazism, but also how similar events are engulfing this country and the rest of the world. We need to talk about the ever-increasing danger of national and international terrorism. About the atrocities committed in Bosnia, about the terror in the subways of Paris and Tokyo, about the bombing of Jewish synagogues and community centers in Buenos Aires and Paris, about the militias, Aryan Nations, KKK, skinheads, and American Nazis. There are over three hundred members of the militia in my small county and over sixty-five hundred in the state of Washington.[3] They and other hate groups are multiplying as fast as some forms of cancer. I would like to suggest that you read a newly published book written by Morris Dees: *Gathering Storm*.[4] Mr. Dees is a veteran in the war against prejudice. Avail yourself to a book written by a young Harvard professor by the name of Daniel Goldenhagen with the title *Hitler's Willing Executioners*.[5] We need to be informed about what happened then and what is happening now.

It was April 1945 that the Germans marched us from Staßfurt Leopoldshall, a town in central Germany, toward the north. We walked about twenty miles a day, and our food consisted of about two pounds of potatoes. Whoever couldn't walk any longer was shot. I remember my birthday on April 22. It was raining and very cold. I was wearing a striped concentration camp suit, and I was freezing. On May 2, 1945, we stopped in a small German village, and the guards locked us in barns. At this point, I was very sick and totally exhausted. I [had] decided that I [was] not going to walk any longer, knowing that [meant] certain death. But I just couldn't do it any longer. By a sheer miracle, the same evening the Swedish Red Cross arrived and distributed food packages to us, something which [had] never happened before. I consumed every food item contained in the package and, with the newly acquired energy, decided to march the next day.

On May 4, we slept in woods, and the next morning, when we [woke] up, our guards [were] gone. We didn't know what to do. But after a while, I got on the road and started to walk, not knowing where I was going and being very sick. A few minutes later, a German sergeant drove by on a bicycle calling to German soldiers who were lying on the roadsides to run because the Russians were five kilometers behind. Hearing this, I turned around and started to walk toward the Russians. I walked only about one hundred feet when a Jeep with two Americans came by, and I was free.

Five years after being told where to sleep, what to eat, where to work, not knowing what to do, I was free. After five years of physical and mental torture, starvation, and being witness to the murder of innocent people, here I was free. Your whole family is gone and you are left alone with all the sadness, fear, and anger, not understanding what is happening and not knowing what to do.

Now, fifty years later, I am trying to understand the nature of prejudice and the consequences resulting from it. In his book, *The Nature of Prejudice*,[6] Gordon W. Allport describes a kind of ladder of "negative actions" that springs from prejudice. This kind of a four-step ladder worked in Nazi Germany and seems to work today in many nations and cultures.

The first rung on this ladder is speech. This [often takes] the form of "ethnic jokes," or talking about a group as if all members of this group were one personality or had one set of features. One Holocaust historian, Raul Hilberg,[7] states that anti-Jewish racism had its beginning in the second half of the seventeenth century when a Jewish caricature first appeared in cartoons. This caricature or stereotype was usually an exaggerated drawing of a face with a long hooked nose, heavy dark eyebrows, a beard that came to a sinister point, and a protruding mole. This devilish looking character was supposed to look like all Jews. The Nazis used this type of caricature again and again in their propaganda posters and media. J. B. Stoner,[8] in an article "The Philosophy of the White Race" published in *Thunderbolt*, a racist paper, stereotyped all blacks as being alike, all criminals violent, and all Jews as being "bloodsuckers."

The second rung of the ladder is avoidance. At this level, people seek to avoid the group which has been stereotyped. Like speech, this seems to be harmless at the beginning. The trouble is that lack of contact with other racial, ethnic, and religious groups leads to ignorance about them. And the more ignorant we are, the more we tend to believe in stereotypes.

Avoidance leads frequently to discrimination. The unwanted group is now kept out of some neighborhoods, shopping areas, social clubs, and public centers. The laws against Jews in Germany were discriminatory—they meant to separate Jews from the rest of the population. Discrimination can be a simple matter of excluding Jews or Afro-Americans or Spanish or Orientals from a fraternity or sorority or a social club. Or, it can be an attempt to cut off entirely an unwanted group and isolate them.

When the Nazis incited riots against the German Jews, they reached the fourth level of "negative actions," namely the physical attack. Physical attack may be a mob's expression of anger and resentment. It may take the form of defacing or burning down places of worship and cemeteries, or it may take the form of a physical attack against a person or group of people. Hate groups such as the KKK, Aryan Nations and skinheads beat and or kill innocent people, be they black, Jewish, Spanish, Asian, or other. Other hate groups under the guise of religion or patriotism don't hesitate to perform acts of violence, including murder against anyone who doesn't agree with their beliefs, political objectives, and goals—or who are different.

We need to be aware of what is happening around us and speak up. We need to educate our children that hating others because they are different from us or because they don't agree with us is wrong. We and they need to be respectful of others' rights no matter if their religious or political beliefs are different from ours. We are a silent majority who have been silent too long, minimizing the dangers around us, hoping against hope that all the hate groups and all the hate will go away and everything will be okay. Our future and our children's future are at stake. When I came to this country, people asked me if I [believed] that what happened in Germany [could] happen here. I said, "Yes." And now I am frightened because what I see is a replica of what I witnessed in Germany in the early thirties. Their name was Sturmabteilung,[9] not militias.

What I tried to share with you today is a lesson I have learned from Holocaust. I do hope that you too will learn this lesson.

NOTES

3   The Southern Poverty Law Center publishes a map showing the number of hate groups currently active on a state-by-state basis. As of early 2015, ten such groups were active in Washington State, including two neo-Nazi groups: the National Socialist Movement and the Creativity Movement. "Hate Map," Southern Poverty Law Center, accessed June 28, 2015, http://www.splcenter.org/get-informed/hate-map.

4   Morris Dees, *Gathering Storm: America's Militia Threat* (New York: HarperCollins, 1996).

5   Daniel Jonah Goldenhagen, *Hitler's Willing Executioners: Ordinary Germans and the Holocaust* (New York: Random House LLC, 1996).

6   Gordon Willard Allport, *The Nature of Prejudice* (New York: Basic Books, 1979).

7   Wikipedia, s.v. "Raul Hilberg," last modified August 15, 2016, accessed August 26, 2016, http://en.wikipedia.org/wiki/Raul_Hilberg.

8   Wikipedia, s.v. "J. B. Stoner," last modified June 27, 2015, accessed February 14, 2015, http://en.wikipedia.org/wiki/J._B._Stoner.

9   *Wikipedia*, s.v. "Sturmabteilung," last modified June 4, 2015, accessed February 14, 2015, http://en.wikipedia.org/wiki/Sturmabteilung.

BELOVED SON

Then God said, "Let Us make man in Our image, according to Our likeness."

~ Genesis 4:7

FRED FRAGNER WAS BORN ON APRIL 22, 1915 to Maurice Fragner and Rosalie (Thieberg) Fragner. He was born in the town of Nový Jičín, which was then a part of the Austrio-Hungarian Empire. It would become Czechoslovakia in 1918. At the time of his birth, World War I was raging in Europe. According to his concentration camp papers, his parents' names were recorded as "Khefrau:: Henia F., Teschen—w.o." But then, it was common to hand over fictitious information to one's captors. Fred also had two older sisters, Helen and Lola.

On this same day, poisonous chlorine gas was first introduced for military purposes by Germany.

Fred described a normal childhood with a successful father and a mother—who he described as "traditional"—a mother devoted to her family. He was the cherished, one and only son. His was a prosperous Jewish family. He was very close to his father, who was in the diamond-cutting business.

His parents' deaths would leave Fred an orphan at the age of fourteen. Several years later, he would lose his entire family in World War II:

> My father moved to Nový Jičín from Austria. So we're kind of a bilingual family. My family spoke German at home. I had two sisters. One was six years older, and one was seven

years older. And at the onset of the war, they were both married. One was married to a lawyer, and one was married to an engineer. My father was in charge of a diamond-cutting outfit. He very frequently traveled to Antwerp.

My mother was a typical European woman who never felt good enough and was always traveling to Carlsbad and Marienbad[10] for a cure. She was a lovely woman, totally and completely in love with my father and totally and completely dependent on him. Very charming woman, very good mother—in her own way.

Then, in 1928—I think—my father decided to open his own place. There were no skilled laborers [diamond cutters] in Czechoslovakia. So, he had to bring in equipment, very expensive equipment. And he had to sign a three-year contract with the laborers. Suddenly, about two weeks after he opened his place, he came down with pneumonia, and one week later he was gone. I remember May 1. It was a beautiful day, and I remember it was May 1, because May 1 in Europe was a big day.[11]

At the time Fred's father succumbed to pneumonia, Fred was twelve years old.

Although Fred had been raised with a governess and wanted for little as a child and young boy, his father's death dramatically impacted the family's economic status. His mother, whom he described so affectionately, was completely devastated by her husband's death. One of her principal occupations became visiting her husband's gravesite every day. Then, just one year after his father's death, Fred found his mother had collapsed on the floor. Although he desperately cried out and ran for help, his mother had succumbed to a fatal cerebral hemorrhage.

In the space of two short years, the adored son had lost both parents. He braced himself to absorb the shockwave from this double loss and moved forward into an uncertain future.

NOTES

10   "The Karlovy Vary Region or Carlsbad Region is an administrative unit of the Czech Republic, located in the westernmost part of its historic region of Bohemia. It is named after its capital Karlovy Vary. The region is world famous for its spas, including Karlovy Vary and Mariánské Lázně." *Wikipedia*, s.v. "Karlovy Vary Region," last modified March 10, 2015, https://en.wikipedia.org/wiki/Karlovy_Vary_Region.

11   Fred Fragner, interview by Shifra Miller and Shirley Davis, July 15, 1993, videotape transcribed by author, 1.

Fred's sister, Lola. This is the only picture of anyone in
Fred's immediate family that survived the war.

ORPHAN

When you beat your olive tree, do not go over the boughs again; the leavings shall be for the stranger and the sojourner; the fatherless, and the widow.

~ *Deuteronomy 24:19* [Amplified]

TO BE HUMAN IS TO STRUGGLE. No one escapes the reality that trials and tribulations comprise the human condition. But the challenge of life is to make from those struggles something beautiful, treasured, and good. Fred Fragner would take hold of this truth and become the master of it.

Although Fred had two married sisters, he basically became a street urchin at the age of thirteen or fourteen. He would stay with his sisters occasionally, but more often he slept on the streets or in a cemetery, and worked in a coal yard. This was his preference. These were the years that toughened him from a pampered child to a youth who thrived on his own ingenuity and ability to make his way under challenging circumstances— sometimes mixed with the beneficence of others.

He would later attribute his survival during World War II in large part to the survival skills he mastered during his youth. Fred observed, during his years at Buchenwald, that those Jews who lived in the easiest of circumstances before the war were often the first to perish during the Holocaust. Fred, on the other hand, developed life navigation skills early on, skills that would help him to endure the long trial that awaited him in his twenties.

There is only one extant picture of any member of Fred's family. It is a picture of one of Fred's older sisters. Only this one picture offers evidence that his family of origin ever existed, since Fred would be the only one in his household who would survive the war. Although there is no official record of such, it is believed that Helen, Lola, and their families died in the Nazi death camps. All efforts to find out what happened to them have been to no avail. Only this one picture remains.

Fred managed to not only survive his years as an orphan, but also to somehow finish his schooling and enroll in Charles University in Prague. Lecturing to an audience at Western Washington University in 2005, Fred joked in characteristic Fred fashion that "Charles University was established in 1346, way before my time."[12]

Fred also told the following story of his time at Charles University: "I had a roommate. He and I, between the two of us (he was about my size), we had one pair of good slacks. So when he went on a date, I had to stay home. We used to go to the opera and to the theatre, standing room only. It was a great time."[13] Of course, they could only go separately.

Fred was close to completing his dissertation in clinical psychology when Adolph Hitler began his annexation and invasion of Czechoslovakia. Appeasement was the mood of the day following the unsuccessful negotiations on the part of the British government to settle the Sudeten Crisis. Hitler held firm that the Sudetenland be transferred to the Reich. "Sudetenland" was the German term used to refer to northern, southwestern, and western areas of Czechoslovakia that were primarily inhabited by German speakers.

On September 15, 1938, Neville Chamberlain and Hitler met in Berchtesgaden and agreed to the cessation of the Sudetenland. Three days later, the French Prime Minister Édouard Daladier agreed to the same. No Czechoslovak representative was even invited to these discussions. Czechoslovakia ceded the Sudetenland to Germany in October, 1938. The Munich Agreement, as it is known, has historically been regarded as an action designed to appease Germany.[14] Unfortunately, it only emboldened the Reich to eventually invade Czechoslovakia.

Shortly after the annexation, the persecution of Jews in the Sudetenland began. Then, a few weeks afterward on November 9 and 10, the Nazis terrorized Jewish communities during *Kristallnacht*, the Night of Broken Glass. Throughout Germany and its annexed lands, the Nazis destroyed synagogues and began their relentless persecution of those they despised. Their list included—but was not limited to—the disabled, gypsies, homosexuals, German socialists, communists, pacifists, and most significantly, all Jews.

The population of Buchenwald concentration camp—where Fred would soon be imprisoned—quickly rose from 2,912 admissions in 1937 to 20,122 in 1938, with the greatest number of admissions (10,098) occurring in November 1938.[15]

In September 1999, Fred and Sylvia visited Prague. Fred found the following inscription on a plaque during his one and only trip back to his former homeland. It documents how far-reaching the Nazis' actions would be for the Czechoslovakian Jews. The following is his translation of the inscription into English:

> On the 15th of March 1939 Germany occupied the Czech and Moravian regions of Czechoslovakia and established the protectorate.
>
> Within its boundaries were more than 118,000 people who according to the racist laws then propagated, were characterized as Jews.
>
> Almost 30,000 of these were refugees from the Sudetenland, the border area occupied by the Germans some months previously.
>
> By the 15th of March 1945 the number of Jews in the protectorate, excluding those in prison or in the Terezín concentration camp, came to 3,030, or roughly 2.5% of the number at the beginning of the occupation.
>
> In all, the war period accounted for the deaths of 85% of Czech and Moravian Jews, 71,000 of whom were murdered in the extermination camps alone.
>
> Fewer than 15,000 people were to experience liberation, of whom barely a tenth are still living today.
>
> Together with the victims from Slovakia and the Baltic republics, the Czech and Moravian Jews are the only ones not to have received any form of compensation, real or symbolic, from Germany.

Due to old age the number of survivors of the "final solution of the Jewish question" is diminishing rapidly.

With their deaths comes closure for the final solution of the question of German compensation for Czech and Moravian Jews.

Four years after his trip to Prague, Fred started receiving money from Germany after a successful legal challenge. He received reparations in Deutsche Marks and later euros for a period of five years up until his death in 2009.

NOTES

12   Fred Fragner. Presentation at Western Washington University on his Holocaust experience, Bellingham, WA, May 4, 2005, videotape transcribed by the author, 1.

13   Fragner, interview by Shifra Miller and Shirley Davis, 2.

14   *Wikipedia*, s.v. "Munich Agreement," last modified June 27, 2015, https://en.wikipedia.org/wiki/Munich_Agreement.

15   *The Buchenwald Report* is a translation of *Bericht uber das Konzentrationslager Buchenwald bei* Weimar, prepared in April and May of 1945 by a special intelligence team from the Psychological Warfare Division, SHAEF, assisted by a committee of Buchenwald prisoners. David A. Hackett, ed., *The Buchenwald Report*, (Boulder: Westview Press, 1995), 113.

BROTHER IN ARMS

If you faint in the day of adversity, your strength is small.

~ *Proverbs 24:10*

FRED WAS A COURAGEOUS MAN. He was also a modest man and would probably be more than a bit embarrassed to be described as courageous or heroic. Nevertheless, he was. While he was working to complete his degree at Charles University, he and some of his friends chose to take up arms to oppose Hitler. He joined a movement that was largely informal and undocumented.

"So we joined in the underground, and for three years, we fought as The Underground," Fred said. "I didn't even know it was an underground. But we did everything we could to make it difficult for them to be in our country." Fred described sleeping in the woods without the benefit of sleeping bags or tents, and he promised himself something at that time. With his relentless sense of humor intact, he observed, "If I survive the war, I'm never going to go camping."[16]

Though he would make light of his trials later in life, he nevertheless lived a life on the run, one with few creature comforts and the need to stay ever mobile because the freedom fighters were constantly being chased by the Nazis. For a short time, he may have eluded the Nazis on horseback as a member of Czechoslovakia Cavalry.[17] Years later, his daughter would confirm Fred's excellent equestrian skills when he pursued her on horseback to rescue her from her runaway steed.

After three years of obstructing Nazi efforts to conquer his homeland, Fred was shot and captured. The Gestapo then proceeded to interrogate and torture him for forty-eight hours. In his own words: "After two days of interrogation—which is a very interesting psychological experience— not for recipients, but for other people, I was unable to stand or sit or lie down. My whole body was totally swollen. Then, I was shipped to Buchenwald."[18]

Fred would remain in Buchenwald for five years until he was transferred—upon his request and successful interview—to a tank-building facility on January 20, 1945. This transfer quite possibly saved his life, as a total of 14,201 Buchenwald prisoners died in the early months of 1945:[19]

January:	2,039
February:	5,661
March:	5,588
April 1–10:	913

This was forty-one percent of all prisoners killed at Buchenwald from October 1, 1937 to April 10, 1945. Buchenwald was a labor camp and not a death camp, as were the Polish concentration camps. However, it became more and more important to the Nazis for the prisoners to disappear as the liberators drew near.

Notes

16   Fragner. Presentation at Western Washington University on his Holocaust experience, 1.

17   The Czechoslovakia Calvary was disbanded September 24, 1938, a few days after the transfer of the Sudetenland to Germany. "Czechoslovakia Calvary Presentation Guidon." *Zaricor Flag Collection*, accessed July 4, 2015, http:// www.flagcollection.com/itemdetails-print.php?CollectionItem_ID=2071.

18   Fragner. Presentation at Western Washington University on his Holocaust experience, 2.

19   Hackett, *The Buchenwald Report*, 112.

PRELUDE TO BUCHENWALD

CONCENTRATION CAMP

He who strives on and lives to strive / Can earn redemption still (V, 11936–7).

~ Goethe's *Faust Part Two*

AT THE AGE OF TWENTY-SIX, THE FAMOUS GERMAN WRITER Johann Wolfgang von Goethe[20] (1749–1832) moved to Weimar, then the cultural center of Germany, where he resided for the remainder of his life. When he first arrived, Goethe lived in a summer cottage, or *gartenhaus*, on the east side of the Ilm River five miles from Weimar to the north. He eventually moved to other quarters, but he frequently visited the cottage, where it is purported he wrote both the first and second parts of *Faust*. According to accounts, Goethe was a frequent visitor to a meadow adjacent to the *gartenhaus*. In the meadow, overlooking the countryside, he frequently paused to rest underneath a giant oak that later became known as "Goethe's Oak," after the esteemed author's purported fondness for the site.

Goethe's Oak maintained its notoriety during World War II, when the area surrounding the oak became the infamous Nazi concentration camp of Buchenwald. So noteworthy was the oak that the Nazis preserved it in the midst of the camp proper. Just as Goethe's character, Faust, signed his name in blood to make a bargain with the devil, so the Nazi reverence for the tree seemed symbolic of a similar bargain struck by the German Reich. This was a bargain that saw not only their ascendency, but also their enactment of atrocities that were beyond imagining, save for the fact that those atrocities were witnessed and documented.

The Allied bombing of the Buchenwald factories on August 24, 1944, symbolically signaled the Nazis' impending demise. Though damage to the camp itself was slight, one of the firebombs that destroyed the camp's laundry also destroyed Goethe's Oak, which was situated just adjacent to the laundry.

Notes

20   *Wikipedia*, s.v. "Johann Wolfgang von Goethe," accessed February 16, 2015, last modified June 20, 2015, https://en.wikipedia.org/wiki/Johann_Wolfgang_von_Goethe.

PRISONER 116:033P

The things I saw beggar description. … The visual evidence and the verbal testimony of starvation, cruelty and bestiality were so over-powering … I made the visit deliberately, in order to be in a position to give firsthand evidence of these things if ever, in the future, there develops a tendency to charge these allegations merely to "propaganda."

~ General Dwight D. Eisenhower

Name:	*Fragner, Ferdinand J*
Date of birth:	*22.4.10*
Birth place/ address:	*Nový Jičín—Möhren (town) Teschen Bahnhofstraße.16*
Occupation:	*Mechanic*
Nationality:	*Pole*
Polit.	*Pole-Jude*
Parents' name/s:	*Khefrau:: Henia F., Teschen—w.o.*
Prisoner #:	*116.033 P*

THIS INFORMATION WAS ON FRED'S ADMITTING PAPERS to Buchenwald. He had a degree in psychology, but he told the Nazis he was a mechanic because he thought he would do better if he did. Prisoners would often give incorrect information, such as the wrong date of birth to try and be in the age range that made them eligible for work. Upon arrival, persons were selected for work, and if they were too young, they were regarded as unfit to work, so they made themselves older. This sometimes explains inaccuracies in admitting records. Fred's actual date of birth was April 22, 2015 (22.4.15) and his nationality was Czechoslovakian. He also had no middle name, so the "J" was fictitious.

As part of his "uniform," Fred wore a red triangular patch with a P inside. This signified that he was a Polish political prisoner based on the information in his admitting papers. Jewish political prisoners wore a red badge with a yellow star. There is no record that Fred wore such a star, even though his admitting papers say Pole-Jude.

Although the camp was originally designed to house eight thousand, it would come to house as many as 89,134 on October 6, 1944.[21]

Buchenwald Concentration Camp was established by the Third Reich in 1937. It consisted of a main camp and many satellite camps, including Ohrdruf. After the liberation, General George S. Patton refused to enter a shed containing the bodies of Ohrdruf prisoners who had died of typhus. Recognizing the possibility that some might deny that these atrocities had occurred, General Dwight D. Eisenhower entered to impress them into his mind and heart so that he could bear witness in the future.

Total number of prisoners incarcerated in Buchenwald: approximately 238,980.

Total number of deaths: approximately 56,000.[22] In contrast, *The Buchenwald Report* states that there were 33,462 official deaths: "Death tolls contain only those registered in the hospital as deaths; not included are the numbers of murdered Russian prisoners of war, executed prisoners, and those prisoners sent on death transports. Also missing is the number of victims who died or were beaten to death on the way to and from Weimar during transports."[23]

One of the individuals who began, and then abandoned, efforts to write about Fred's life became frustrated with the effort because Fred refused to talk about his Buchenwald years, only speaking of them in the barest details. One likely reason was that these years were of such profound sorrow and struggle that he hid these memories away so they had no power to rob him of present or future joy. Having endured the unendurable, he would not waste a moment more reconstructing for the curious what never should have been in the first place.

Another reason, however, may be of a more philosophical bent: why give glory to darkness?

That he was willing to talk at all about his years at Buchenwald can be credited to a desire to encourage thoughtful reflection on how to prevent such atrocities from happening again. And, like Eisenhower, he became dedicated to preserving the historical record of what had happened.

On November 20, 2008, Fred was interviewed by Western Washington University students and graduate assistants Dave Morrin and Jamie Daniels.[24] These students planned to be teachers, and they wanted to know the most important thing that young people, kids, should learn about the Holocaust. Fred told them that students should study the forces that led to the Holocaust during World War II, as well as the holocaust in Rwanda and those in other parts of the world. When Jamie asked him why there is so much hate in the world, he responded that it was a question of great value, "a hundred thousand dollar question."[25] He continued, "There is much hatred because people haven't yet learned how to respect each other, how to love each other sometimes in spite of each other, to respect [their] rights, to respect differences and respect and find ways of resolving troubles in talking with each other." When Dave asked, what the best life lesson was that he had learned, Fred paused for a while and then answered, "I think, be considerate to others is probably the best life lesson I have learned."[26]

It is likely that this conclusion was either formed or cemented during his five years at Buchenwald, a place that was the antithesis of regard for others. At the entrance into the camp was a sign that, translated into English, reads, "To each his own." The sign did not face outward as a greeting, but rather faced inward as a warning to prisoners. There has been much speculation about the meaning of this phrase. In light of Fred's observance to regard others well, the Nazi dictum was one promoting insularity and fear—the antithesis of regard for others and the building of community.

A prisoner residing in Buchenwald was not treated as a human being, but was regarded as an object to be utilized as the Nazis saw fit. For instance, Commandant Koch's wife, Elsa, was a great admirer of lamps. According to Fred, "Mrs. Elsa Koch liked lampshades. And once in a while, we were assembled, and we were told to strip from the waist up. And anybody who was lucky enough to have a nice tattoo, this person disappeared, and there was another lamp for Mrs. Koch."[27]

Fred was quick to point out that Buchenwald was not a death camp. He observed, "Buchenwald was a concentration camp. In Buchenwald, we had forty thousand people at any given time of all nationalities, and the Germans asked us to work hard and work hard and work hard until we drop dead from starvation and exhaustion."[28] This largely accounted for the estimated fifty-six thousand prisoner deaths that were attributed to Buchenwald.

After the November 1939 attempt on Hitler's life, twenty-one Jews at Buchenwald were taken to the quarry and shot, even though they had absolutely nothing to do with it. By 1940, a crematorium existed on the site to dispose of prisoner remains. Previously, a crematorium at Weimar had been used. By 1944, the camp population was 63,048, and there were 8,644 deaths that year, followed by the 14,201 deaths reported in the first months of 1945.[29]

Prisoners were given little to eat, they were asked to endure roll calls that sometimes lasted for hours even when temperatures plummeted to below freezing, and were often exposed to typhus from a sanitation "system"—actually an open trench—that was designed for eight thousand prisoners, not the actual numbers that came to be imprisoned.

During one of his public lectures on the Holocaust, Fred recounted the wonders of the Buchenwald diet:

> Our diet was very simple. In the morning, we got so-called coffee. We got up in the morning about four or five a.m. The coffee was called coffee. I don't know what it was, but it wasn't coffee. And yet we got a slice of bread that I swear was made out of clay, because it tasted that way. And this was our breakfast. And then we went to a stone quarry and worked there until lunchtime. And then we went and had lunch. For lunch, we usually would get the same menu—a cabbage soup. And if you were lucky, you'd find a lonely leaf of cabbage floating in the rest of the so-called soup. And then we worked until late evening, and then we went back to our barracks.[30]

According to camp records, prisoner rations as of September 1939 were listed as five hundred grams of bread a day and a liter of watery soup.[31]

And when describing camp roll calls, Fred was always bitingly sarcastic about the Nazis' ad infinitum enthusiasm for counting prisoners. "Before we went to work, we had to assemble in one big place because everybody had to be counted to make sure nobody was missing. There was no ghost of a chance to escape from Buchenwald." Fred said the next statement with a gesture of his right hand circling around again and again to show the way camps were situated within other camps: "There were camps in camps in camps in camps with dogs and Gestapo. There was not a chance. But the Germans were very methodical, very methodical, so they were counting."[32]

Fred was willing to talk about only a few specific incidents that he witnessed or that happened to him during his years at Buchenwald. As he shared these stories, he said,

> I'm not telling you just to make you feel bad or to present a gruesome story. I'm telling you for one purpose. Try to place yourself in my place and what would happen to you as a man or woman who at this point meant nothing, absolutely zero. And I think that's very important, at least to me. I'm very important to myself, and if you take that away from me, there's not very much left. And this is one of the things I've learned as I grew up. I'm precious to myself. I like myself. I like people, because if you can't like yourself, how can you like anybody else? But I always dealt with people with respect, but they were stripping me of this respect. They were stripping me of everything.[33]

Think back on a time in your life when someone was abusive to you. Perhaps you were in a situation where someone took out his or her own discontent with life on you. And perhaps their anger burst forth in an unpredictable rhythm that made you nervous, jumpy, or sick to your stomach, not knowing what was next. Now, multiply that feeling exponentially with no breaks, no rest, no escape from the onslaught, and add in the horrors of seeing others abused or even killed, and then you would still have only a fraction of understanding as to what life was like in a concentration camp. Fred went on:

> I remember a sixteen-year-old boy who had to hang his parents. I don't know where he is now. I don't know what's happened to him. I doubt very much if he is what, as we call it, sane.

> I had a very close friend, very close friend, my best friend. We stood together, and an SS man came and shot him. No reason. And I forgot about it. But when I came to the United States and I went to the University of Chicago, they sent me to the medical service because I was screaming every night. My late wife got tired of my screaming, so she told me to go and see somebody. So I did. I went to a psychiatrist who dealt with what we used to call in those days combat fatigue. Now we have more scientific names. And he put me under hypnosis, and I found out I couldn't accept that my best friend died in front of me this way, and I just rejected that's what happened. And every night I was recounting this. I still have nightmares every six months or so. In my nightmares, I know I'm going to be killed. I was never killed in all those years, but I ... it's a very frightening experience every six months—anticipating being killed.[34]

Fred would move forward, summoning the same strength that moved him to fight for his beloved homeland. Yet with each step forward, the memories would pull him backward in these subterranean moments of sleep when the night terrors could overwhelm him in the twilight between sleep and consciousness. Then, he was again in Buchenwald, standing in the never-ending roll call line. A soldier approached. He raised his pistol and fired, and Fred's best friend fell dead. And Fred was next; in his dreams, he was always next. And so he endured these night terrors for sixty years.

In 2009, President Obama was the first US president to visit Buchenwald while in office. He stood outside the entryway to the camp alongside German Chancellor Merkel, his friend Elie Wiesel, and Bertrand Herz, both of whom were camp survivors like Fred. Obama spoke of the survivors and the perpetrators:

> ... but still surrounded by death they willed themselves to hold fast to life. In their hearts they still had faith that evil would not triumph in the end, that while history is unknowable it arches towards progress, and that the world would one day remember them. And it is now up to us, the living, in our work, wherever we are, to resist injustice and intolerance and indifference in whatever forms they may take and ensure that those who were lost here did not go in vain. It is up to us to redeem that faith. It is up to us to bear witness; to ensure that the world continues to note what happened here; to remember all those who survived and all those who perished, and to remember them not just as victims, but also as individuals who hoped and loved and dreamed just like us.
>
> And just as we identify with the victims, it's also important for us I think to remember that the perpetrators of such evil were human, as well, and that we have to guard against cruelty in ourselves.[35]

In the midst of his internment, Fred was confronted by this reminder that his captors were humans, humans doing inhuman things, yet human nevertheless. According to Fred,

> A German took me to do some domestic chores, like clean his room, etc., and the logic of those people—who were drunk a good part of the time .... One day, he called me into his room, and he said, "I got a cake from my mother, and I want to share it with you." This guy, who could kill me without an excuse, [says], "Sit down." I was scared, of course. I don't know. I never knew what was going to happen next. But I sat down and he was ... showing me about his mother.[36]

Moments such as these could quickly turn dangerous, however. That same night, this SS officer invited Fred to the officer canteen to participate in the conviviality of a drinking session. One of the Germans asked Fred if he knew what schnapps was.[37] He put the bottle of schnapps to Fred's mouth, his gun pressed against Fred, and said, "Drink it." Fred said that he passed out, but it wasn't clear whether he fainted from fright or passed out from guzzling down the bottle of schnapps.[38]

Because he spoke fluent German, it is likely that his language skills gave him an advantage over other prisoners. German language skills, combined with the survival skills he developed as a youth, perhaps gave him the edge he needed to survive. And then there was a bit of good luck, or perhaps divine intervention, thrown in.

When speaking to a class of middle school students in 1995, he offered a few more details on what it was like to be a prisoner of the Third Reich and all the questions raised by his ordeal:

> In the five years in Buchenwald Concentration Camp, I have seen a lot and I have experienced a lot. I have seen Jews being forced to dig their graves and then being shot. How can one understand the loss of a family, including uncles, aunts, cousins, etc.? I don't know where their ashes or bodies were buried. I don't know if they were killed. I don't know if they were gassed in crematoriums. I just don't know. How can one explain the sense of powerlessness and hopelessness and anger and frustration? How can one convey the brutality and the daily violence to the human spirit and dignity? How can one convey the sense of emotional and spiritual disintegration living only with a biological urge to survive?[39]

Fred was extremely clear about this last point. He felt strongly that it was only the biological urge to survive that kept prisoners alive under the slave state perpetuated by the Nazis. Years later, he would meet another liberated prisoner, the famous psychologist Viktor E. Frankl, who wrote *Man's Search for Meaning*.[40] In 1963, Fred and Frankl were both invited to participate in a debate panel following Frankl's speech at Earlham College, a college founded on the perspective of the Religious Society of Friends (Quakers).[41] During the discussion, Fred would openly and vigorously challenge Frankl's premise that it is finding meaning—even in the most horrific of circumstances—that provides the will to live.

Frankl's philosophical premise in his book was this: "Between stimulus and response there is a space. In that space is our power to choose our response. In our response lies our growth and our freedom."[42] Fred said that while Dr. Frankl had "the luxury of being able to think, to use [his] brain" during his stay in Theresienstadt,[43] this was not the case for prisoners in the worst of circumstances. The majority of those imprisoned in the Nazi concentration camps had been stripped of everything except a purely biological imperative to go on. Within Fred's Buchenwald experience, the power to choose was muted.[44] Right or wrong, he took a hard stance against Frankl's philosophy and maintained it throughout his lifetime.

Fred also maintained that the camps were particularly deadly for the Hungarian Jews who came to Auschwitz. "I understand they were dying like flies, simply because many of them were middle class, upper middle class."[45] They didn't have the physical toughness that poverty builds.

In his video response to questions from middle schoolers, one student asked Fred if he ever gave up hope in the camps. Fred threw his head back in response, and a grimace flashed across his face for a brief moment. Then he responded,

"One never believes that one is going to die, no matter what. But it doesn't mean that one has hope. I don't think that I had hope. I just had nothing, and I felt nothing."

"We just were existing. We went to work. We ate whatever little food we got. And then we went to sleep. And yes, our greatest entertainment was to delouse [ourselves] once a week—which means to try to get rid of lice, which were leading many of us to be sick with typhoid fever."[46]

Fred thought it was a very interesting question as to why he survived so long without being killed, but he didn't have a definitive answer, and he didn't feel it was because he necessarily willed himself to go on. "I think that I was tough kid, raised in tough conditions, and maybe this gave me some physical strength to survive. I guess I was very lucky. I'm very determined and very stubborn, and this helped too. But only God knows why I survived and how I survived."[47]

By contrast to the fifty-six thousand souls lost at Buchenwald, the following are approximate death counts for those lost in the Nazi death camps—all located in occupied Poland:[48]

Auschwitz-Birkenau	1,100,000
Belżec	600,000
Chełmno	320,000
Majdanek	80,000
Sobibór	250,000
Treblinka	800,000

Captured in Czechoslovakia and tagged as a Polish political, Fred's chances would have been severely diminished had he been sent northeast from the Czech Republic into Poland, rather than west into the heartland of the Reich. It is also possible, though unlikely, that Fred was not readily recognized as a Jew (although his camp admittance paper does say Pole-Jude). *The Buchenwald Report* states, "Many, especially foreign Jews, had survived in camp unrecognized, that is, not recognized as Jews by the SS."[49]

Likewise, his chances for survival would likely have become negligible had the plans to build a gassing facility at Buchenwald not failed. Fortunately, daring individuals destroyed the telegram that was sent near the end of 1943 ordering this new construction. This and other circumstances resulted in the project's dismantling.

As Fred stated, he was very lucky to be alive.

During the July 15, 1993 video interview,[50] Fred was asked if he had a special skill that helped him survive. He answered:

> Yeah. I spoke fluent German, which helped a lot. And, I think there's a bit of sociopath in me. This was the end of 1944, beginning of 1945. The Germans started to liquidate some of the camps, and they started to bring people to Buchenwald. I decided that if I'm going to stay there, I'm going to die. And one day they announced that they were looking for auto mechanics—believe it or not. [He makes

this last statement with a huge grin on this face.]

So there was one guy who was an auto mechanic. So for three days, he was instructing me, and we all appeared before three civilians, and I guess I overloaded them in fluent German, and they were very impressed—didn't ask me any questions, and I knew that this group [was] taking two thousand people out to a brand-new smaller camp—which [meant] getting out of Buchenwald. And I was one of the two thousand people sent there, and this was in a place called Stassfurt.[51]

According to *The Buchenwald Report*, "To be a skilled worker was in any case to have a life insurance policy. Anyone who had the courage and presence of mind to present himself as some sort of skilled worker, and was able to withstand with boldness and inventiveness any difficulties that developed later, had at least a chance."[52] That was Fred—inventive and a very good actor.

When he and the others arrived at the repair center, there was nothing being repaired, as it turned out. According to Fred,

The Germans were not interested in repairing anything, because they were afraid that if they were out of work they'd be shipped to the Russian front. So not one [of them] was motivated to do anything.

However, we were working in a big building like airplane hangars, and the hunger was getting to us. There was no food. Not far from us was the German canteen where the SS was eating, and behind the canteen were garbage cans with what they threw out. And we knew also that if any of us was caught outside the hangars, no questions asked—dead! And yet we were willing to risk our life to get some garbage out of the garbage cans. So this is hunger.[53]

Fred also talked about somehow getting into the facility's kitchen and hitching a ride on a truck used to pick up carrots.

I was sitting on top of the truck and stuffing myself with carrots. I'm a survivor, you know! Well, everything was risky. To be alive was risky. I took a lot of risks, a lot of risks. Then, I come here now to the whole issue of preliberation, because when the Russians started to come close and the Americans started to come close, we were told we are marching. They told us one day that we are going. Where are we going? Who knows? At this point, there were a lot of Hungarians, what they called Hungarian Germans—about sixty years old, sixty-five years old—and they were marching us, and we had not the slightest idea of where we were going. First of all, we were grossly undernourished, and we had to walk every day.[54]

After about two weeks of marching some fifteen miles per day, the group Fred was part of was very close to Annenberg, Germany. At that time, the Nazi guards told the prisoners that Annenberg was already in Russian hands, so they changed course and started to walk toward Libec. The date was April 22, Fred's thirtieth birthday.

Here Fred gave a bit more detail on his day of liberation: "I will never forget because it was pouring and freezing, and I was walking in the striped suit and shoes with wooden soles, and I was sick and feverish, and we walked probably about fourteen hours, and there was rain coming down, and I'll never forget that birthday."[55]

Then, at the beginning of May 1945, the Nazis brought the prisoners up to a barn and ordered them inside. They then locked the doors. The prisoners did not know what was next, and some, including Fred, were too exhausted and sick to go on.

He continued, "I had edema from the waist down, and I'd had it. And I said to myself, 'That's it. I'm dying.' I cannot go on. I knew what it meant, 'cannot go.' But I couldn't go any longer. Didn't care. And then a miracle happened—if you talk about miracles."

Fred's miracle was the arrival of food packages from the Swedish Red Cross—something that had never occurred in all the years he had been a prisoner:

Are you kidding? Jews? And they give us each a package and, of course, most of us consumed the whole package—except for a few things. And so, next morning I had more pep and everything, and so we marched. We marched into a woods, and the American artillery was shredding the woods. [He says this with a huge smile on his face.] Fortunately, nothing happened to anybody. And we came to another village, and there was a river—not a big river—so we stopped to delouse ourselves and to bathe and wash with sulfur provided in the packages. And then two German officers came in a car and followed the guards, who took us because it was a bunker zone. So they marched us again, and we came to woods. This was about May 4.[56]

We came to woods, and the woods were full of Germans who run away from the Russians, and there were plenty of German soldiers who got lost from their regiment. Who knows? Anyway, they allowed us to make a fire. This was the first time in the war that we were allowed to make a fire, that anyone was allowed to make a fire at night. So we slept in those woods, and I woke up in the morning, and our guards had gone. They were gone, and we were here!

And some of the guys from the group were gone too. So here I was in these woods and what to do? And I saw German soldiers, wounded soldiers on both sides of the road. And as I said, I had edema from the waist down, and I was feverish. Some of these Germans stopped in on a bicycle. Right there they called the Germans around because the Russians are five kilometers behind.

When I heard this, I turned around and went toward Russia, and I walked maybe two hundred feet and a Jeep came with two American GIs, and the war was over.[57]

In the retelling of this most momentous moment in his life, the video recording shows that Fred is clearly overcome with the emotion of that incredible memory. He has his glasses off, and then puts them back on and stares silently into the camera for a seemingly infinite length of time.

The interviewer finally responds with the statement, "Pretty heavy duty. Pretty heavy duty," and then, "Did you find any of your family?"[58]

Fred puts his finger in the air in response. He looks up, and it is clear that he needs a break as he struggles to not be overcome by the recollection. He then moves out of the video camera, except for this left shoulder.

In response to the interviewer's question, Fred begins to say, "No, but ..." Overcome again, he removes his glasses and wipes his eyes quickly with his handkerchief and looks up once again.

"You are standing in the road, you know, and you are ... free."

"Yes," replies the interviewer.

"And you don't know what to do. You are standing in, you know, in a strange country. You don't know anybody, and you are free. What to do? I didn't know what to do."

"How long had you been in captivity?"

"Five years."

A second interviewer repeats, "Five years in captivity."

"I am free. In a strange county, a strange road, and sick like a dog. And I've not the slightest idea what to do with myself."[59]

Fred's confusion was all the more poignant because he never once imagined during all those years of imprisonment that this moment would ever come. "You know, the only way I can put it is that your psyche stops functioning. Your body continues to function, and suddenly my psyche has to function. It's not ready for it."

Notes

21   Hackett, *The Buchenwald Report*, 109.

22   This number is an estimate based on the *Histories of the Holocaust* documentary film series. *Histories of the Holocaust: Buchenwald 1937–42* and *Histories of the Holocaust: Buchenwald 1942–45*, DVD, directed by John Moore (2010; London: Artsmagic Limited), documentary film.

23   Hackett , *The Buchenwald Report*, 109.

24   A transcript of this interview can be found on the university's website: https://wce.wwu.edu/nwchgee/fred-fragner. The transcription used in this book was made by the author based the audio recording provided by Sylvia Fragner. Fred Fragner, interview by graduate assistants Dave Morrin and Jamie Daniels, Northwest Center for Holocaust, Genocide and Ethnocide Education, Woodring College of Education, Western Washington University, November 20, 2008.

25   Ibid, 4–5.

26   **Ibid**, 1.

27   Fragner. Presentation at Western Washington University on his Holocaust experience, 2–3.

28   Ibid, 2.

29   Moore, *Histories of the Holocaust: Buchenwald 1937–42* and *Histories of the Holocaust: Buchenwald 1942–45.*

30   Fragner. Presentation at Western Washington University on his Holocaust experience, 3–4.

31   Moore, *Histories of the Holocaust: Buchenwald 1937–42* and *Histories of the Holocaust: Buchenwald 1942–45.*

32   Fragner. Presentation at Western Washington University on his Holocaust experience, 2.

33   Ibid, 3–4.

34   Ibid, 3.

35   Barack Obama, "Buchenwald Speech." *The World Post.* Accessed July 4, 2015, http://www.huffingtonpost.com/2009/06/05/obama-buchenwald-speech-t_n_211898.html.

36   Fragner. Presentation at Western Washington University on his Holocaust experience, 3.

37   Schnaps (schnapps in English) is a "strong alcoholic drink resembling gin and often flavored with fruit." *Wikipedia*, s.v. "Schnapps," accessed July 4, 2015, last updated April 13, 2015, https://en.wikipedia.org/wiki/Schnapps.

38   Fragner. Presentation at Western Washington University on his Holocaust experience, 3.

39   Fred Fragner, answering questions provided by Ann Jester's middle school students, February 1995, video transcribed by the author.

40   Frankl's book was originally published in 1946 under the title *Trotzdem Ja Zum Leben Sagen: Ein Psychologe Erlebt das Konzentrationslager* (translated as *Saying Yes to Life in Spite of Everything: A Psychologist Experiences the Concentration Camp*). It was translated into English in 1959. Viktor E. Frankl, *Man's Search for Meaning* (Boston: Beacon Press, 1959).

41   Fred Fragner, Colorado, Indiana, and Ohio scrapbook titled "Next Stop Denver," compiled by Fred and Anita Fragner, covering the years 1951–1963.

42   In the preface to one of the iBook editions of Frankl's book, Harold S. Kushner, rabbi emeritus at Temple Israel in Natick, Massachusetts, cited this basic premise in this way: "Finally, Frankl's most enduring insight, one that I have called on often in my own life and in countless counseling situations: Forces beyond your control can take away everything you possess except one thing, your freedom to choose how you will respond to the situation. You cannot control what happens to you in life, but you can always control what you will feel and do about what happens to you." Viktor E. Frankl, *Man's Search for Meaning* (Boston: Beacon Press, 1959). iBook edition.

43   Frankl had been imprisoned in Theresienstadt initially. This camp was acknowledged as a propaganda tool by the Nazis to hide from the world what was going on in the other labor and death camps. Fred was adamant that Frankl had not experienced the worst the Nazis had to offer and, therefore, was not in a position to know that choice was irrelevant in the worst of circumstances. Frankl, however, was only initially at Theresienstadt. In October 1944, he and his wife were transported to Auschwitz for processing, and then

he was sent to Kaufering, a camp associated with Dachau. He would do slave labor there for five months, after which he was offered a move to "the so-called rest-camp, Türkheim." His wife, Tilly, was transported to Bergen-Belsen, where she died. Frankl and his sister Stella were the only survivors of his entire family. *Wikipedia*, s.v. "Viktor Frankl," accessed July 5, 2015, last modified June 11, 2015, https://en.wikipedia.org/wiki/Viktor_Frankl.

44   More on the Fragner-Frankl disagreement in the "Mental Health Professional" chapter.

45   Fragner, interview by Shifra Miller and Shirley Davis, 5.

46   Fred Fragner, answering questions provided by Ann Jester's middle school students, February 1995, video transcribed by the author, 7–8.

47   Ibid, 7.

48   *Wikipedia*, s.v. "Extermination camp," accessed July 4, 2015, last updated June 24, 2015, https://en.wikipedia.org/wiki/Extermination_camp.

49   *The Buchenwald Report* is the definitive report on the Buchenwald Concentration Camp. The foundation of the report was contributed by Eugene Kogon, the author of *The Theory and Practice of Hell*. (New York: Farrar, Straus and Cudahy, 1950) is revered as one of the great historians and sociologists of the twentieth century. The full report itself was organized under the leadership of Albert Rosenberg's SHAEF psychological warfare team, and the book is dedicated "to the twenty-eight members of the Rosenberg family who died in the Nazi Holocaust." The edition used for this book was translated by David A. Hackett with a forward by Frederick A. Praeger, whose father was interned in Buchenwald from 1939–1945, at which time he suffered a head trauma during an altercation with a communist trustee in the camp. His injury led to his transport and subsequent death in the Auschwitz gas chambers. David A. Hackett, ed., *The Buchenwald Report* (Boulder: Westview Press, 1995), 76.

50   Fragner, interview by Shifra Miller and Shirley Davis, 8–9.

51   In an April 14, 1985 article in *The News Tribune* of Tacoma, Washington, Fred refers to the location of the "German Army tank repair station" as in "the little town of Strassfurt-Leopoldshal." In this article, he refers to being sent with one thousand other prisoners, rather than the two thousand mentioned in the video interview. It was difficult to make out what Fred was saying. On the recording, its sounds like "Stattsford." According to *The Buchenwald Report*, as of March 25, 1945, there were three listings for a factory producing tank parts:

Reh, Stassfurt (387 workers), G. Walzer & Co., Stassfurt (235 workers), and Kalag, Stassfurt (forty-seven workers). While these numbers don't match the "two thousand people sent there," there isn't another factory name or function that is as close to Stassfurt. Hackett, 307.

52 Hackett, *The Buchenwald Report*, 51.

53 Fragner, interview by Shifra Miller and Shirley Davis, 9.

54 Ibid, 9.

55 Ibid, 10.

56 The taped recording sounds like "Weistadt." There is a town in Germany fifteen kilometers east of Stuttgart with the name "Weinstadt." Ibid.

57 Ibid, 10–11.

58 Ibid, 11.

59 Ibid, 11.

POSTSCRIPT TO BUCHENWALD CONCENTRATION CAMP

There may be times when we are powerless to prevent injustice, but there must never be a time when we fail to protest.

~Elie Wiesel

THE FOLLOWING EXCERPTS ARE TAKEN FROM the final months and aftermath of Buchenwald as portrayed in the second half of the documentary series *Histories of the Holocaust:*[60]

- Himmler left it to the discretion of the camp commander whether to liquidate the communist and criminal prisoners. However, he wanted the Jews left untouched because he felt that at a later stage he would use the remaining Jews as a bargaining tool—perhaps even convincing the Allied Forces that he should be put in charge of a defeated Germany.

- Buchenwald was the first camp to be liberated, and the Allies were unprepared for what they found. The ovens were still hot and burning bodies. The Allied Forces hunted down the seventy or so guards who had fled and killed them.

Some stats:

- A total of 250,000 prisoners had been incarcerated at Buchenwald during the war.

- 8,000 Soviet prisoners were shot.

- 12,000 were sent to death camps, mostly Dachau.

- 1,000 were hanged.

- 33,462 deaths were recorded in camp records.

- Total deaths: approximately 56,000.

- German citizens from Weimar were "invited" (an invitation that could not be refused) to visit Buchenwald to see what had happened.

- Those put on trial for atrocities committed at Buchenwald were put on trial at Dachau rather than Nuremberg. Trials for the 793 defendants began April 11, 1947; 273 were executed.

- Weimar and Buchenwald became a part of the German territories taken by the Soviets. Under Soviet rule, Buchenwald continued to function as a camp, this time for German prisoners. The prisoners under Soviet control died at an even higher rate than did their counterparts under the Third Reich.

Notes

60   *Histories of the Holocaust: Buchenwald 1937–42* and *Histories of the Holocaust: Buchenwald 1942–45*, www.artsmagicdvd.com.

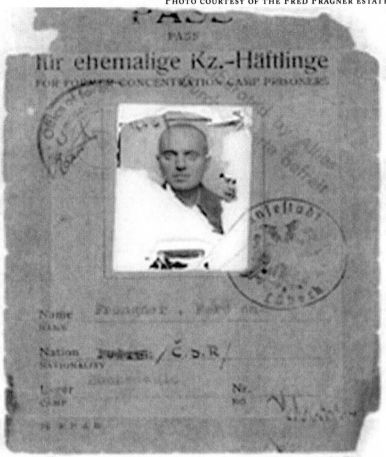

Fred's photo was taken immediately after his liberation to create this identification card, as it says—"FOR FORMER CONCENTRATION CAMP PRISONERS." Fred's "lager/camp" is listed at the bottom as Buchenwald.

FREEMAN

Freedom is what you do with what's been done to you.

~Jean Paul Sartre

THE DEATH OF HIS PARENTS AND HIS IMPRISONMENT in Buchenwald twice cast Fred in the role of orphan. The war had robbed him of the remainder of his family, the completion of his education, and all external accouterments. It also left deep psychic wounds, as evidenced by recurrent night terrors that lasted for the remainder of his life.

The liberation, though, provided a startling and amorphous new beginning. He remembered standing on the road and crying. What next? "You don't know what to do."[61]

While the GIs he encountered urged him to go back to Germany, Fred stubbornly continued on in the direction he had chosen as the rain poured down:

> I kept going, and I ended the first night of freedom in an
> open field with the German soldiers. Finally, the second day
> [we were] close to the German border where the Americans
> and Russians met. And so, they [started] to organize us, and
> they put us in [a] village—us and ten thousand Russian

prisoners. The Russian prisoners, they were tough. They lost a lot of people, more than [the] Jews.[62]

We were in those villages two days, three days, and there was one guy who was a cook, and the GIs were running Jeeps and confiscating food and bringing it to us. Anyway, they got meat and he gave me a chunk of hot meat like this.

At this, Fred holds his hands up to describe the length of a piece of meat, about twelve inches across. He then talks about the intestinal repercussions of eating so much meat in one sitting after having been without dense food for such a long time: "[The meat] almost killed me because I had severe diarrhea for three weeks. But I survived this too."[63]

Still in very fragile physical condition, Fred was temporarily dependent on those around him who were stronger and/or who had the resources he needed to get stronger. "They transported us to another place which used to be an SS camp. And they gave us American white bread—which I hate now—white bread!"[64]

Gradually, he made his way to Lübeck, Germany, where he and others displaced by the war stayed in SS housing. He described Lübeck as a very old German port on the sea, "a beautiful place."[65]

During his transport to Buchenwald, Fred met a young woman and her father. Because even short courtships were impractical, Fred and Kazhmeira (Kay) were secretly wed within two weeks of meeting. They were then separated just as quickly when she was moved to another concentration camp. Kay's father—whom Fred liked very much—was also imprisoned at Buchenwald and killed just days before the liberation. His name was Peretz Wilner.

While staying in Lübeck, Fred would often journey the distance of forty-two miles to Hamburg to search for his wife. Finding Kay became an important focusing activity for Fred, and a challenging one at that, considering the hundreds of thousands with this same goal—to find loved ones, or at least attempt to find out what had happened to them.

"One day, there was an announcement that a bus was coming from Prague and taking all the people back to Prague," Fred said. And because Fred was close to finishing his degree at Charles University, it would be only natural for him to return home to Czechoslovakia to complete his education. "So I had an assignment—five o'clock a.m. buses are leaving, and I had a seat on that bus. So, quarter to five, I'm in my seat on that bus. Five minutes before five, I said 'I'm not going.' No rhyme or reason. There's nothing. I just decided I'm not going back. I don't know why. Sometimes an irrational decision is a good decision."

Because he stayed in Lübeck, he was finally able to get some information on Kay's whereabouts in southern Germany. For Holocaust survivors, the process of finding lost loved ones involved searching makeshift boards where people posted information. It also involved telling strangers their stories and the stories of their loved ones—what they looked like, their age, where they were last seen. The process was very much like searching for the proverbial needle in the haystack.

Fred also searched to find out what had become of his two sisters and their families. He would never find a definitive answer.

Many years later, on May 18, 2007, his good friend, Dr. Ray Wolpow, would journey to Germany to go through the ITS archive in Bad Arolsen to try and find evidence of their deaths, but there was no trace of what had become of them.

Once reunited with his wife, Fred and Kay journeyed to Stuttgart where they were housed in an apartment building that had formerly housed German officers and SS. While in Stuttgart, Fred found that he began to have influence. Although he wasn't quite sure why this was the case, it is likely that his magnetic and outspoken personality was somewhat to blame.

> I have not the slightest idea how. Anyway, what happened is that we were getting packages. And one day this German who was in charge of this whole area decided that nobody would get packages, we are going to eat in common dining rooms, and all those packages would be commingled. And our buildings were on top a hill in Stuttgart. So we said no way. Hunger strike! We hoisted a black flag, and so two days later Eisenhower came.[66]

After an unsuccessful negotiation with General Eisenhower, Fred was approached by the United Nations Relief and Rehabilitation Association (UNRRA) and offered a job at Aglasterhausen, a residential facility and school for war orphans.

"We need a school principal," they said.

Recounting his answer with a big smile on his face, Fred told them, "That's fine."[67]

With that simple answer, he entered into a new and brighter world that forever changed the course of his life and those of the many children for whom he would come to care so deeply.

NOTES

61   Fragner, interview by Shifra Miller and Shirley Davis, 11.

62   A study published in 1993 by the Russian Academy of Sciences estimated Soviet losses during World War II at 26.6 million, including military dead of 8.7 million calculated by the Russian Ministry of Defense. *Wikipedia*, s.v. "World War II casualties of the Soviet Union," last modified July 6, 2015, accessed July 11, 2015, https://en.wikipedia.org/wiki/World_War_II_casualties_of_the_Soviet_Union.

63   Fragner. Presentation at Western Washington University on his Holocaust experience, 6.

64   Fragner, interview by Shifra Miller and Shirley Davis, 12.

65   Ibid, 14.

66   "The black flag, and the color black in general, have been associated with anarchism since the 1880s. The uniform blackness of the flag is in stark contrast to the colorful flags typical of most nation-states. Additionally as a white flag is the universal symbol for surrender to superior force, the counter-opposite black flag would logically be a symbol of defiance and opposition to surrender." Symbols.com, STANDS4 LLC,2015. "Black Flag." Accessed July 11, 2015. http://www.symbols.com/symbol/160.

67   Fragner, interview by Shifra Miller and Shirley Davis, 15.

Fred's beloved Aglasterhausen.

KIND CARETAKER

As many leaves are on the trees as many stars are in the sky, I wish so much happiness in your life, to my beloved and kind caretakers.

~F. Siedlik, Aglasterhausen orphan

FRED WAS OFFERED THE POSITION OF PRINCIPAl at the Aglasterhausen Children's Center in Germany. The United Nations Relief and Rehabilitation Association (UNRRA) established these schools immediately following the end of World War II. He described his time there as "fantastic." From the depths of despair under Nazi domination, he had emerged triumphant!

Although the war had interrupted his quest for a PhD from Charles University, he was well-educated and had already completed several years of study in the field of psychology. Of course, his intelligence, life experiences, and language abilities were priceless in terms of what he would bring to this position.

The school housed and cared for non-German children who had survived the war, but had been orphaned or separated from their families. The schools provided shelter and schooling until each child could be placed with a new family or reunited with their family of origin.

One of the saddest facts of the Holocaust is that only one percent of all Jewish children survived. One percent. Yes, one percent. Estimates of the number of children who died during the Holocaust range as high as 1.5 million, including more than 1.2 million Jewish children. Aglasterhausen and the other UNRRA schools housed the surviving Jewish children, as well as children of other religions and nationalities.

Most of the narrative in this chapter is Fred's own words describing his time at the school. His words are taken directly from a scrapbook that he created to preserve his memories of Aglasterhausen.[68] Generally, edits were kept to a minimum, so the reader may notice the absence of a few hyphens and some unconventional word use or sentence structure. The scrapbook was a 14-by-12.5-inch bond book with an embroidered cloth cover that displayed items sacred to Judaism—The Torah, a Star of David, and a Menorah. On the inside front cover in the upper left-hand side of the page is the name of the owner, written in gold foil: Fred Fragner.

In many ways, Fred's time at Aglasterhausen was the most miraculous and memorable time in his entire life. Having just been liberated from the Nazi hell, he was about to share a miraculous healing and rebirth, experienced in the fellowship of those who had known the same suffering and lived, not only to "strive on," but also to flourish. The scrapbook that was to chronicle the brief seven months he spent as principal of Aglasterhausen begins with his description of the journey to the center and a description of what a visitor would find there, and then it continues on to describe every facet of day-to-day life at Aglasterhausen.

Unterschwarzach is a colorful little village. As you drive through it you notice about one hundred yards to the left of the road, a quadrangle of buildings surrounded by trees. You will see white laundry drying in the wind in the front of the buildings. A group of children are playing on the banks of a narrow stream nearby. To your right is a large athletic field where boys and girls are playing soccer and volleyball. And when you pass the field, turn your car to the left and you will find yourself on a road, shaded on both sides by trees, and ending fifty yards further in the heart of the "United Nations Relief and Rehabilitation Administration" (UNRRA) Children's Center. You cannot miss the center, because it is at the end of the road, and also because it is announced by a large gateway, or arch, on which is a sign—UNRRA District Children's Center.

At the gate you will be stopped and greeted by a Polish guard. The guard is there to protect the center against hostile Germans, to check German employees, and to check anyone entering the center. The children are always free to leave without any questions from the guard. They understand that the guard is there not to limit their freedom, but to protect them. A meeting with the children, in which the reason for guarding our center was discussed, helped them to accept it and to see it as a protective measure for the security and welfare of the center. So don't misunderstand it and feel bad about it; just tell the guard your reason for entering the center and he will lead you to the office. Someone there will locate the person with whom you wish to talk.

I am quite sure that our director or our welfare officer will be informed about your visit and will greet you with the kindness and hospitality offered all visitors to our center. You can be sure that you will be invited to the UNRRA quarters and offered a cup of coffee. You will be invited to stay with us for a day or two if your time allows; you will be offered a nice, clean room and meals with the UNRRA staff or with the displaced persons[69] (DP) staff and children, as you wish. And as soon as you are ready, a discussion of the needs and problems of our children will begin in a relaxing and encouraging atmosphere. But in order to understand the needs and problems of our children, you should know a little about our institution, the service it offers, the children it accommodates, and the people it employs.

Certainly our institution is far from being a perfect one. But in order to understand the effectiveness of an institution you must first understand the total situation in which it functions. Our situation is a very peculiar one for many reasons. Our center is a rehabilitation center, an educational center, and an emigration center. It serves children of different nationalities, with different religious and cultural backgrounds. It serves children of all ages from newborn babies to adolescents of eighteen. It serves children who have suffered the most traumatic experiences, which have greatly disturbed normal development of their personality, children with serious medical defects. Every type of physical and mental disability which only war can produce is evident not only in the children, but also in the staff who instructs and serves the children in all of their needs, including understanding, affection, and love.

Another aspect of our situation, caused by the total material destruction of Europe, is the constant lack of supplies necessary in maintaining any kind of an institution. I must tell you that we are able to offer everything but complete material security. This is a rather peculiar situation as far as an institution is concerned and it is deplorable in our case, where we deal with children who have a much greater need for this kind of material security than the average child.

But in spite of all the handicaps and shortcomings you will sense an unusually high morale, an atmosphere of kindness and understanding, of love and brotherhood, created only, and I underline, *only* by the mutual understanding on the part of the staff as well as [the] children, for what is being done. I will never forget as long as I live, the understanding, the love, the friendship, the cooperation, the trust and confidence, which made up our unforgettable relationships.

Aglasterhausen is a block of buildings, built in a quadrangle with a pavement in the front of each building, with a lawn, trees, and benches in the middle of the quadrangle, surrounded from all sides by trees.

A large, three-story building with three entrances faces the road from two sides. The second flank of the quadrangle is made up of the two buildings; one rather old two-story building which faces the garden, the center, and overlooks the waving corn fields of Unterschwarzach; and not far away but withdrawn somewhat, another building, three-storied, which overlooks the center, the school, our garden and the road and fields. The third flank is made by the school and the UNRRA building. The school is a two-story modern building with a carpenter shop, a garage, and an auto repair shop on the first floor. The UNRRA building is a two-story building overlooking fields from three sides and the center from the fourth. The fourth flank is made by an old barn.

Aglasterhausen was until the year 1946 a German institution for "feebleminded" children and adults, but mostly for children. It shouldn't be surprising to anyone who knows the mentality of Nazi Germany and their methods of perfecting the German "race" that most of the poor creatures who were unfortunate enough to be fished out by the SS and put in the institution were usually in a "humanitarian" way removed from this world in order to save the German race and in order to save food "wasted" for their nourishment. Doctors and professionally trained nurses were in charge of this mass murder. That was Aglasterhausen as it was.

Aglasterhausen is now a children's center, or we can call it a children's institution for children of other than German nationality, who don't have or don't know anything about their parents. Although this was the rule, we also have children whose DP parents are for some reason unable to care for their children. We have approximately 105[70] Polish, Czechoslovakian, Latvian, Lithuanian, Estonian, Yugoslavian, Hungarian, Romanian, and Ukrainian children. We have babies, preschool children, children in the age of puberty and adolescence. We bring the children from DP camps; we find them in German families, and some of them are new refugees from territories occupied by Russians. They arrive in groups large and small or singly. They are undernourished and usually in great need of good medical care. They have no property and the clothing they wear is a mixture of all types of old uniforms, from German cloth to Russian military clothing. Some of them have lice; others are very clean, but all of them show years of neglect and deprivation. Some of them come from a high cultural background and have no education at all. Some bring an understanding and love for freedom, democracy, and brotherhood and are readily able to establish good relationships. Others, poisoned by the Nazi propaganda, carry hatred and distrust to everybody and to anybody. All are in need of good care and much affection.

Our staff is composed of three groups of people: UNRRA staff, DP staff, and German helpers. UNRRA (about eight in number) is composed of Americans, English, and one French girl. UNRRA is considered a "millionaire class" because they have plenty of everything and a country of their own (USA) to which they can and plan to return. The duties of the UNRRA staff are mostly of administrative character. Their staff is composed of a director, welfare worker, secretary, medical officer, supply officer, food distributing and meal planning officer, and drivers. The DP staff numbers thirty and is composed of myself (a school principal and liaison between UNRRA and DP staff), teachers, shoemakers, tailors, carpenters, auto mechanics, and a cook. The German staff are cleaning men, dressmakers, laundry women, kitchen helpers, etc. And I should add to the DP staff a part-time Catholic priest, a Protestant pastor, and a Rabbi.

When a new child or a new group arrives, the first step is a medical examination. The next step is usually taken by myself. I try in a very kind but firm manner to explain to every child what kind of institution we have (or I should say rather what kind of group of which he will become a member), emphasizing the fact that we are an international center, and that children of different nationalities and religions live happily together. We offer every newcomer a hearty welcome and promise him assistance in his needs. But what is even more important is the welcome he gets from the groups and the interest shown by the groups. Although they do not accept the newcomer right away, they show their willingness to accept him eventually. The houseparents take charge of the boy and girl, and try to make them feel that here they will find a place where someone will care about them and where they and their feelings will be respected by everybody.

But now let's speak a little about our services and the organization of those services. I shall start with our nursery, because it covers the most important period in development of personality. Our nursery is placed on the second floor in the UNRRA building, across from the hospital.

Right now we have about fifteen infants in our nursery, and they are placed in a very large, well-heated, and well-ventilated room. The room has a high ceiling and windows on two sides, three to a side. The other two walls are covered with paintings done by one of our children. Next to this room is the nurses' room and the next is the kitchen.

In charge of the nursery is an American-trained nurse. As for the rest of the personnel, they are rather few in number and untrained. Our past experiences with the nursery staff convinced us that we should choose kind women with an interest in children and train them in our center rather than nurses who are overly efficient and not humane enough. Although the number of nursery staff is limited and so is the training, the interest shown and the work done by that staff is remarkable. With the staff shortage we are not able to give as much individual attention to each child as would be ideal, and certainly we are not able in those circumstances to give the infants in our nursery complete emotional security, but we do our best within limitations. From the medical viewpoint and from the point of view of general care our services are superior. They are superior as far as institutions in Europe are concerned, and I think that even in the United States not many institutions can offer better care in these aspects. We have a feeding schedule for each child and we have a chart for each child above his bed, which shows and which gives instructions to each staff as to all medical, feeding, and training problems. The chart is a picture of daily changes in almost all aspects of the development of the infant. Temperature is taken twice daily, because our infants have low resistance and we have to be extremely careful in checking their physical conditions. If an illness is detected soon enough we are able to prevent it, or at least arrest it and if we are careful we can better prevent the spreading of a contagious disease all over the nursery.

Each infant is, in addition to those protective measures, seen every day by our doctor, and given a periodic thorough medical examination. The preparation of food is carefully supervised. One person is responsible for preparing food and we have a special kitchen for that purpose.

As for the food, we are using all resources available to us and go even far beyond those resources, sometimes as far as black market, to get food for our infants. It takes much imagination, a good deal of ability to make friends in the army, and to use them properly it takes days of driving a jeep on not exactly the best roads, in not exactly friendly environment, in not always pleasant weather; it takes sometimes even enough courage to do things not in accordance with the regulations of the military government to secure a minimum of milk and other food needed for our children. But we have the strength to go on, and we go on. We get all we need, and the infants get all they need. We are happy to see the results—the changes in the physical constitution of our infants, to see at last some life coming into their undernourished bodies, to see some movement of their hands and legs, some interest for the outside world shown by the, until now, apathetic little human beings. We are happy to hear a baby crying or screaming. This is the reward to the people who give their days and nights, their love and understanding to the infants. It is the only reward for their work, because their salaries range between $1.50 and $2 monthly.

It is a reward because it brings a new hope that from the physical and emotional ruins of the victims of the past war, a new, healthy, relatively secure, happy child will be transformed. It is almost impossible, after a period of several months, to recognize in the well-nourished, smiling, and full-of-life baby, the motionless wreck of a human being brought to us from a German institution. It is hard to believe such a change because it seems to be a miracle. We are happy that our nursery is not a quiet, well-organized, and scientifically sterile place, but rather a noisy playground, full of laughter, crying, and screaming, full of life and children's activity. We are glad that our infant is able to cry when he needs it, able to scream when he feels like screaming. We are glad that he is able to express his feelings and needs, able to play, to act, and to respond like an average child.

From our nursery we move to the kindergarten. The kindergarten is located on the second floor in the school building. It is not the best location since the schoolrooms are on the same floor, but the large, airy rooms and good system of central heating had to be taken into consideration.

The kindergarten consists of a large bedroom with windows on two walls; a washroom with what we consider in Europe modern wash basins, two bath tubs, and with a space for each child's towel, toothbrush, toothpaste, and glass; a very large light playroom with all kinds of toys; a dining room with little tables and chairs; and a room for nurses located next to the children's bedrooms.

We have at present eight children in the kindergarten and two nurses. The nurses are not trained for this kind of job. They have, however, a good understanding of our children and their needs. They are all called upon to offer a great amount of kindness, affection, and attention to each individual child. They are supervised and instructed by an American-trained kindergarten teacher, and their work is satisfactory.

The somewhat limited number of toys, most of which came from our director's friends in the United States, and some of which were made in our carpenter shop or even tailor shop, give the children a good opportunity to express their feelings, abilities, and interests. Our playroom is a good place for our children to fulfill their needs for exploration and gives the staff the opportunity to watch and learn to understand our children.

Little things like a toothbrush, a personal towel, give the child the feeling of possession, of owning something. The common washroom makes the training easier for some children, because some of them seeing other children washing or bathing try to imitate them. As for the toilet training, although each child is being trained individually, an occasional "group session" gives the children a great "kick" and speeds training. Every effort is made to help the children to become as independent as possible, to learn to wash, eat, and live in a socially accepted manner. No one interrupts them in play, and all quarrels, fights, and misunderstandings between them are handled with much patience, understanding, and kindness.

Although their food is prepared in the common kitchen, everything is done, within our very real limits, to give them as much variety in meals as possible. The children are seen every day by our doctor and given excellent medical care. They are not separated from other children in our center, but see them daily and on many occasions play with them. They move freely around the whole center but are always supervised. They take an active part in our parties, see our movies, and enjoy outdoor activities all year round.

These children are the most confused ones, the most sensitive ones; it takes a great deal of understanding, kindness, and goodwill to help them understand and accept the world that is, for them, a new and often confusing experience.

We move now to the large "front" building. Although it is one building, it is composed of two units, which are connected only by a common dining room. On the left side on the second floor are a few small rooms which accommodate three to four boys aged twelve and thirteen years, a large dormitory which accommodates about ten boys [aged] six to ten, a room for houseparents, rooms for some of the teachers, and washrooms. The second floor is composed of about ten small rooms, each for two boys in ages from thirteen up, rooms for teachers, houseparents, and some of our maintenance staff.

The rooms for the girls are larger than the boys' rooms and more attractively furnished. On the second floor is one large room which accommodates little girls from six to ten years. Each floor has a large washroom with one bathtub, which is rather inadequate for twelve girls.

All children had a choice in selecting their own roommates within certain limits. The limits were age difference, possible sex problems, etc.

Naturally, boys live only on the boys' side and girls on the girls' side. This freedom of choosing their own roommates reveals so vividly that all nationality and religious prejudices and hatred are artificial, man-made products. Our children, against all principles of prejudice, choose in most cases roommates of different nationality or religion.

When you come to our center you will notice not only a display of flags in all rooms, but you will find on the tables the New Testament and a Hebrew book. The religious and nationality differences are not at all a problem in our center. If we have a problem, we have it with the outside Catholic, Jewish, or Protestant groups, but never with children, and very seldom with the staff. Don't understand me and think that we try to deprive the children of their religions, or that we try to weaken them in their faith. On the contrary, we provide them with religious education through a priest, a pastor, and a rabbi or Hebrew teacher. We encourage them to take part in religious services. We also help them to understand each other's customs and beliefs and to understand everyone's right to have their own nationality or religion. In order to achieve this, we, the staff, and all the children celebrate all holidays together. We celebrate all Catholic, Protestant, and Jewish holidays. We celebrate together all national holidays, and on a national day of each national group you will see all the flags fluttering in the wind over our center. Don't be too surprised if you meet Catholic and Protestant children in a Jewish synagogue or Jewish children in a Protestant church. And do not be surprised if you march into one of our rooms for boys and find on the wall a picture of the Madonna and around her, pictures of pinup girls! Do not be surprised, like Mrs. S (director of JDC)[71] who once asked us, "How come that last Sunday so many blond Jewish boys came to the service in the Army Synagogue of Heidelberg?" The large group of "Jewish" boys was a group of our Protestant Estonian children. And you certainly missed something if you were not at the midnight service on Christmas Eve in the Catholic Church in Neunkirchen. There you would have found a real mixture of all faiths and all nationalities of our center's staff and children.

In all the world religion is a tough subject, many being afraid to discuss it, to avoid any misunderstanding or hurting someone's feelings, yet in our center everybody is proud of his own religion but at the same time respects what everyone else believes. We are not afraid to talk about our beliefs and feelings. Our harmony is complete and our faith is one, the faith in one peace-loving world, in one brotherhood, in a world without hate.

Let's talk a bit about our houseparents. Everything is not always congenial between the children and houseparents. Many repressed feelings about the loss of their own parents cause frequent outbursts of hostility. However, it is the general agreement among the children that the houseparents spend all their time, all their energy for the children's welfare, and that all their love and understanding is transferred to them. They awaken the children and they are last to go to bed. They change or supervise the change of linens. They eat with the children and are always present to help them in any possible way. They do not work a limited amount of time, nor do they rest on holidays or Sundays. They do not work for money. Their salary is enough to buy one package of American cigarettes on the black market. They work day after day, night after night. Their only aim is the welfare of "their" children.

Let's see what goes on in the Center during a normal weekday. Life in the Center begins to stir at 7:00 a.m. That is the waking time for the children of school age. However, the cooks and the houseparents wake up almost one hour earlier. At 7:00 a.m. the Center is full of life. The children get up, some of them promptly; some of them like to stretch out for fifteen more minutes. The time between 7:00 and 8:00 a.m. is used for washing, cleaning, and sweeping bedrooms, done by the children. At 8:00 a.m. everybody congregates in our big dining room. The dining room is decorated for all kinds of holidays, and the decorations last from one holiday to another. Six children are seated together, and here again they choose their own company. In the meantime, our kitchen staff, which consists of two DPs and four German men and women, prepares breakfast.

The kitchen itself is a very clean, airy, and modern one. Next to the kitchen is a small room from which all meals are served through a window. Each table provides two waiters and waitresses. The waiters and waitresses change automatically every day. The tables are set by the boys and girls, whoever arrives first. Usually the boys are down first. The setting of the table is not a routine, and the children were never asked to do it, but we have always had many volunteers.

After breakfast, the children go to their rooms and prepare for school. School begins at 8:45 a.m. We have one class for beginning Polish children, one for the more advanced, and two high school classes. We also have one class for Estonian children and one for Latvian children. The Czechoslovakian and Lithuanian children who understand a little Polish join the Polish classes. Other children who don't understand either of these languages are given individual instruction by me. Our teaching staff consists of the school principal (myself), two Polish teachers, one Latvian, one Estonian, one art, one handicraft, one priest, and a part-time Protestant minister. The program, which is a rather difficult one, is planned and set up at the staff meeting. We teach writing and reading separately in nationality groups, mathematics and geometry, national geography in the lower grades, international geography in higher grades, national history in lower, world history in higher grades, physics and chemistry in higher grades, and what may seem rather strange—democracy. Yes, we really teach democracy in school. We have instructions in art and singing, and we have gym. At 12:00 noon we have lunch. After lunch at 1:00 p.m., the school continues on to 2:30. At 3:00 p.m. our vocational program begins. We try to encourage everyone to take part in this program, and we expect everyone to choose his line of interest. We have instructions in auto mechanics, electricity, mechanical drawing, plumbing, cooking, knitting, bookkeeping, typewriting, commercial art, and individual instruction in music. Twice weekly we have religious instruction or Hebrew lessons for Jewish children.

I would like to tell you about the problem of religious instruction, which is rather complicated. Some of the Polish Catholic girls and boys refused to attend religious instructions. A staff meeting with UNRRA was called, and the question was discussed. Some staff members insisted that the children should be forced to attend, and if they refused, [they] should be punished. Especially the Catholic priest insisted that strong disciplinary measures should be taken. It was for many of us, not Catholic, a very touchy subject. We wanted to cooperate with the Catholic priest, and yet we were unable to convince him that children should not be forced to attend religious services, that it would only make them more resentful toward religion, and that no child should be punished, especially our children who had behind them years of punishment. After a long debate, feeling that no compromise could be worked out and no understanding achieved, the demand of the priest was flatly rejected by the entire group: [by the] UNRRA director and welfare officer, by the teachers' staff, and by the houseparents' staff. It was agreed we should encourage our children to attend the instruction classes, but that no punishment should be given. A meeting of Catholic children was called and the matter discussed.

At another time the Hebrew teacher complained that a group of Jewish boys refused to attend Hebrew lessons. He did not ask for punishment, but he asked for help. Again a meeting of Jewish children was called, the importance of Jewish education was discussed, and the children [were] encouraged to attend classes.

Twice weekly we have a choir and band rehearsal. Five thirty p.m. is the dinnertime. After dinner the playrooms are open. Although there are two playrooms, one for the younger and one for the older children, they are allowed to play together if they wish. The playrooms are supervised by staff members, but the children are in charge of keeping them clean and in order. They do their best, although the rooms often look like a mess. There are all kinds of games in the playrooms, from children's billiards to ping-pong, and all kinds of table games. The walls are covered with murals done by one of our boys.

At 8:00 p.m. a snack is given, and at 10:00 p.m. the playrooms are cleaned and closed by the child in charge. After 10:00 p.m. we expect everybody to be in his or her room. The lights are turned off by the children themselves, except in the dormitories for younger children where the houseparents have to take charge.

At the same time the school begins, the German maintenance workers start to clean the buildings; cooks are washing dishes and kettles and preparing for lunch; shoemakers, carpenters, tailors, dressmakers, electricians, and plumbers start their daily work. What with the Center's 150 children, thirty DP staff, and eight UNRRA staff members, it takes a lot of work to maintain such a large group.

At the same time, in the nursery, the nurses have a full day's work on their hands. In the kindergarten the children are starting to play; in the hospital the doctor starts to examine children, and the dentist gives help in emergency cases. In the UNRRA quarters the day also begins. Supply officers prepare trucks and cars and get traveling orders. The welfare officer is already in her office and so is the secretary. The food supply officer is in the kitchen discussing meals and menus and food problems with the cooks. The director is on her rounds around the Center. The Center is at work. Everybody works hard, everybody gives their best to secure and provide the best for the children.

I would like to tell you more about our recreational program and about the many parties and outdoor recreations we have. As I said before, we have good playrooms, and our children make fairly good use of them. But during the summer afternoons, the children spend most of their free time outside, playing soccer, volleyball, playing all kinds of games, or just lying on the grass in the garden and relaxing. Very often when we have a truck available and enough gas, a large group of children goes to nearby Neckarburken for swimming.

Fred with Aglasterhausen volleyball players.
Fred is pictured second from the right.

Once a week we have movies. The projector and pictures come from the American Army in Mosbach. Almost every Saturday afternoon, the children have a party and a dance with refreshments. And on every national holiday, we throw a big party with the entire population of the Center participating. We have a library and a printed weekly newspaper. You will say that almost all children's institutions in the United States have some kind of newspaper. Yes, it is simple in the United States but not in Germany. Let us see. We were thinking about some kind of paper, which would serve the children and the DP staff, something which would have educational value, something which would allow the children to express their interests and their feelings. So we decided to have a weekly paper. But as I said before, it was not so simple. First we had to get permission from the army. In order to get permission, we had to get an American officer who would help us. Finally, we found such an officer and got the permission. Then we went to Heidelberg to find a printer who would agree to print our paper. We spent several days looking for such a printer, and each time we had to ride about thirty kilometers from our Center to Heidelberg. With some luck, and with the help of good Chesterfields[72] and some Hershey's, we found a printer, but he told us we would have to get paper. You cannot buy paper in Germany without a requisition from the military government. So again, we had to find an army officer who would help us. We got the necessary requisition, but we still did not have the paper. We went through all the wholesale and retail paper stores in Heidelberg before we found one where we could get paper. So, we have a paper! The Christmas issue was published in English, Polish, Latvian, Lithuanian, Estonian, Hungarian, and Yiddish—all in one. It also included pictures.

Aglasterhausen children celebrating Christmas.

Our children have plenty of physical activity. Usually some of the staff members take part in these activities and instruct the children in them. The interest in sports is great; both in winter and summer, we encourage the children to play and to be active. In the winter the whole Center is empty. Life is concentrated in the nearby hills, where the children enjoy sleighing and skiing, building snowmen, and fighting with snowballs. We also have boxing. Or perhaps I should say we had boxing. When we got the boxing gloves, the fighting spirit was so high that on the next day our doctor was busy. It did not discourage our boys, but it did discourage us, and we are now more careful with this particular sport. The majority of children, especially older ones, expressed a wish for organized soccer and volleyball teams and requested some kind of uniform. We realized what it would mean to fulfill their wishes and what it would mean for them to become members of a team, wear uniforms, and represent the Center. We also took into consideration the psychological effect it would have on the rest of the children, the importance of group competition in the development and strengthening of the children's egos. So now we have a soccer team and a volleyball team. I wish you could have seen the children training every day, working hard, discussing each player on the team, trying to help each other to improve, arranging and rearranging the teams.

One day one of our girls on the UNRRA staff came back from Mosbach with the news that she had been able to arrange a volleyball match with the XX Infantry Division of the American Army[73] stationed in Mosbach. Five minutes later the whole Center knew the news. Everyone was excited, and most of all the children who played on the team. If you could have gone through the Center on this day, you would have heard only one topic of discussion: "Have we a chance?" "Maybe a miracle will happen and we will win," and so forth. Everybody was talking about this great event, and everybody was discussing the chances. It was their first contest, and it was their first chance. Our boys trained twice as hard as before, went to bed at 9:00 p.m. Finally, at a special meeting they decided who would play on the team. The great day came. UNRRA provided trucks and cars for all children of school age, and for all staff members who wanted to go. Mosbach is about twenty-five kilometers away from Aglasterhausen. When we arrived in Mosbach, it was about 8:00 p.m. To tell you the truth, when I saw the six-foot-tall Americans, I became pessimistic about the outcome of the match. I also was worried as to what effects losing their first game would have on the children. And I saw that everybody else was also rather upset. However, when the game started, everybody, all our children and staff, all the American GIs who had come to watch the game, were cheering our team, and the spirit rose higher every minute. Our children became more and more confident and played better and better. The first game was won by us 17–15, the second 15–3, and the last one 15–0. You should have heard the screams of our children. It was a great event. It was a great evening. It also was something more for them. A new spirit, a new, hitherto unknown feeling of security and strength entered into them—a willingness to fight and to win, a belief that they have an equal and fair chance. Even the fact that one of our trucks broke down on the way home did not change the atmosphere. This night on the German road, with a broken truck after the first won battle in their new lives, was a new and wonderful adventure after the many years of misery and fear.

But this was only the beginning. Our soccer team went ahead with their plans and arranged a match with the German soccer team in Unterschwarzach. The German soccer team was an adult team, and when we heard about it, we were again concerned about the difference in physical strength and about the possible defeat, which could have a bad effect on the feelings and growing self-respect of our children. When the day of the match came, many of us felt apprehensive. We were not playing Americans, but Germans. We did not face a cheering audience of GIs, but rather hostile Germans. The whole German population of Unterschwarzach came to cheer their team. But also every living soul in our Center went to the match to cheer our team. And our team put up a real fight and won 2–1. This was not a victory anymore. This was a triumph. They had won against adults, they had won against Germans, and they had proven to themselves and to the whole world that they were on the march again, on the march to life.

PHOTO COURTESY OF THE FRED FRAGNER ESTATE

Three girls who played for the Aglasterhausen band.

One day we received musical instruments from the YMCA in the United States—plenty of new, good instruments…enough to provide [for] a small band. There were more children who wanted to learn music than there were instruments, and the music teacher, who arrived shortly afterward, divided the group into classes and started individual and group instruction. After six weeks, our band played one song. After two more weeks, two more songs, and so on. The band was of mixed sex and ages. They took their work very seriously and practiced studiously. When they knew several songs and marches, the whole group requested special fancy suits for the band. It was quite a problem to make special suits for about ten children, and when I went to UNRRA to discuss this problem, I was a little skeptical. However, our director and our welfare officer understood that the suits meant something more for our children than just suits, and they agreed to make them. Our girls helped considerably. The band played at all occasions—birthdays, holidays, parties, and so forth. I will never forget the birthdays of our UNRRA officers. When an UNRRA officer had a birthday, the members of the band woke them up at 5:00 a.m. by themselves (or asked the houseparents to wake them up) and marched toward the UNRRA quarters. Then they would line up in the hall on the third floor, where the bedrooms are located, and here everything broke loose. First "Jingle Bells" and then all the other songs they knew. Even today, I cannot understand why they always chose "Jingle Bells." Anyway, everybody was awakened and came out in the hall in pajamas and bathrobes. And when the celebrant came out, everybody sang "Happy Birthday."

You should also not miss our movies, shown every Friday evening. Everybody in the Center quits for Friday evening. Cowboy pictures, musical comedies, and gangster movies get the best reception. About two hours before the movie is to be shown, a group of children starts preparation in the dining room, setting up chairs and benches. There is plenty of excitement and fun when the pictures are being shown. Laughter, remarks in all languages, whistling, screaming, and when kissing takes place on the screen the children, with a special delight, imitate every kiss. They enjoy movies as much as a normal child enjoys them or maybe even more. Many of them saw movies for the first time in their lives at the age of sixteen or seventeen.

Food comes through UNRRA. The children are supposed to get about 2,700 calories daily. However, our UNRRA staff, and many friends in the army who become interested in our Center, try to help our children in every possible way. Also, UNRRA's friends in the USA send food packages for our children, so as a result, instead of 2,700 calories, they get 3,500 to 4,000 calories daily. Also, when military or Red Cross units were moved away from a certain district our UNRRA was able to get supplies from them. We have our own garden, but the seeds have to be secured on the black market. The menus are prepared with great care. A special committee consisting of the houseparents, a cook, and the UNRRA officer plan the meals. The houseparents are informed by the children about the kind of meals they would like to have. In every institution, the meal planning is an important part of the overall program. In our Center, it is even more important because of the undernourishment of our children, because of their need for tasty and nourishing meals, because of their desire for a great variety in meals, and because of their different tastes, due to their different national and cultural backgrounds.

The laundry is done by German women under the supervision of a DP girl. Once a week every child takes their laundry and brings it down to one of our supply rooms. The laundry supervisor receives the soiled laundry, marks each piece with the child's initials, and gives the child a receipt. Several days later, on a specific day and during certain hours, the clean laundry is returned to the children. Not everything went so smoothly in the beginning, because of the many thefts by German employees. However, our guard checked them very carefully, and everything possible was done to prevent it.

Once a week, the teachers and houseparents have a meeting with all children of school age. In these meetings all problems, events, and happenings in our Center are discussed with the children. German is the language used because the majority of the children understand and speak German. If a child does not understand, we always have someone who is able to translate into the child's own language. Most of the children like the meeting and take a very active part, but not all of them. Some just sit and sleep, and it takes a great deal of understanding and patience to make them talk and express their feelings about what is going on in the Center.

Almost every week a DP staff meeting takes place. All kinds of problems regarding our work, children's behavior, staff relationships, [and] children's relationships are discussed. Besides those meetings we also have meetings with the UNRRA staff, teachers' conferences, and individual conferences between the UNRRA director or welfare officer and staff members, not to speak of the regular interviews with the children, done by the UNRRA welfare officer, and informal interviews and talks between teachers and children.

These frequent meetings make it possible to iron out large and small problems as soon as they arise, making for more understanding and cooperative relationships between all those concerned with the Center. As for the children, the meetings have a much more significant meaning. It gives them a picture of the work done by UNRRA and DP staff and an understanding of the many problems involved in maintaining our Center. It gives them a chance to participate in this work and to accept responsibilities. They have a chance to express their thinking and feelings about every stage of our life in the Center. It gives them a feeling of self-respect, an opportunity to learn democracy, and an assurance of their rights within certain unwritten social laws and socially accepted limitations. They learn to trust people with whom they live and work, and understand better some of their own problems and needs. It helps them to accept help and to make good use of it.

These meetings help the Center as a whole, because without everyone's understanding and cooperation, the work done would be unsatisfactory. The existing good relationships give everyone at the Center a great deal of satisfaction and gratification.

The relationship between the children and the staff is rather a good one, thanks to good understanding on the part of the staff. It is a relationship of mutual understanding and respect—mutual cooperation and affection. Everything is not always so beautiful, but of course if it were, it would not be normal.

The relationship between the children and the UNRRA is a little different. The UNRRA represents to the children a mystic fairy tale, which they had heard at home as young children, a fairy tale about a country with plenty of everything for everybody, a land of millionaires, cowboys, and gangsters. UNRRA represents to them a country whose army liberated them from long years of slavery. They have a kind of admiration for the UNRRA staff; they have some sentimental, romantic, irrational feelings, and some unreasonable awe for them. But the uniforms UNRRA officers are wearing remind them too much of the uniform which represented hate, punishment, and deaths of their loved ones. And thus, their feelings about UNRRA are rather conflicted. They still, in spite of the great admiration and good individual relationships, have some reservations, some mistrust, and some anxiety toward the people in uniform. To them, they are strange people who came to a strange continent to find them, people who "cannot understand what we went through." They have a need to be helped, but they wonder with a great deal of anxiety as to why, for what reason the help is offered, what will be the price they will have to pay, and if they should really accept it. They are accustomed so much to the fact that they must pay, and pay plenty, for everything they get.

The relationships between individual members of the DP staff are in general satisfactory. A good understanding of their functions, of the need for cooperation in order to fulfill those functions, similar past experience, similar hopes for the future, make the relationships constructive. Personal daily contact and a well-developed social life help a great deal. But one feeling, common to all the staff members, dominates all other feelings and helps to settle all misunderstandings and creates a good, cooperative relationship. I may describe the feeling as "everything for the children." The feeling, as I said, is common and dominating. And in spite of all differences in national, religious, and cultural backgrounds, in spite of differences in their thinking and feeling as to what and how it should be done for the children, everyone agrees that everything should be tried and done if possible. Everyone is ready to do his best for the sake of the children and their future.

UNRRA is doing an outstanding job in our Center. Perhaps it is because we were fortunate in getting a good staff. They are few in number, but their responsibilities and their work is great. They know no limits to work hours or in distance if something must be brought for our children. They have a wonderful understanding of children in general, and especially our children. They are ready to do everything to help them. They understand the mistrust they have to face. They know about the conflicted feelings of our children and DP staff toward them. They have, however, confidence in our children, in the DP staff, in their own work, [and] in the final outcome. They offer their time, their energy, and their efforts. They give their love and understanding. And if one could measure their work and the results of it, it could be measured only by the amount of love and response on the part of children and the DP staff. Is it a big loving family? No. It is an institution where everybody respects and tries to understand everyone else, where everyone works for a certain goal and tries to give his best. We are a happy community, and although it is a slow and not always encouraging process, in the long range it works. It must work.

You see, I do not think that you will really have the best understanding of Aglasterhausen from what I have told you. To understand and appreciate it, you would have to be in Aglasterhausen. You have to see our children, how they live and how they play, how they love and how they hate, how they laugh and how they cry. You have to witness the change from physical and mental disability to physical and mental health.

There is something in Aglasterhausen, in its children and staff, in the work and hardship, its happiness and sorrow, its hope for new, brighter futures for everyone, that makes Aglasterhausen unforgettable to everyone who has been in our Center. It is as the first glimmer of the rising sun.

Many, many times Fred recounted to friends and family that it was his time at Aglasterhausen that gave him back his life. Having lost his own childhood when his father died, Fred felt that his time with the children of Aglasterhausen refreshed him and provided a setting where his own inner child was resurrected in all of his mischievous and optimistic glory.

Kay and Fred during happy times at Aglasterhausen.

Fred and Kay would certainly be missed by the Center. The Center director for UNRRA, Rachel Greene, wrote the Fragners the following note on their departure:

> To Mr. and Mrs. Fragner,
>
> The Center which you have helped to build will seem a different place without you both. But we all hope, as I know you do that the need for it will not last much longer and that others like yourselves will soon have an opportunity to leave. I am glad that you are able to go with our first group of children to America and hope that you will have a full and happy life in your new country.
>
> Signed, Rachel Green, April 21, 1946

Fred also received a typed letter signed by G. Larson Sperry, the principal welfare officer, on an UNRRA letterhead and dated June 27, 1946:

To Whom It May Concern

This is to certify that Mr. Fred Fragner was with us here from October 1945 until he left for the USA in May 1946. Mr. Fragner came here as our school principal, as a teacher, and with his wife, as a houseparent.

Mr. Fragner did an excellent job in all three of these capacities. As the school principal he was responsible for setting up a program which included teaching in Polish, Estonian, Latvian, Lithuanian, English, Hebrew, German, and occasional tutoring in other languages when we had only one or two of some other nationality. The program also included vocational training in carpentry, shoemaking, baking, tailoring, auto mechanics, [and] electricity. Mr. Fragner managed, in spite of the problems of such a program, plus a constantly moving school population, to have an orderly school set up. He was just as efficient in his own teaching as in his duties as principal. His teaching staff had great respect and liking for him.

In his contacts with the children, both as teacher and houseparent, Mr. Fragner showed unusual understanding and tolerance. He was so imbued with the hope of an international world, a peace-loving world, that he tried to teach this assorted group of children the importance of living together amiably, and he succeeded. Mr. Fragner was the person most responsible for the fact that we had no friction among or between national or religious groups. He was a splendid teacher and personal example of his teaching. As in the case of his teaching staff, the children and the rest of the staff had real respect for Mr. Fragner as well as love for him.

Mr. Fragner had no limits in his working day, or his duties.

He enjoyed his work and spent many hours at it, both day and night. He organized a newspaper and followed through on all of the publishing details of it. He also planned and carried out many observances of holidays—all done with good detail and good thought.

We can recommend Mr. Fragner highly for his relationships with adults and children, for his good organizational ability, for his ambition in his work, and for all of the abovementioned qualities that prevailed during his stay with us.

Signed, G. Larson Sperry

What were likely the most important messages from Fred's perspective were the notes of gratitude and fond farewells that came from the Aglasterhausen children—*his* children:

"To my dear parents as evidence of sincere appreciation for good times in our school."—Ursula Janton

"To our unforgettable 'parents' Mr. and Mrs. Fragner. As evidence of sincere appreciation wishing all the luck in the years ahead." —Lilka Bornsztajn

"To my dear parents to remind them in the future, well wishing."—little Haneczke

"To my dear foster parents to remind them of pleasant days in our school in the future."—Jadzia Zmidek

"To my dear pop and mom, my best wishes in life."—little Halinka Goldszlager

"To my dear parents with appreciation for all the days in Aglasterhausen."—Sincerely, Sojkiewicz

"To my dear caretakers before we say good-bye to remember our days in Aglasterhausen."—Abram Frydman

"To my dear parents!!! As evidence of my sincere appreciation for all the kindness to us in our school. From the troublemaker who brought so much troubles."—L. Frydman[74]

"To my dear parents!!! As evidence of my goodwill for giving so much kindness in our school!!!"—Druszkowski Roman

"To my dear mom and dear dad to remind them of pleasant days in Aglasterhausen."—Hanna Starkman[75]

"To our best caretaker and teacher with deepest appreciation." —Janusz Andrej

"To my kind caretakers, I wish all the happiness and joy on their new road."—Rapaport Molelr

"Remembering: love, honesty and hope are your future." —V. Naujokaite

"To my beloved and always remembered parents."—their student Antoni Kasprazak

"To my dear parents, I wish you a long life and happiness."—Matek Wajsbordy

"To my dear caretakers, I thank you for all the good times we had in our school."—Zalia Rusin

"To my dear parents for all their kindness to us in Aglasterhausen."—Dina Frydman

"One never forgotten, Mom and Dad Fragner, forever indebted, I wish that your future fulfills all your dreams."—S. Musrkatblat

Notes

68   Fred Fragner, Aglasterhausen scrapbook. Date unknown.

69   During World War II, millions of individuals were removed from
their native surroundings due to the circumstances of the war. These people
became known as "displaced persons" (DP) and were housed in displaced
persons camps or DP camps. Even two years after World War II, there were
still 850,000 displaced persons living in DP camps across Western Europe.
Wikipedia, s.v. "Displaced Persons Camp," last modified June 28, 2015,
accessed June 28, 2015, http://en.wikipedia.org/wiki/Displaced_Persons_
camp.

70   Fred's scrapbook contains an apparent discrepancy regarding the
approximate number of children at Aglasterhausen. While this part of his
account references 105 children, later he refers to 150 children. It is also
possible that these numbers merely refer to two separate points in time and
that the number of children had grown. The commendation letter to Fred from
G. Larson Sperry of UNRRA—found at the end of this chapter—supports the
notion of a fluctuating population, because Sperry references as problematic a
"constantly moving school population."

71   The American Jewish Joint Distribution Committee (JDC) shipped
critically needed supplies to Europe from US ports. Their mission after the
Holocaust was to ensure that all "newly liberated Jews would survive to
enjoy the fruits of freedom." The organization was founded during World
War I. "History of JDC," *American Jewish Joint Distribution Committee
(JDC)*, accessed February 21, 2015, http://archives.jdc.org/history-of-jdc/
history-1940.html.

72   Chesterfields were a common cigarette brand at the time.

73   There wasn't a Twentieth Infantry Division that served in World War II.
There was, however, a Twentieth Armored Division that activated on March
15, 1943, at Camp Campbell in Kentucky and served in Central Europe. It is
difficult to determine if this is the division Fred was referring to in this context,
if the "XX" was meant to designate something else entirely, or if it the "XX"
was meant as a redaction of the actual division number. *Wikipedia*, s.v. "20th
Armored Division (United States)," last modified March 10, 2015, accessed
July 11, 2015, https://en.wikipedia.org/wiki/20th_Armored_Division_(United_
States).

74   Additional information is presented on brothers Abram and Lolek Frydman in the chapter "Voyager."

75   Additional information is presented on this child in the chapter "Voyager."

These youth were at Aglasterhausen during the time Fred and Kay were caretakers. Many of them came to the United States with Fred and Kay as their chaperones on the USS *Marine Flasher*.

VOYAGER

Then I Myself shall gather the remnant of My flock out of all the countries where I have driven them and shall bring them back to their pasture; and they will be fruitful and multiply.

~Jeremiah 23:3.

IN APRIL OF 1946, FRED RECEIVED A CALL from the American Consulate in Stuttgart: "Look, the first boat to the United States is leaving very soon, and we are sending sixty kids. Would you mind supervising them on the trip?"

Fred replied, "Not if I can stay in the United States."

"I'm sure we can arrange it."

As he described it, Fred had been "emotionally tempted" to go to Israel. But he was physically and emotionally exhausted and didn't think that he was ready for more hardship. So, Fred escorted sixty of the Aglasterhausen children to America, where many of them would receive blessings and honors they could not have imagined when they left Germany. And many of them would remain friends with Fred for the remainder of his life.

Fred recounted the journey to the United States during his interview in the early 1990s:

> I'll never forget it. It was an army transport ship, which means it was horrible, and we embarked at Bremerhaven in

the evening, and everybody was unhappy. [But] at dinner [we] ate oranges and hot dogs and real butter—all this stuff ... unbelievable![76]

He also recounted the food provisions with a huge smile on his face:

Unbelievable stuff, you know. We had nine hundred people on the boat. At night, we hit the British Channel, and it wasn't a good night. And next morning, we come for breakfast, and we had twenty people—everybody was seasick! But one of the characteristics of the children in the Children's Center was that they were hoarding food. Here, we had so much food you couldn't imagine yet.[77]

Fred explained that he was still finding the children squirreling away food under their beds even on the boat: "They still didn't believe it that it's going to last!"

The other characteristic Fred noticed about the children was that their love of learning continued during their passage to the United States, as he would find them thirsty for more learning. Even after the eight o'clock lights out call, he would walk about to check on the children and find them still reading and studying.

On the ship of nine hundred souls, sixty were children—Fred's children. The others were crew and adult refugees. However, Fred didn't have time to find out about the others, because he was constantly busy taking care of his often seasick children. Even Kay was sick and saying, "I want to go back. I want to go back!" So it was up to Fred to make sure that all sixty-one had their needs met during the voyage.

One of the children Fred brought to the United States was Dina Frydman Balbien. Her daughter, Tema N. Merback, would later write a book on Dina's life called *In the Face of Evil*. In the book, Dina describes her experience on the voyage:

The days fly by like the springtime clouds that glide across the sky. Our departure day has arrived. John is driving us to Bremerhaven to the *USS Marine Flasher*, which will sail her cargo of immigrants to the hallowed shores of America. Sixty students from Aglasterhausen are sailing as are many of the teachers. Our dorm parents and teachers Fred and Franka [Kay] Fragner, concentration camp survivors from Czechoslovakia, will be our chaperones, continuing their dedication to the orphaned children they call "our children." The buses are lined up to leave, our small cache of belongings stowed in the storage racks on the top. Tearfully we bid our good-byes to those that will remain. Soon Aglasterhausen will be filled with the voices of a whole new group of children. In fact, Aglasterhausen under the austere guidance of Rachel Greene will remain open until February 1948, rehabilitating the lives of orphans who lost everything during the Nazi era.[78]

Dina's experience of the voyage was a bit different from those of many of the children, as she was assigned a cabin next to the captain's quarters with a woman refugee. And generally, she described the voyage as having "idyllic conditions, balmy sunshine, and clear black evening skies that glitter with millions of stars."

Our passage across the Atlantic seems to me to fly by and the night before our arrival the Captain gives a wonderful speech wishing us success in our new lives in America. He announces that we will be arriving in the morning and encourages us to get a good night's sleep so that we can all be topside when we arrive. That evening we are so excited that I don't think any of us sleep a wink.[79]

As the ship lands, the ship's loudspeaker recites the poem written by Emma Lazarus,[80] a Jewish girl from a distant time. The ending lines ring out, so familiar to so many—and perhaps never ringing so true as with this arriving remnant—a few of the very few child survivors of the Holocaust.

> Give me your tired, your poor,
>
> Your huddled masses yearning to breathe free,
>
> The wretched refuse of your teeming shores.
>
> Send these, the homeless, tempest-tossed to me,
>
> I lift my lamp beside the golden door![81]

During his 1993 video interview, Fred was asked about what happened to the children once they landed in the United States:

> The Catholic organization in New York took the Catholics. The Protestant Church took the Protestants, and the Jewish took the Jewish. One of the Jewish kids, I forgot what was her name. Anyway, she was shot by the Germans just days from liberation. She was put in a German hospital. She was sixteen years old, and her whole family was wiped out. And she was adopted by Joshua Liebman. He was a famous Rabbi who wrote this book, *Peace of Mind*.[82] He was the first Rabbi, the first person who wrote about combining psychoanalysis and religion. She was adopted by him. And his wife was a social worker, and there was a lot of conflict. She was an only child and [*Fred smiles while recounting this*] I think the wife resented [the young girl]. It was funny, but on their way to Hollywood in 1947, they stopped in Chicago and took us to a very fancy restaurant, and he was calling waiters and saying "my daughter this" and "my daughter that," and I don't think his wife liked it.
>
> But in 1966, we had a twenty-year reunion with most of the kids, and they did extremely well—most of them.[83]

Many of the children continued studying, learning, and establishing a new generation with their own families. Dina was reunited with a family member and established a happy life in southern California with her husband Leo Balbien, a *Kindertransport*[84] survivor from Vienna, Austria. They had four children and seven grandchildren. Her daughter Tema described her as "vibrant and healthy, and she often speaks at schools, temples, and organizations of her experiences during the Holocaust." Many of the other children also went on to lead very fulfilling lives.

They were all voyagers to a bright new continent. The experiences of three of the Aglasterhausen children—brothers Lou and Abe Frydman, and Hannah Kent—are provided in greater detail. For Fred, their stories would have brought him the greatest joy because he loved them so. In many ways, what happened to these children was the centerpiece of Fred's life, and he would always be so proud of the lives they created and the good that they did in the world.

Pictured are Abe Frydman on the left and Lou Frydman on the right. The boy in the middle may have been their friend Moniek Wollman whose grandfather lived in Israel. Moniek considered telling his grandfather that Abe and Lou were his long-lost cousins so that they could immigrate to Israel and live together but it wasn't meant to be.

LOLEK AND ABRAM FRYDMAN

Brothers Abram and Lolek Frydman[85] were born in the city of Łódź, Poland, on January 3, 1929, and July 1, 1930, respectively. Later in life, they would be known as Abe and Lou.

Their father was an accountant for a textile company, and he was killed at the time the Warsaw Ghetto was dismantled. They were then shipped with their mother to Majdanek—one of the four largest death camps near Lublin, Poland, where 78,000 people were killed, about 60,000 of them Jews.[86] It was the camp from which the US Holocaust Museum got a gift of many, many shoes. Museum director Sara J. Bloomfield called the shoes "iconic symbols of the Holocaust since ... each represents an innocent life. Our millions of visitors tell us overwhelmingly that the display of victims' shoes was the most unforgettable part of their Museum experience."[87]

Upon arrival at Majdanek, the newcomers sat for a day or two in an open field. Then, the Nazis made an announcement that they were looking for experienced metalworkers. Although Lou was only twelve and Abe fourteen at the time—and they had no such experience—their mother told them they were to raise their hands and volunteer. The boys never saw their mother again, but suspected that she was killed in November of that year, along with another eighteen thousand souls all killed within a twenty-four-hour period. The "Bloody Wednesday" killing at Majdanek on November 3, 1943, was the largest single-day, single-location massacre during the Holocaust. Had their mother not had the wisdom to make the boys volunteer, their lives would likely have been lost.

Just as Fred had masqueraded as an auto mechanic to escape Buchenwald, Lou and Abe were sent to a subcamp called Budzyn. By mid-April 1943, the camp's population had risen to three thousand, including three hundred women and children. The boys were supposedly making airplanes during their stay at Budzyn, but they never saw a single plane. Although it was a truly horrible place, it was the *only* subcamp where the inmates were not killed on that fateful day in November.

Lou and Abe were shipped to several camps over the course of the war but somehow managed to stay together until about two or three weeks prior to their liberation. At that time, they were on a death march toward the east, toward Dachau. Abe was the older and stronger of the two. Lou eventually was not able to get up, and that should have been his demise. So, he urged Abe to continue on without him. This most certainly would have broken Abe's heart. Unbeknownst to Abe, however, Lou caught a break and was not shot. He found that his short rest and the gift of an apple had revived him and enabled him to continue.

Meanwhile, Abe also had a close call with death, and he was convinced that Lou had already met his end and never looked for his brother.

Lou, however, felt strongly that Abe had survived, and so he set out to look for him. They eventually met up, and shortly afterward they were approached by an UNRRA officer and asked if they would like to go to a school for orphaned children. The woman was Rachel Green, and the school was Aglasterhausen.

At ages fifteen and sixteen, the boys agreed to the offer once the woman gave them an affirmative answer to the question they posed: "If we come to your school and if we don't like it, will we be able to leave?"

Their decision to enroll in Aglasterhausen rewarded them abundantly with friends, learning, and an eventual trip to the United States. Lou always said that the philosophy at Aglasterhausen seemed to be that the kids should be kids and that they should have fun. The children were also discouraged from telling each other about the horrors they had experienced. Aglasterhausen was a place for restoring the joys of youth and commencing the healing process.

The decision to send children to the United States was not a clear choice. After the children had been in Aglasterhausen for about a year, there was much ado about where they would go. The Israelis were interested in the Jewish kids and wanted to take them to Israel. The British, in the meantime, stepped forward and said, "No." They didn't want children to be trained as soldiers.

And then the Israelis said, "Well, if you wouldn't let them come to Israel, we won't let them go to England." This spat was resolved when both sides chose the United States as an acceptable compromise.

Abe was one of the sixty children Fred escorted to the United States. Unfortunately, Lou was ill at the time the ship was scheduled to leave and had to take a later transport. This was only the brothers' second separation. The separation continued, however, when they landed in the states because they were put in separate foster homes. Abe lucked out with his foster home, and he maintained a [lifelong] relationship with his foster family. Lou's situation, however, was not a happy one. Lou always suspected that the family he stayed with took him in for the money rather than in the spirit of altruism. Lou attended James Monroe High School in the Bronx. He could barely speak English and got no real help learning. If he asked his foster mother for sugar to put in his coffee, she replied, "Sugar? They send sugar to Europe. We don't have any!"

Fortuitously, as soon as the boys turned eighteen, they were free to live wherever they wanted. They lived together until Lou married his wife, Jane, in December 1954. Eventually, the boy who spoke only broken English graduated from Columbia University with a degree in sociology and a commitment to work a minimum of eighteen months for Jewish Family Services in Cincinnati, Ohio. This was the agency that had paid his full tuition and most of his living expenses to assist Lou in finishing his master's degree.

Ironically, Fred and Kay were also in Cincinnati at this time, and this gave them the opportunity to reconnect. Lou and Jane lived only about a mile and a half from the Fragners, and Lou and Fred liked to play cards together.

Abe would eventually get a law degree, and he became both a lawyer and accountant while Lou went on to get a PhD in social work in 1968. Lou was offered three academic teaching positions and would choose the third offer in Kansas, where he had a rich and rewarding professional life.

Collectively, the two brothers went on to have five sons and five grandchildren. Lou died January 24, 2012—about eighteen months after his brother Abe.

Even after Fred and Kay moved from Cincinnati, Fred and Lou maintained their friendship over the years, and there were several reunions of the Aglasterhausen children, whose brief, but especially happy, postwar experience at the Aglasterhausen school had created deep bonds.

A picture of Hannah Starkman taken at Aglasterhausen.

HANNAH STARKMAN-KENT

Hannah Kent was also one of the Aglasterhausen children that Fred and his wife, Kay, escorted to the United States. The following is a transcript of her interview[88] with the author.

SUSAN.   So, I was wondering, Hannah, did you know Fred Fragner?

HANNAH. Yeah, I knew him. Sure, because he was like the father figure. The United Nations arranged it that, like, there was a father-mother. He had a wife, but I don't know if it was the same wife he had here, but I know he had a wife.

SUSAN.   Yes, that was Kay Fragner.

HANNAH. Yeah, Kay Fragner. And they both lived there, and we had girls and boys, and there was Leyla Leibman, who died since—who was a friend of mine—was there in that camp. Leyla Leibman, she was adopted by Rabbi Leibman who was the head of the reform movement at that time.

SUSAN. Oh, yes. And she was adopted by Rabbi Leibman?

HANNAH. Yes. At that time, I think he was the head of the reform movement of Judaism.

SUSAN. I think I had heard about her.

HANNAH. Yes, she was very bright. She was a graduate of … I forgot the school. She was very bright and very nice. She died very young.

SUSAN. Oh, she did?

HANNAH. Yes, she had cancer of the blood, I think. And she told me that she would die within two years, and I was with her all the time. The last few weeks of her life, I was with her because we were very close.

SUSAN. I'm so sorry to hear that. That must have been a huge loss to you.

HANNAH. Yeah, and I think that he liked her too—Fragner.

SUSAN. That Fred liked her also?

HANNAH. Yeah, I think so. Too much, I think.

SUSAN. I heard that Fred liked the girls very much but not in a bad way.

HANNAH. No, no. He just liked her very much.

SUSAN. Yeah, but he was appropriate. He seemed to have a fondness for women throughout his life, but was always faithful to his wife, I think.

HANNAH. Yeah. I remember her too. I didn't know her as well as I knew him, but I knew them both.

SUSAN.   Could you tell me if you remember any stories about Fred during the time you were at Aglasterhausen?

HANNAH.   Not really. When we were at Aglasterhausen, we were children, and the first time after the liberation we could be children, because we couldn't be children during the war.

SUSAN.   So you were able to be a child when you went to Aglasterhausen?

HANNAH.   Yes. The rest of my childhood [was gone], and I was already fourteen, and I don't know how because I was born in 1929 and we were liberated in 1945, I think.

SUSAN.   I know I read some writings that Fred did on Aglasterhausen. Did you know that Fred was an orphan?

HANNAH.   I didn't know that he was.

SUSAN.   Yes, he had been orphaned before the war when his father died when he was thirteen and his mother when he was fourteen. And so, I think that he had never had a childhood really.

HANNAH.   I see that. I was separated from my father at the beginning of the war because my brother and my mother went to Radom,[89] which was part of the protectorate, and thought it would be better than Łódź where I was born. My father and my sister were supposed to join us, but Łódź became part of the Reich as soon as they came into Poland, and they could never join us. I was orphaned because I didn't have any father. My sister also. I saw her in Auschwitz through the wires, and she disappeared. I don't know what happened to her.

SUSAN.   You don't know what happened to your sister?

HANNAH.   I was the youngest of three children, and when the war ended, I didn't know whoever survived, but I found out my brother survived, and I have a brother in Michigan.

SUSAN.   And what is his name?

HANNAH. Henry Starkman.

SUSAN. And so he was the only other member of your family who survived?

HANNAH. He was seven years old, and I had an older sister who I saw through the wires, and I don't know what happened to her.

SUSAN. Do you know what happened to your mother?

HANNAH. My mother was with me. She went through Auschwitz, and after there we went—when the Russians were coming close by—they sent us to Bergen-Belsen, which was a concentration camp, too, in Germany. And over there it wasn't so difficult, but my mother was very weak. Even so, we were there, but she died.

SUSAN. Oh, I see. I'm so sorry.

HANNAH. And she was buried in the mass graves with the people who died at that time in the concentration camp at Bergen-Belsen. And then I found out, after the war ended, a lot of the young men our age started traveling from different camps to others to find out who survived. I was supposed to go to Sweden, because Sweden was the first country that opened their doors for survivors, because I didn't know that I had family in the States. I found out from one of the young men, who knew my brother and knew me. My brother had survived, so I didn't go to Sweden. My brother found out that I survived and came for me. At that time, there was no transportation from place to place. There were no cars. There were no streetcars. There was nothing.

SUSAN. When you say that your brother came for you, did he come to Aglasterhausen?

HANNAH. No, he came to the place where I was at that time. I think Aglasterhausen was after. Later on, I found out also that I had a cousin. One day I was walking, and somebody who knew me said, "A soldier is looking for you." I didn't know what they were talking about, and this is a cousin of mine who lives in Michigan. So anyhow, I found my brother, and I found out that I had relatives here [in the United States]. I didn't know that, because I was a child before the war.

SUSAN.   You were very young. [*Hannah would have been about nine years old at the start of the war.*]

HANNAH. Very young.

SUSAN.   Do you have any fond recollections of Aglasterhausen?

HANNAH. It was wonderful because we could be children there again. I have kind memories of it. I cannot tell you anything special of him [*Fred*] because I didn't see him much after that. We had a ten-year reunion. I think he was there. But I didn't see her [*Kay*] ever again.

SUSAN.   Did you happen to know about a band at Aglasterhausen? I know Fred said that there was a band.

HANNAH. The band. I didn't play in it, but there were some people who knew how to play instruments. They had all kinds of things for us. It was nice. And they had teachers who taught us English. There were teachers who taught people who wanted to go to Israel after that, and it was a nice place where young people ... at that time when we didn't know what to do, where to go or what to do ... it was very nice. Yeah.

SUSAN.   So, were you one of the children who came over on the boat with Fred and Kay?

HANNAH. Was that the first boat that came over with children?

SUSAN.   Yes.

HANNAH. I don't remember. He [*Fred*] came on the same boat. Maybe we came on the same boat. But it's such a long time. I just don't remember. Don't forget, I have a daughter who is fifty-four! It was many years ago.

SUSAN. And it sounds like you have a wonderful husband.

HANNAH. I do. I was lucky.

SUSAN. You are blessed.

HANNAH. Yes, I am. It made up for all the other years.

SUSAN. Yes.

HANNAH. I cannot complain.

SUSAN. That's wonderful. I'm so happy to hear that.

HANNAH. I have two children. I have a daughter.

SUSAN. And her name is Susan?

HANNAH. Susan, and she has three children.

SUSAN. Oh, you have grandchildren.

HANNAH. Yeah.

SUSAN. So, besides your daughter Susan, you have a son also?

HANNAH. Yes. He lives here in New York.

SUSAN. And what is his name?

HANNAH. Jeffrey. I just saw him this morning. We had lunch together.

SUSAN. Oh, wonderful. Good to have family close by.

HANNAH. Uh huh. So, this is the story. And Fragner I saw ... we had the ten-year reunion.

SUSAN. And so where did your ten-year reunion take place?

HANNAH. In New York. I think it was in New York, in a hotel. I think it was in New York. At this point, I don't remember.

SUSAN. Uh huh. And someone told me there was another more recent reunion in the Catskills. Do you remember going to that one?

HANNAH. I may have, but I don't remember it.

SUSAN. Uh huh. So, you didn't know that Fred was an orphan?

HANNAH. Maybe this is why he was interested in orphans and the whole thing.

SUSAN. All his life he was very interested in children.

HANNAH. We were all orphans. We didn't know that anybody else survived.

SUSAN. His father was a diamond cutter in Czechoslovakia. His father died, and his mother died about a year later, and Fred was an orphan, and he became a street child.

HANNAH. Oh my.

SUSAN. He put himself through school, and he put himself through university, and he became a resistance fighter with the Czech underground. And then he was captured, and he was wounded, and they sent him to Buchenwald for five years.

HANNAH. Uh huh.

SUSAN. Then after the war, because he had a degree in psychology and he knew about five or six languages, they asked him to be principal of Aglasterhausen.

HANNAH. This is a story I didn't know exactly. As I said, I saw him once or so. We all went our own way, but a few of us somehow stayed close together, and we knew each other. We knew each other's families with their own children and grandchildren.

SUSAN. Yes, life goes on.

HANNAH. That's right.

SUSAN. Happily.

HANNAH. You cannot bring back the ones that are gone and you have to go on.

SUSAN. Thank you, Hannah. It was a pleasure talking with you.

HANNAH. Bye-bye.

SUSAN. Bye-bye.

Notes

76   Fragner, interview by Shifra Miller and Shirley Davis, 15.

77   Ibid, 16.

78   Readers interested in what life was like for the children of Aglasterhausen would be well served by reading this moving account of Dina's experiences. This book was a 2010 National Jewish Book Awards finalist. Tema N. Merback, *In the Face of Evil* (Victoria, BC: Friesen Press, 2010), 373–374.

79   Ibid, 376.

80   Emma Lazarus was one of the first successful Jewish American authors. She penned the famous poem "The New Colossus." She was born July 22, 1849, and died at the age of thirty-nine on November 19, 1888. Sixteen years following her death, a bronze plaque commemorating her poem was placed in the pedestal of the Statue of Liberty. "Women of Valor," *Jewish Women's Archive*, accessed February 21, 2015,, http://jwa.org/womenofvalor/lazarus.

81   The poem, in its entirety is presented in this article. *Wikipedia*, s.v. "Emma Lazrus," last modified June 16, 2015, accessed July 11, 2015, https://en.wikipedia.org/wiki/Emma_Lazarus.

82   According to *Wikipedia*, "*Peace of Mind* was still on the best-sellers list when Liebman died at age forty-one on June 9, 1948. Although Liebman's death was attributed at this time to a 'heart attack' or to a 'heart ailment,' writer John Bear later stated that Liebman had died 'in mysterious circumstances.'" *Wikipedia*, s.v. "Joshua L. Liebman," accessed February 21, 2015, http://en.wikipedia.org/wiki/Joshua_L._Liebman.

83   Fragner, interview by Shifra Miller and Shirley Davis, 17.

84   Kindertransport was an organized rescue mission that took place during the nine months prior to the outbreak of the Second World War. The mission transported ten thousand children to homes in Britain just before the start of World War II. Often these children were the only members of their families who survived the Holocaust. One organizer of a Kindertransport project was Nicholas Winton who rescued 669 mostly Jewish children from Czechoslovakia. As coincidence would have it, Winton was honored with Fred many years later for their work on behalf of the children of World War II. *Wikipedia*, s.v. "Kindertransport," last modified July 12, 2015, accessed August

23, 2015; also, "Nicolas Winton," last modified August 15, 2015, accessed August 23, 2015, https://en.wikipedia.ord/wiki/Nicholas_Winton.

85   Lou died in January 2012. This account of Lou and Abe was graciously provided by Lou's widow, Jane Frydman. Readers interested in finding out more about the friendship of Dr. Lou Frydman and his friend, Polish resistance fighter Jarek Piekalkewicz, should read their story in *Needle in the Bone*, by author Caryn Mirriam-Goldberg. Jane Frydman (wife of Lou Frydman) in discussion with the author, March 17, 2012. All subsequent quotes from Jane are taken from this interview.

86   The reader will note that estimates of the number killed at Majdanek vary widely. It is thought that this estimate is more realistic than the initial estimate of 360,000 provided in 1948 by Judge Zdzislaw Łukaskiewicz. *Wikipedia*, s.v. "Majdanek Concentration Camp," last modified July 5, 2015, accessed July 11, 2015, https://en.wikipedia.org/wiki/Majdanek_concentration_camp.

87   In the summer of 2010, a fire at the camp destroyed approximately ten thousand of the shoes that were on display. One commentator was attributed with the following summary of the event: "The shoes went the way of their owners. The saddest part is that the shoes were saved, but their owners were not." Conference on Jewish Material Claims Against Germany, "Majdanek" *A Page in History—Our Story: A Look at the Holocaust Today*. Last modified August 12, 2010, accessed February 21, 2015, http://blog.claimscon.org/tag/majdanek/.

88   Hannah Starkman-Kent (former Aglasterhausen resident) in discussion with the author, March 18, 2012. All subsequent quotes from Hannah are taken from this interview.

89   Radom was one of four administrative districts in Poland after the German invasion. The city of Radom was occupied by the Germans on September 8, 1939. In addition to thirty thousand local Jews, several thousand additional Jews were sent to Radom, where in early 1941 the Germans established two ghettos. "Radom," *Holocaust Education & Archive Research Team*, accessed February 21, 2015, http://www.holocaustresearchproject.org/ghettos/radom.html.

IMMIGRANT

*Remember, remember always, that all of us, and you and I especially,
are descended from immigrants and revolutionists.*

~Franklin D. Roosevelt

UPON HIS ARRIVAL IN THE UNITED STATES and the dispatching of the
children in his charge to those who would find them homes, Fred and
Kay journeyed to Chicago, where Fred would soon enroll in college, and
together they would establish their first home as houseparents at the
Marks Nathan Orphans Home in 1946. It was a Jewish boys' home.

Although Fred was fluent in several languages, English was not
among them. So he began to conquer the tongue of his new homeland
and acquire the education he would soon need to move forward in helping others who were facing physical and mental challenges. Of course, he
already had a degree in psychology from Charles University in Prague,
but those credentials would likely not be enough to open doors for him
in the United States.

As with many situations that he encountered in life, he had an en-
trenched core belief that he could do whatever he wanted to do. There
was, apparently, no way to say "no" to Fred, because he was so utterly
convinced that he could do whatever he set his mind to do. Who could
argue?

Fred would say that *chutzpah* is akin to pooping on someone's lawn and then ringing his or her doorbell for toilet paper. He had real guts.

Still, even armed with an ample measure of *chutzpah*, he would never fully recover from the harm he had suffered at Buchenwald. While in Chicago, he would awaken night after night to the same terrible dream. He would once again find himself at Buchenwald, running from the Nazis who wanted to kill him. Then he would wake up.

It is no wonder that he turned to social work and behavioral health as a profession. He was a natural—someone who had been through the worst the world had to offer and lived through it to bring his understanding and support to others. He was perfectly positioned to help not only the children of the Holocaust, but also children and adults who had experienced other types of physical and mental trauma. He would be there with a kind word, the understanding that only experiential knowledge can teach, and the knowledge and resources for healing and moving forward.

Eventually, Kay admonished Fred that he should seek professional help. During their stay in Chicago, he went to a Freudian psychiatrist and underwent therapy. It helped, but it certainly was not a cure-all. To his dying day, he would always consider himself to have a mental illness.[90]

But to his credit, he probably supported those with mental illness with more caring and savvy than many among us who call ourselves sane.

By the time Fred and Kay left Chicago, Fred had acquired a master's degree in social work from the University of Chicago. This degree increased Fred's professional opportunities, and in 1951 he accepted a job at a Jewish hospital for the treatment of tuberculosis—the National Jewish Hospital in Denver, Colorado. The couple loved the Rocky Mountains, and Fred was able to ski again while Kay enjoyed shopping for fashionable skiwear.

Fred on a Colorado ski slope.

The hospital in Denver was an excellent facility, and patients came from all over the country to be treated for tuberculosis. There was no fee for services. The motto of the facility was, "None may enter who can pay, none can pay who enter." The hospital still exists as of this writing and is a top respiratory research and treatment center,[91] still attracting patients from far and wide.

Fred's impact on the clients he served is reflected in the following letter from one of his patients, Ida Nakashima:[92]

Dear Mr. Fragner: (dated 10–30–51) 9:30 p.m.

It is curious to me at this moment that I am neither tense, nor anxious, nor excited. After all the days of suffering through ascending and descending waves of feeling, like a temperature, I can better enjoy this small pocket of relative calm. It gives me time to collect a few thoughts together in a preoperative perspective.

First of all, I should like to express again my profound appreciation for the patient and conscientious work you have done with me. I feel very fortunate in having acquired as my *first* experience with a social worker someone as intelligent, as sympathetic, as understanding, and as persistent as you. As a future physician, I will very likely have occasion to ask the help of social workers—and you see what a high standard you have set for others in your profession!

Then too, I am very much comforted by the fact that you are one person who knows me thoroughly—my faults, my weaknesses, my abounding egoism—and yet accepts me as I am and even likes me. It is a new and, as you know, a painful business to me to see myself in the objective light you show me, and you have seen me wince frequently at what I see. Whether it is compassion, or forgiveness, or a wide understanding of human nature, the fact that you never condemn me for past acts is something that I am very grateful for. And not only in not condemning, but in helping me to understand why—this broadens *my* understanding and views of other people, too. Because I understand myself better, I understand others better. I think that I have become a more mature person because of the work you have done with me. I can never thank you enough for helping me to grow.

I am far from having enough perspective about the whole of this hospital experience to say that it was the best thing that ever happened to me—what a silly statement!—but I am hoping that the price I am paying in anguish and disappointment and fear will buy for me greater sympathy and understanding for sick people, both as a physician and, as you would add, a human being. I think I know now why a truly profound sympathy and understanding are comparatively rare qualities—they come at a great cost.

In the fairly recent "permissive" attitude which you have noted in me, I can say, as I couldn't have been able to say four months ago, that I am glad you will be here when I come back from surgery, even though I will be in anesthetic coma and probably look awful. Since my family won't be here, it comforts me to know that someone will. Regression, no doubt!

I look forward to being able to see you, however hazily, in the very near future.

Many of the friends who knew Fred throughout his life would equally praise him for his kindness and attentive acumen. However, he had a demanding persona. Several of those who knew him closely would say that people either loved Fred or couldn't stand him. There was nothing lukewarm about him. He was intense, and he intensely clung to his friendships.

It was during his employment at the National Jewish Hospital that he met someone who would become a lifelong and very dear friend— Leni Markell. This is how she described their first meeting:[93]

Well, my husband and I moved to Denver, Colorado in 1949, and I'm not sure, but I think I met Fred in 1950 or 1951. And he had just come to Denver with his wife Kay, and I started a new job at the National Jewish Hospital as the director of volunteers. I'm a social worker, and Fred came in as a social worker for the patients. And I remember it very clearly. I was sitting on the steps having lunch, and he came over and sat down next to me and said [*with a very heavy accent*]: 'I'm Frrred Frrragner.'" [*She laughs.*] "I remember it very clearly. And he told me that he had come from Chicago and had just finished school and that he had a wife. And so, I invited them to the house that night for dinner. And we became friends. And that's how it started.

Although Fred was quite a bit older, Leni said, "we just clicked. As a matter of fact, my parents came out, and I guess because [the Fragners] were survivors of the Holocaust it meant a great deal to my parents, and they kind of took them in as well."

As with many of Fred's friendships, it stuck over the years. Fred was persistent if he was anything. Some of Fred's closest friends from a later time in his life—Eric Wilson and Melenie Fleischer-Wilson—described what a friendship with Fred was like. As Eric said:[94]

> What was so striking about Fred was his intensity about things. And at first, I think we were a little bit taken aback by him just because he was so, um, in earnest. Very personable, of course, but when you get to that next step of developing a friendship with someone, you know, he was very, very—I wouldn't say aggressive, but he was—he would emphasize that part of him that wanted to connect with people.

And this need to connect wasn't something superficial. It was, as Eric described it, "intense. It seemed a little bit like a responsibility almost."

Melenie described it this way. First of all, just like Leni, she had a very vivid recollection of her first encounter with Fred when they were taking classes at Temple Shalom in Vancouver, British Columbia. "I remember meeting Fred in the hall upstairs—I guess maybe during one of our breaks or at the very end of classes one time. And almost like, we felt like the *chosen* people." She and Eric laughed loudly together in recalling this memory. And then Melenie added,

> He pursued his friends, not just us. I think he just … when you were his friend you were one hundred percent his friend. He wanted to see you over and over again, and he could never get enough. You know, in that way because he wanted to look forward to the next time. And I think that's part of Fred. You know, the conversations were never finished. They were always ongoing and ongoing. He always said, "You have to peel the layers," you know—like the layers of an onion—you just peel it and peel it and he kept always saying, "Ask a question and ask another question, and another question."

And for Fred, disagreeing with a friend was not a threat to the relationship. Perhaps, as with Ida Nakashima, those closely connected with Fred had a sense of security in his need for connectedness.

Leni Markell explained that although she and Fred were very, very good friends, they also had their professional disagreements:

> When we worked together at National Jewish Hospital, he would behave in a way with his clients that I really didn't approve of! And I'd say to him, "How can you treat them like that?'
>
> And he would say, "Well, that's what they understand."
>
> So, we had a lot of arguments, but that didn't stop our friendship. And I remember saying to him, "What about expectations? Don't you have expectations about your clients?"
>
> And he said, "You have expectations, then you have disappointments. So, I don't have expectations." That always remained with me, because I never felt that way. I always had expectations.
>
> But I think he was good as a clinician. I just didn't appreciate the way he operated, but I think he was good as a clinician. I think his clients liked him.

Leni noted that many of their patients with tuberculosis could be hostile. Whether or not they were hostile before their tuberculosis diagnosis, she didn't know. "I think they were angry because they were there, and it seemed like they were there forever." For Fred, understanding the very real everyday consequences of confinement was a proverbial piece of cake.

Confinement during treatment? Check.

Angry? Check.

Frustrated? Check.

Ready to climb the wall? Check.

Urge to run away? Check.

Allowed to run away? Nein.

For Fred, it was everything he had known for five years multiplied by a number. Two? Five? One hundred? No telling, really. Fred had the perfect combined life experience and education to fully understand what it was like to be a tuberculosis patient confined to an institution. Further, his degree in psychology from Charles University and his degree in social work from the University of Chicago gave him the skills he needed to help.

Despite the extreme hardship he had suffered as a child and young adult and, in large part because of it, he was making a wonderful life. And it was indeed wonderful.

Notes

90   Fred is likely describing post-traumatic stress disorder (PTSD), which today is considered more a response to a traumatic event or series of events than an anxiety disorder or mental illness. PTSD has been moved to a new chapter on trauma- and stress-or-related disorders in DSM-V. It had previously been addressed as an anxiety disorder in DSM-IV. American Psychiatric Association. "Postraumatic Stress Disorder Fact Sheet," *American Psychiatric Publishing*, accessed July 12, 2015, http://www.dsm5.org/Documents/ PTSD%20Fact%20Sheet.pdf.

91   The *US News & World Report* has ranked National Jewish Health as the nation's number one or number two hospital in pulmonology ever since that category was included in the rankings. *National Jewish Health*, accessed February 22, 2015, http://www.nationaljewish.org/.

92   Fred Fragner, Colorado, Indiana and Ohio scrapbook, 5.

93   Leni Markell (lifelong friend of Fred Fragner) in discussion with the author, February 5, 2012. All subsequent quotes from Leni are taken from this interview.

94   Melenie Fleischer-Wilson and Eric Wilson (friends of Fred Fragner) in discussion with the author, January 11, 2013. All subsequent quotes from Eric or Melenie are taken from this interview.

This photo may have been affixed to Fred's naturalization papers.

CITIZEN

The Holocaust illustrates the consequences of prejudice, racism, and stereotyping on a society. It forces us to examine the responsibilities of citizenship and confront the powerful ramifications of indifference and inaction.

~Tim Holden[95]

ON MAY 4, 1953, FRED ACHIEVED U.S. CITIZENSHIP according to Petition No. 12786, Certificate No. 7057404. Fred's Certificate of Naturalization displayed the following information:

- Date of birth: April 22, 1910
- Male
- Complexion: medium
- Color of eyes: brown
- Color of hair: brown
- 5'7", 138 pounds
- Mole by left eye
- Married
- Former nationality: Czechoslovakian

To the certificate, Fred had affixed his signature, and there was also a picture.

The papers said, "In testimony whereof the seal of the court is hereunto affixed this 4th day of May in the year of our Lord nineteen hundred and fifty-three, and of our Independence one hundred and seventy-seventh." Signed Walter Bowman, Clerk of the US District Court.

Fred had just turned thirty-eight the previous month,[96] no longer either an orphan or an immigrant without a permanent home. He had been adopted by the United States of America. He was not only a free man, but he was also a son of liberty.

NOTES

95   Tim Holden is a former US Representative from Pennsylvania's seventeenth congressional district. He served in Congress from 1993 to 2013. *Brainy Quote*, accessed February 22, 2015, http://www.brainyquote.com/quotes/quotes/t/timholden324754.html.

96   Based on his correct birthday of 1915.

A picture of Fred and Anita with a cookie sticking out of her mouth.
It is one of her favorites of her and her dad.

DEVOTED FATHER:
THE EARLY YEARS

I remember my father as being a strong, tanned, and very loving person who always had a smile on his face when he was with me.

~ Anita Fragner

IN 1953, FRED TOOK A POSITION IN ST. LOUIS, MISSOURI, with the Jewish Child Welfare Association. From then until July 1956, he served as Institutional Superintendent of the Jewish Children's Home, Acting Director of the Jewish Child Welfare Association, and eventually Executive Director of the Jewish Child Welfare Agency.

Fred and Kay lived on the grounds of the home, where they had their own apartment. The following year, their daughter, Anita Lynn Fragner, was born. From all accounts, Anita was the apple of her father's eye. Anita's birth announcement read:

KAY and FRED FRAGNER
Proudly present
ANITA LYNN
Tuesday, September 28th, 1954
Weight—7 lbs. 7 ozs.
6630 Oakland   St. Louis, Mo.

The birth announcement also said, "Kay is fine. Fred is still weak." It seems that Fred was in meetings at work when Kay went into labor. He went racing over to the National Jewish Hospital in St. Louis. Unfortunately, he was going a bit fast and got a speeding ticket while en route.

The year Anita was born, Dwight Eisenhower was president, a loaf of bread cost seventeen cents, a first-class stamp cost three cents, the average income was $4,684, minimum wage was seventy-five cents per hour, a car could be bought for $1,950, and a house could be bought for $17,500,[97] and in the case of *Brown v. Board of Education* of Topeka, the Supreme Court unanimously banned racial segregation in public schools.[98]

While in his position at the home, Fred also became a father figure to many of the children who lived there. Thirty years later, a reunion was held, with Fred flying back to St. Louis to meet with many of his charges. One of them wrote:[99]

> Fred, you need to know my memories are very clear of life at the home before and after you were there. That includes feelings, emotions, self-concept, etc.; everything a growing child experiences. Until recently, I had given very little thought, if any, to that portion of my life. As I look back (and I've done more of that since the idea of the reunion evolved), I realize what a positive impact you had on my life and how fortunate I was that you appeared when and how you did. The fact that you wouldn't compromise our well-being, and the fact that you created a climate where we thrived and where our self-concept and self-respect was foremost, has remained with me. With the confidence you encouraged, I recognized when it was time for me to leave the home and get on with my life. Even if given the chance, I wouldn't change any part of that either.

Another wrote:

> For me, the memories associated with you include: how you got the money for my first formal dress by having the kids paint the fence silver, then giving us the money meant for the painter; how you decided it was indeed important to

provide funds so I could join a sorority at school; how you used to visit in the evening and hug the kids that needed hugs as much as they needed food to survive; how you were the only person who came to see me graduate from high school, etc. I remember the excitement when Anita was born! I was the youngest in my family, so Anita was the very first baby I ever held.

A couple of months before Anita turned two years old, Fred resigned his positions in St. Louis when he decided to relocate the family to Cincinnati, Ohio.

The president of the Jewish Welfare Association of St. Louis wrote a glowing recommendation for Fred to take with him on his journey:

Jewish Child Welfare Association of St. Louis
6630 Oakland Avenue Mission 5–4601 St. Louis 10, Mo.

Mrs. Hyman C. Weisman, President
Norman Bierman, Vice-President
Mrs. Irving Edison, Secretary
Harry L. Franc, Treasurer
Fred Fragner, Executive Director

July 23, 1956

TO WHOM IT MAY CONCERN:

It has been my privilege and pleasure to work with Mr. Fred Fragner for almost three years.

During that time he served in the capacity as Institutional Superintendent of the Jewish Children's Home, Acting Director of the Jewish Child Welfare Association, and then took on the dual role of Acting Superintendent of the Jewish Children's Home and Executive Director of the Jewish Child Welfare Agency.

He served the Institution and Agency at one of the most difficult and critical times of its history, as we were going through the transitional period of giving custodial care to serving emotionally disturbed children. In addition to this, we were, and still are, in the process of a remodeling program of the physical facilities of the Institution.

Mr. Fragner showed a remarkable aptitude to meeting these changing situations and under his direction, and the goals that he set, we feel we are making unusual progress in meeting the needs of the community in childcare insofar as budgets and policies permit.

His relationship with the children is outstanding. There is devotion between them that merits great commendation. [I have] also found that his relationship with the personnel and staff leaves little to be desired in that direction.

Above all, Mr. Fragner is one of the most conscientious men that has ever come to our Institution or Agency. He is honest in all his thinking and works far beyond his own physical strength. I am sure he will give completely of himself in any endeavor.

He is leaving our employ of his own desires and is taking with him the profound respect of our board of directors and our gratefulness for the sincerity he has manifested during the years, for the achievements that are now obvious and will continue to develop, through the high goals he has set.

He should do well in almost any other welfare field of his choice.

Cordially,

Gertrude Weisman, President

Over the years, the accolades piled high, then higher, and then higher still as the world's testimony to a man who believed in a bright future and who rejoiced in the first glimmer of the rising sun.

From Anita's standpoint, she knew her dad's worth in a way no one else would, and he was, in many ways, the center of her universe. And she was the center of his. Throughout their relationship, it would be very close, very intense, and marked by more than a little thunder and lightning.

Anita has very clear recollections of their early years together, which are presented in the following section.[100]

I was born on September 28, 1954, in St. Louis, Missouri. My parents had moved there a year or two earlier from Denver, Colorado. My father was the director of a Jewish children's center there, and it was a residential center for children (I think) and adolescents to age eighteen, who came from troubled home situations. I believe it was only for females. Some of the girls/women actually managed to find my father years later when he was already in Bellingham, and they brought him to St. Louis for a reunion. They were absolutely thrilled to have found him, and all of them remembered special times when he went out of his way to enrich their lives.

I remember some funny stories that my parents told me about my birth and infancy. Apparently, my mother was quite anxious about caring for me just the right way, so she hired a nurse to help her for the first couple of weeks. I had my days and nights mixed up, and according to my parents, they both took turns walking with me at night. My father said that he took me for rides in the car, which usually put me to sleep. Some of the teenage girls who were residents in the facility loved to come and help my mother and eventually babysit, and I am still in touch with one of them.

My mother also was very concerned that my bottles were sterilized and was always reminding my dad to make sure to sterilize the nipples and bottles when he was feeding me. My dad told me that sometimes while carrying all the supplies he would drop the nipple on the floor and just pick it up and stick it on the bottle and feed me. Obviously, I survived! Maybe that's even why I have such a strong immune system! He didn't tell my mother until I was a teenager.

I had a little wading pool, and my parents would put me in the water, which I loved, and sit with me while I splashed. They couldn't figure out why the water in the pool kept getting so low, and then they realized that when they would turn their heads for a moment, I would fill my pail with water and water the lawn! My father was always taking pictures of me, so I have lots of photos of me in my little pool and also of me on my tricycle (or falling off of it).

The residential facility also had an African American gardener named Cliff, and I can still picture him. He was my buddy, and he fixed my toys for me if they broke. I was told that when I first starting talking, one of the most frequent things I said was, "Cliff, fix it."

We lived there for the first two years of my life. I remember my father as being a strong, tanned, and very loving person who always had a smile on his face when he was with me. He also had more hair than in his later years! My mother was beautiful and loving, although more anxious (Jewish mother says it all). She took me for walks, played paper dolls with me, and read me stories. She also used to sing to me in Polish.

When I was about two years old, we moved to Cincinnati, Ohio, to a very Jewish neighborhood. I remember the adults would sit outside in lawn chairs while the kids played. I can still picture them sitting outside on warm evenings. I had a boyfriend, Aaron, and was deeply in love with him. My mother said he was always creating mischief and blaming me. Once he made some cardboard boxes on top of one another and a chair on the top and told me to sit up there like a queen. Luckily, it fell down before I could attempt it. Another time, he hugged me so tight I threw up. With boyfriends like that, who needs enemies!

I went to Sunday school in Cincinnati at a reform synagogue, and we went to services on Friday nights. The only thing I remember about Sunday school back then is that I won a prize for my collage of Joseph and his many-colored coat. My dad saved it and gave it to me when I was an adult. I still have it.

We were also very actively involved in the Jewish Community Center, and that's where I learned to swim at a very young age. I was quite active and apparently once decided I should jump off the diving board (before I learned how to swim). My mother caught up with me when I was almost to the end of the diving board. Our summer days were spent at the pool there, and the mothers would all sit on chaise lounges tanning while we played in the water. My mother told everyone I swam like a frog. I think she meant "fish"—hopefully. Apparently, I was very social as well, and my parents told me that at a formal dinner dance at the club there, I danced by myself next to all the tables and introduced myself to everyone. Since I loved to dance, my parents put me in ballet lessons when I was three, but I was kicked out. According to my dad, I got the whole class to follow me climbing on chairs and tumbling on mats, and the teacher was not happy. I was readmitted, however, when I was four, and my parents attended many recitals. Of course, my father had to take pictures of me in my tutu. He was definitely the photographer of the family. When my mom would try to take pictures, she somehow managed to leave out the subject of the photo!

Also during our Cincinnati years (about 1956–1960), my parents had some close friends who were from Poland and Czechoslovakia, and we would go to gatherings at their homes, where everyone was speaking Polish or Czech. My parents frequently spoke in those languages at home when I was young, when they didn't want me to know what they were talking about. Unfortunately, that was a time when people wanted to assimilate rather than celebrate their cultures for the most part, so I didn't learn either of those languages. Both parents actually spoke a number of languages, but alas, I just speak English. Once in a while, my mom got a kick out of trying to get me to say a Polish word with about ten consonants in a row, and both parents would laugh at my pronunciations.

Notes

97   "Television History—The First 75 Years," TVhistory.TV, accessed February 21, 2015, http://www.tvhistory.tv/1954%20QF.htm.

98   *Wikipedia*, s.v. "Brown v. Board of Education," last modified July 6, 2015, accessed July 17, 2015, https://en.wikipedia.org/wiki/Brown_v._Board_of_Education.

99   Fred Fragner, Colorado, Indiana and Ohio Scrapbook, 9.

100   This entire section was written by Anita and sent to the author as an e-mail attachment. Anita Fragner (daughter of Fred Fragner) email message to the author, December 13, 2011.

MENTAL HEALTH
PROFESSIONAL

*True heroism is remarkably sober, very undramatic. It is not
the urge to surpass all others at whatever cost, but the urge to
serve others at whatever cost.*

~ Arthur Ashe

IN CINCINNATI, FRED HAD BEEN OFFERED a three-year contract as
Director of the Children's Unit at Longview State Hospital, a psychiatric
institution. He was specifically brought in to completely overhaul the
unit due to problems they had been experiencing.

The following article ran in the *Cincinnati Times-Star*.[101]

A man who resurrected his life from five years of man's inhumanity to
man at Buchenwald concentration camp is now rebuilding the lives of
children in Longview Hospital.

Fred Fragner, forty-two, has headed the hospital's children's unit, the
only such separate organization in Ohio, since last October.

Mr. Fragner has a simple definition of his job: "It is to rehabilitate
the child as quickly as possible, so he can function adequately in his community. That's all."

Carrying out these aims is not so simple.

The children's section at Longview is a strange mixture. It has teachers, whose main job is not to teach; young children, who are old in the pressures of living, and child minds eager for understanding and acceptance, yet unwilling to take the first step.

"We have six teachers here," Mr. Fragner explained, "but we are not so much concerned with instructing the children as we are with providing them with a motive to learn."

The school, with ungraded sections, concentrates on social sciences, teaching the children how to meet with others, play, and intermingle.

The last is superlatively important to mentally injured children. Now, they are not capable of ordinary interactions with others.

Most of the thirty-seven children attending the school have a form of "childhood" schizophrenia—the adult "split personality" disease.

Boiled down, this means that the children were put here because society could not tolerate their behavior, Mr. Fragner said.

The children are social in some instances, and antisocial in other cases. They were sent here as fire setters, window breakers, and being "unreasonably mean," to quote some of the complainants.

Actually, these children are proof that their parents failed to give them love, understanding, and "a certain reliable firmness" during the first year of their life.

Late, but perhaps in time, Mr. Fragner and the staff are trying to bring these children the ingredients they need to sweeten life; ingredients not supplied by their parents.

Until now the children have felt unwanted, burdensome, and even contemptible for being so much trouble. They consider themselves—in some vague manner—as "unworthy" of life.

Thirty-seven of these ill children are being cared for at Longview. Another three to five hundred wait for admissions.

"We could fill five hundred beds in a week—if we had the space and facilities," Mr. Fragner said. Now there are seventeen beds at the school, a brightly painted, light place. The twenty other students must stay in the wards. Only the younger ones can stay in the school overnight. The children range from seven to thirteen years in age.

"To fill the immediate needs of Cincinnati alone, we need another sixty-five to one hundred beds right now," Mr. Fragner declared. "To function adequately as a state hospital, we would need another five hundred beds," he added.

Following his three years at Longview, Fred accepted a position as Chief of Probation and Director of Treatment Services for the Cincinnati Juvenile Court System. Anita fondly remembered one of the many judges Fred worked with—Judge Swartz. Although she recalled that he was terrible to work with, Anita really liked him because whenever she visited the court with Fred, Judge Schwartz gave her toys.

Fred was very active in the community while in Cincinnati. He was invited to join a group of psychiatrists and psychologists who met monthly to discuss difficult cases. He also spoke at the annual meeting of the Ohio State Nurses' Association and had numerous other speaking engagements.

In December of 1961, Fred accepted a position as the administrative director of the Guidance Clinic of Wayne County, Inc., a child guidance clinic in Richmond, Indiana, and the family moved from Cincinnati to Richmond. The Guidance Clinic was an outpatient treatment center for "emotionally disturbed" children, but the focus was on treating the family as a whole. As Fred noted in an interview, the clinic staff felt "a responsibility toward the entire community in a much greater degree and expected to furnish broad guidance to families within the framework of parent-teacher groups, church organizations, and other civic groups."[102]

Richmond was a very friendly community, and the family made friends quickly. They became members of a synagogue, and Kay became very active in the temple sisterhood and Hadassah. Kay also had a gorgeous rock garden in the backyard, which had beautiful flowers in bloom almost year-round. Anita spent Saturdays at the YWCA taking such classes as swimming, acrobatics, tap, water ballet, modern dance, etc.

She also attended YWCA camp in the summer and attended numerous slumber parties during the year. She and Kay frequently spent summer days swimming at the Elks Country Club.

While in Richmond, Fred also taught at Earlham College, which was a Quaker school. He was well-known in the community and was a popular speaker for various organizations both in the community and statewide. In 1964, the Fragners marched in a civil rights march in Richmond, and Fred was one of the distinguished speakers. He represented the Jewish community at this event.

A scrapbook page from this period shows a picture of the Fragner home in the top right-hand corner. In the bottom left-hand corner, there is a picture of Anita in a ballet tutu with some ballet shoes and a tutu outfit glued to the area around her picture. A box under the picture of their home says, "There is no place like home." And around it are a number of scrapbook stickers, including individual stickers saying the following words and phrases: entertainment, joy, warm places, great fun, life, grow, welcome, I'm home, and cherish the memories.

As previously mentioned, Viktor Frankl, the famous Austrian neurologist and psychiatrist, as well as Holocaust survivor, gave a speech and participated in a debate at Richmond's Earlham College in 1963. Earlham was affiliated with the Religious Society of Friends—the Quakers. It supported the premise that all truth is God's truth and emphasized in their mission pursuit of truth—wherever that pursuit leads—lack of coercion, letting the evidence lead that search, respect for the consciences of others, openness to new truth and therefore the willingness to search, veracity, rigorous integrity in dealing with the facts, and application of what is known to improving our world.

Fred was on the debate panel, and he spoke loudly and clearly that he thought Frankl's premises to be false.

FRANKL'S ASSERTIONS[103]

In his 1946 book, Frankl writes about experiences he had at a prison in a "concentration camp" and describes his "psychotherapeutic" method of finding a reason to live. Frankl states that the book answers the question, "How was everyday life in a concentration camp reflected in the mind of the average prisoner?" He identifies three psychological reactions that he says are experienced by all concentration camp prisoners to one degree or another: (1) shock during the initial admission phase to the camp, (2) apathy after becoming accustomed to camp existence, when the prisoner values only that which helps him or her or others survive, and (3) reactions of depersonalization, moral deformity, bitterness, and disillusionment after being liberated.

Frankl asserts that life never ceases to have meaning, even in suffering and death, that a prisoner's psychological reactions are not solely the result of the conditions of his or her life, but also from the freedom of choice he or she always has even in severe suffering.

Frankl also writes that prisoners in the camps face an increasing chance of survival if they make efforts beyond self-preservation and try to help other prisoners, that this increases their "inner resistance." He states his opinion that helping other prisoners gives a goal and meaning to one's life other than just "self-survival," stating, "In spite of all this enforced physical and mental primitiveness of the life in a concentration camp, it [is] possible for the spiritual life to deepen .... They [are] able to retreat from their terrible surroundings to a life of inner riches and spiritual freedom."[104]

FRED'S RESPONSE[105]

Dr. Frankl was a well-known Jewish psychiatrist and neurologist in Vienna, Austria, before the Holocaust and was Director of the Neurology Department at the University of Vienna. His first "camp" was Theresienstadt,[106] which was a ghetto in Czechoslovakia where certain categories of Jews were taken, such as the famous and wealthy and those with special talents. Throughout his "concentration camp experience," he was given preferential treatment and didn't have to experience the suffering that most of the other prisoners experienced. Initially, when deported, he worked as a general practitioner in Theresienstadt, in a clinic. Frankl himself states that when he was deported to other camps, he did such jobs as "establish a special unit to help newcomers to the camp overcome shock and grief."[107] Where was this unit? Fred and other survivors/victims certainly never saw it. Frankl also reports having headed a neurology clinic in one of the camps and lecturing on such topics as "Sleep and Its Disturbances," "Medical Care of the Soul," "The Psychology of Mountaineering," etc. Who heard these lectures? Not the other prisoners. Fred pointed out that most of the concentration camp victims were not able to think about their suffering as being a "challenge of self-realization." How can anyone care about self-realization when they are a virtual skeleton, stealing potato peels to eat, seeing friends and family mutilated and killed? Life was viewed by prisoners "in the moment," and literally being able to take a step, to put one foot in front of the other, required major physical effort while being beaten and starved to death. The ability for abstract thought is vastly diminished when one is starving to death, and survival each second is more an instinct than a thought, much less finding the meaning of life. Frankl grossly underestimates how drastically the horrific conditions affected most victims of Nazism (hunger, cold, hostility, lack of hygiene, no privacy, hard labor, humiliations, stark terror, constant, extreme physical and emotional trauma, random death, and unspeakable acts of torture, etc.). Fred felt that Frankl, when discussing survival as related to conscience and self-realization, didn't stress at all the unpredictable luck, coincidence, and continuously changing and varying circumstances that considerably affected the chances of survival of the victims (nationality, wealth prior to the war, social standing, professional standing, knowledge of foreign languages, intellectual development, ability to do various forms of manual labor, appearance, number of prisoners in ones' group, character of their direct supervisor, the moment of their arrival at the camp, the weather of the moment, etc.). Fred was angry that, in his opinion, Frankl in a sense used the Holocaust and concentration camp experience to advance his own psychological theories and therapies.

After Frankl lectured at Earlham College, Fred wrote the following satirical speech from his biting perspective on what Frankl might say and believe.

"Viktor Frankl's Happiness Tonic, or: Psychiatry as a New Tool in Christian Science"[108]

It was with great fear and reluctance that I have accepted the invitation to come to the United States, where people are basically primitive, the food is terrible, the coffee outrageous; a country with a political system bordering on anarchy, with people allowed to express their beliefs and opinions, even against their own government. A country where children are encouraged to think independently and where colleges and universities are infested with intellectually acting-out students.

Now at home in Vienna, which was the place where the poor misguided fool Freud got his education and which produced the greatest leaders of the Nazi establishment, you get a real sense of culture and civilization. There is an atmosphere of *Gemütlichkeit,* and one can enjoy eating good Wiener schnitzel while listening to the music of the "Blue Danube" or Horst Wessel, reminiscing the good times not so long ago when an Austrian corporal became a German emperor. Twenty million people in extermination, concentration, and slave labor camps should give you a real sense of living; the end result of many years of searching for the "meaning of life." But if this emotional experience fails to bring you peace of mind and answers to the Holocaust, you can always engulf yourself into a new search, which may prove to be a very fruitful spending of your time, but which can prove to be an ongoing, intellectually stimulating, erotic experience never culminating in an emotional orgasm; and so in itself providing with a reason for continued search for the "meaning of life."

And so, while I am most reluctant to leave my *vaterland,* which was kind to me and my family, I have no choice, since I have a mission to fulfill. In coming to Earlham, an insignificant college, I see the fulfillment of this role for me, the only person intellectually equipped to show you the light, to guide you out of the darkness of your ignorance, to help you do some right searching, to help you—to become like us.

Today, as always, in books and lectures, I am attempting to convey to you the thesis that "a person who feels miserable can be happy, if he only searches his soul and mind" and "realizes how happy he really is in his misery." On the other hand, a happy person can in reality be miserable without being aware of it. All he or she needs is a little bit of searching. Social conditions, economic problems, poverty, racial and religious prejudices are all a product of your lazy, unmotivated and poorly integrated *ego*. And it is very unfortunate that we still have people who are longing for such things as enough food to eat, decent housing, or racial justice, without first understanding the underlying meaning of their miserable existence. If you fail to see the logic of my arguments and follow my advice to continue searching for the meaning of life, then you are sicker than I thought you [were]. All you have to believe is that your grim reality is not real, but a fantasy. You can even believe that you are Napoleon, Hitler, President Johnson, or even God. It is a painless, inexpensive, easy and at times, pleasant therapy.

And so my friends, take it from me. Take if from someone who knows. Just look at me. Here I am, having a great professional status, a nice income, living in the midst of what is being considered the ultimate in culture, having a great mission to travel to the culturally underdeveloped countries to help the poor, ignorant, uneducated, unhappy, maladjusted, primitive people like you, to take time out for a search in order to find the relatively easy way to ultimate happiness. I do hope you appreciate the honor I have bestowed on your small college by coming here and giving you the benefits of wisdom acquired through many years of searching. And if you don't feel better within two weeks after my lectures, please don't call me. Write to Ann Landers. And if this won't help you, go and see a real psychiatrist. Thank you, and God help you!

It is interesting that Frankl was such a lightning rod for Fred. On the surface, they had so much in common—both were interested in psychology, both saw their families destroyed by the Holocaust, and both had suffered personally during the Holocaust. Obviously, Frankl's six months of hard labor at Kaufering cannot be compared to Fred's five years at Buchenwald. Fred was obviously resentful of Frankl's preferential treatment during his incarceration, something that Fred and his fellow Buchenwald inmates didn't experience. Aside from his fervent rebuttal of Frankl's precepts, only Fred knew the basis for his extreme reaction to this man.

There is one statement of Frankl's, however, that Fred might have agreed with: "For the meaning of life differs from man to man, from day to day, and from hour to hour. What matters, therefore, is not the meaning of life in general but rather the specific meaning of a person's life at a given moment."[109] Each life is relevant, each life is uniquely formulated based on unique experiences, unique paths. And Fred's life was soon to come upon yet another fork in the road.

By 1966, Fred was once again ready for new challenges. So in that year, he moved his family to Delaware, where Fred was offered a position as director of Fernhook Mental Hygiene Clinic.

NOTES

101   Don Young, Jr, "Slave Camp to Child Care—Former Buchenwald Inmate Has Job of Rehabilitating Children at Longview," *Cincinnati Times-Star* (Cincinnati, OH), March 22, 1957.

102   Fred Fragner, Colorado, Indiana and Ohio Scrapbook, 23.

103   These notes are taken directly from Fred's scrapbook "Next Stop Denver!" and appear to be Anita Fragner's documentation of what Fred knew about Frankl and his thoughts on Frankl's speech and his philosophical writings. Fred Fragner, Colorado, Indiana and Ohio Scrapbook, 29.

104   Viktor E. Frankl, *Man's Search for Meaning* (Boston: Beacon Press, 1959), from "Experiences in A Concentration Camp" chapter. iBook edition.

105   Fred Fragner, Colorado, Indiana and Ohio Scrapbook, 29.

106   It seems that Fred may have been a bit hard on Dr. Frankl. It is true that Frankl, his wife, and his parents were deported to the Theresienstadt Ghetto, where Frankl worked as a general practitioner in a clinic and where later he was assigned to the psychiatric care ward in block B IV. However, Frankl's subsequent experiences were not so pleasant. First, his father died of pulmonary edema and pneumonia at Theresienstadt. Then, in October 1944, Frankl and his wife were transported to Auschwitz, where he was processed and moved to Kaufering, a labor camp affiliated with Dachau. There he was a slave laborer for six months. Finally, he was moved to the so-called "rest camp," Turkheim, where he worked as a physician until his liberation on April 27, 1945. His wife and everyone in his immediate family—with the exception of his sister Stella—died during the Holocaust. *Wikipedia*, s.v. "Viktor Frankl," accessed July 5, 2015, last modified June 11, 2015, https://en.wikipedia.org/wiki/Viktor_Frankl.

107   It is somewhat unclear where this Frankl quote comes from. A search of Frankl's book does not turn up this quote. Again, this appears to be Anita Fragner's documentation of what Fred knew about Frankl and his thoughts on Frankl's speech and his philosophical writings. Perhaps this particular quote came from Frankl's speech at Earlham College. Fred Fragner, Colorado, Indiana and Ohio Scrapbook, 29.

108   Fred Fragner, Colorado, Indiana and Ohio Scrapbook, 30.

109   Viktor E. Frankl, *Man's Search for Meaning* (Boston: Beacon Press, 1959), from "The Meaning of Life" section in the "Logotherapy In a Nutshell" chapter, iBook edition.

A photo of young Kazia.

HUSBAND

Two are better than one, because the reward is great when they toil together. If they fall, one can lift up the other; and if it is cold they can warm each other. One alone is easily cast down, but two standing together will withstand. And a cord of three braided strands is not easily broken.

~ Ecclesiastes 4:9–12

FRED WAS MARRIED TWICE. He likely met his first wife, Kay, at Bergen-Belsen en route to Buchenwald. They knew one another a brief two weeks before their secret marriage by a rabbi. They would only be reunited following the end of the war.

KAY[110]

Kay came from a very wealthy Jewish family in Poland. Her name in Polish was Kazimiera Wilner (the first name is pronounced like "cashmere" with an *a* on the end). She was called Kazia for short. Her father, mother, sister, and brothers were all killed by the Nazis, either directly in the gas chambers or indirectly as a result of malnutrition, overwork, and disease. Kay had started university at eighteen and a half and already had a master's degree in business administration at the time of her capture. Her last year at the university was in 1938, and the persecution of the Jews had become so bad that she only went to school when she was required to take her exams because "the situation was very, very bad."

She also studied at a music conservatory and played the piano beautifully. She loved gourmet cooking and was known especially for her hors d'oeuvres and European-style gourmet desserts. Anita said that this came in very handy, because she and Fred loved to entertain. Anita also said, "She was a great mother and wife and very devoted to us, but she was damaged by her experiences, and I think underneath the surface she was very depressed."

One morning in 1939, the family was having an early breakfast when the bell to her father's office rang. Her father, who was a physician, went to answer it, and he came back "white as a sheet," according to Kay. There were two people in the office who said they had been injured in a bombing. This was nine in the morning on a Friday. By eleven, the war announcement came over the radio.

Kay remembers the following Sunday as a gorgeous day. A captain in the Polish Army arrived and told the family it would need to leave because the Germans would be coming soon. The family then crossed over the river to its summer cottage on the other side. Kay's father had obtained a large wagon and horse to load whatever of their possessions could be taken. At this time, thousands and thousands of people were evacuating.

At one in the morning, German airplanes flew overhead and began shooting at the fleeing Poles and killing everyone on the road. She especially remembered a man holding a lifeless baby. He came to the cottage to find out whether her father could do anything for the baby.

Kay's father was eventually taken prisoner by the Germans. For a while, the family didn't know if he was dead or alive because every night the Germans were taking busloads to the cemetery, where prisoners had to dig their own grave before they were killed.

One day, her father returned. He had been forced to sign a paper saying that the family would leave town, but at the same time there were signs outside the city saying that no one was to leave.

Kay recounts the night when a German soldier came to their door accompanied by a Jewish fiddler. He roamed the house going room to room with the fiddler until he came to Kay's room, where she was in bed. He entered the room with the fiddler, locked the door behind them, and began shooting as he sat at the foot of Kay's bed. Though the family pounded on the door, he would not let them in. Kay passed out, and her mother fainted during the incident. Then, just as quickly as it had begun, the solider got up and left the house. Kay was physically uninjured.

A week later, at nine o'clock in the evening, soldiers rousted the whole family, and they were taken to the railroad station and loaded into cattle wagons that were open at the top. They were taken from one town to another, and no one wanted to accept them. They spent two weeks in the cattle wagons and got no food from the Germans, only the food they had carried with them when told to leave their homes. Other Jews would also offer them food at the towns where they stopped.

At first, they were allowed to leave the train once a day to take care of bodily needs, but then this stopped altogether. It was then that the dysentery began. People began dying, and the bodies were thrown off the train.

Kay didn't remember how they ended up in a camp, but they eventually did. Especially traumatic for her was the moment when she had to choose whether to go with her mother or her father. According to Anita, "I don't think she ever got over that guilt. She was very close to her dad. He was a doctor, and she would be his nurse and go on house calls with him and things like that. She chose her dad, but they were taking her mother and brothers to the gas chamber. She chose to go with her dad, and they were killed."[111]

A couple of days before the liberation, her father was shot when he couldn't get up during a death march. Her younger sister died of typhus.

Even though Fred and Kay made a go of their marriage for many years, it would always be the union of two people who married under extraordinary circumstances and struggled for the remainder of their lives with devastating scars. Anita recounted:

> As I said, in the camps there weren't really long courtships, and they were two very different people. They really were. And also, I think the war affected them, the camps affected them differently. And they were at different stages of their lives when they got put in the camps. My father had already

been independent for years because he had to be. My mother was very sheltered and really had, you know, everything she wanted. So, she was raised to believe she was going to have a certain style of life too. It wasn't so much that as that she was really scarred by what happened.

Kay had also been engaged to a young doctor before the war broke out, but the war brought an end to their relationship. The doctor, whose name was Heniek (Henry), managed to avoid capture and escape to Israel.

PHOTO COURTESY OF ANITA FRAGNER

This is a photo that Kazia sent to Heniek in 1935.

Kay and Fred also had very different thoughts about sharing their experiences in the camps. While Kay spoke often about her experiences, Fred did not. It was only in his later years that he was even willing to talk about it at all, and he did it sparingly and only because he felt it was the only way to prevent such atrocities from happening again. He had no personal desire to talk about things that were best buried, in his opinion, but unfortunately only possible to bury in a very shallow grave. "I think what he repressed when he was younger really came out more and he started talking a lot more about it. I think he was having more frequent nightmares. He always had nightmares about every six months," said Anita.

When *Schindler's List* came out, Fred and Anita both saw it separately but on the same day. She remembered calling him as soon as she got out of the movie to ask him what he thought about it.

> I was worried about him. But he handled it, actually. I think he was still repressing things more, but he handled it pretty well. And I asked him, "Is this what it was like? Is this movie realistic?"
>
> And he said, "To a point it is. But there is no way they could ever show how bad it was. There's just no way they could even ever portray that and especially in a movie." But, he said the basic details were accurate.

For whatever other personal reasons may have entered into their decision, Fred and Kay separated in 1977, at which time he moved into an apartment in Newark, Delaware. The separation and divorce were devastating to Kay and angered many of their mutual friends. Fred, however, was miserable in the relationship and vowed that he'd had enough misery in his life. It wasn't that he didn't care about his wife. They just had so little in common from his perspective.

Pictured are Sylvia and Fred (center) under the chuppah on their wedding day.
On the far left and right are their very close friends Tony and Kathie Roon.

Sylvia[112]

And then there was Sylvia. She was his second wife, but the love of Fred's life, and she inspired the writing of this book.

Sylvia met Fred when he was a consultant for public health nurses for the State of Delaware. She was a public health nurse and so would sometimes receive help from him when she worked with families experiencing complicated issues. This was in 1975 or 1976, just before Kay and Fred separated.

Around this same time, Sylvia and her first husband were having problems in their relationship and had decided to end their five-year marriage. She was twenty-seven at the time.

> And so, there's a social worker in my office, Leni Markell. I said to Leni that I was having some trouble and would she give me the names of three therapists. I needed to talk to somebody. And she gave me three people, and Fred was one of them. And I didn't know he had a private practice or

anything, I just thought that he worked for the state. I didn't know anything else about him. So, when I called all three of them, he was the person who I said, "I really like what he has to offer."

His approach was that he needed to meet with the couple, and then there were options for ongoing individual therapy. He had a group of women who he was working with too. And so if that worked out, I'd go into that support group or whatever. So, he met with my [soon-to-be] ex-husband and myself. And he was really to the point. He looked at him and he said, "Do you really want to be married to Sylvia?" And he said, "No." Of course, this was devastating.

Fred then asked the same question of Sylvia, and she responded that she wanted to be married and make the relationship work. But it takes two.

So after that, I knew it wasn't going to work. And so I think it was about a week later, I moved out because my ex-husband was actually having an affair. So he was very involved with this other woman, and he was with her. So, I said, "Okay. That's it, and I'm moving out." The next day, I called in sick and I moved.

Anyway, I left that relationship and was in counseling for about once a week for about at least a month, and then Fred said, "You need to be in this group."

There was a nun in it. There were several women who were married. It was just an interesting mix of people, and he was such an amazing facilitator. Just really got us talking.

Sylvia met with the group for about nine months starting about May 1977. About three months after she joined the group, Kay and Fred separated. It was some time after the separation—but perhaps before her participation in the group ended entirely—that Sylvia and Fred began to meet periodically for lunch. They then began to get to know more about one another, and what they learned, they liked. "He talked about his life, and he was really unhappy. He had been for many years. So we just decided to move in together!"

On their first Christmas together, Fred recorded the following audio message for Sylvia:

> My message to you on the eve of Christmas 1977:
>
> The past few months have been the most significant ones of the many years of my life.
>
> Since I have met you, my life has developed a new meaning full of joy and happiness. You have provided me with an incentive to free myself from the stagnation of a dead relationship. And you have given me a reason for changing into something I always wanted to be.
>
> My new life is full of excitement, peace, and serenity, anticipation and fulfillment, love and compassion.
>
> You have become my love object, my guiding star, my source of ultimate happiness.
>
> You are indeed a beautiful person, Sylvia. And for all of what you are and for all of what you are giving me, I am eternally grateful.
>
> I love you, Sylvia, with all my heart, with every fiber of my body, with all my soul. You are indeed my princess, my queen. I am high on you, with a wonderful high.
>
> I believe that God has given me you and your love as His ultimate gift. It is indeed worth waiting for you.
>
> My only dream, on this day, is to spend the rest of my life with you—to be allowed to love you and care for you and to feel your love as I do today.
>
> Thank you Sylvia for being you, for giving me so much of yourself. Merry Christmas, Sylvia.[113]

Fred was thirty-five years older than Sylvia. And Jewish. She was young, and her family background was North American Baptist. Sylvia recalled that her family was very conservative:

> I moved very much away from that. I realized that this was not meeting my needs at all. What I learned all my years of

growing up didn't match with what my experience was in the world. And my family had many prejudices, that blacks are somebody to be wary of, Jews, you never know, they killed Christ. All these kinds of things that ... Japanese bombed us in the world war. My dad fought against them. So many prejudices that were ever engrained in my upbringing that when I met my first black person, it was like, "Wait a minute. This person's really cool. There's nothing wrong with this person." You know. And Fred was Jewish.

Although she had not been looking for another intimate relationship, "Fred was just such an amazing person. And the power of his persona was maybe some of it, was just ... maybe I just needed to be cared for and really loved."

Sylvia and Fred were married on Halloween, October 31, 1977, by a justice of the peace. Much later, they were married by a rabbi in a traditional Jewish ceremony—under the chuppah[114]—on March 18, 1999, after Sylvia's conversion to Judaism.

It was a very happy time for the couple when they studied Judaism under a reformed rabbit at a synagogue in Vancouver, British Columbia. Sylvia wanted to understand Judaism, and Fred's upbringing was not particularly religious. In the small community where he was raised, the men went and prayed, and the women focused on keeping the accouterments of the Jewish faith alive.

His dad wasn't a rabbi. His dad was a diamond cutter. A businessman. Fred didn't understand a lot about Judaism *per se*. So we just checked out books and bought a bunch of books, and every time we were in the car, he'd read for hours to me, and I just remember having these feelings that *this* is who I am. That is *exactly* what I believe. This is my experience that validates who I am. This feels right to me! And so I just thought over time of converting, and Fred never asked me to convert. Never asked me ever, "Do you think you want to be Jewish?" I didn't need to get married under the chuppah. It was just how I felt.

Their life together was generally very wonderful. Sylvia is a very kind and cheerful individual, and her nature was likely balm for Fred's soul. And while he continued to carry a great deal of baggage, Sylvia's load was a bit lighter and certainly not marred by the types of loss and abuse Fred had suffered. Sylvia related this in her bat mitzvah speech: "Fred not only loves me, but he likes me." How many couples can say that? Fred's love for Sylvia was unconditional. Tearing up, she recounted, "And that is how he loved me—total acceptance."

When she wanted to go to graduate school, he was one hundred percent behind her. "Yes you can!" was his attitude. "Absolutely, and everything we can do we're going to make that happen!"

"He just supported me through that whole time," she said.

"Yeah," she recalled Fred saying. "It's tough and I'm not going to like it when you're studying and you have to be away all day and study at night when you come home. I'm not going to like that. I'm not going to be happy. But I want this for you."

On the occasion of her fiftieth birthday, Oprah Winfrey said that her beau, Stedman, was happy with whatever made Oprah happy. This was Fred's definition of happiness also, and he brought as much joy to Sylvia as she brought to him.

They shared many adventures traveling to distant places. Their first trip was to London and Paris. Then they went to Switzerland and Italy in 1981. And he was a good travel partner. According to Sylvia, he relished planning the trip as much as traveling. He'd say, "We're going to do this, and we're going to do this, and ..."

Sylvia said that she learned a great deal about being a confident traveler. "He would plan everything, and I'd write the check and pay for it." She added quickly that the check was out of their joint checking account because "we shared everything."

Fred liked the predictability of having everything planned out so that they would know that where they were staying was wonderful and that they were going on wonderful mini-adventures within each trip. Of course, there was room left for spontaneity as well.

They went on a ten-day trip to Athens and Israel in 1994 with their dear friends Tony and Kathie Roon and their children. Their visit to Yad Vashem[115] in Israel was a particularly poignant experience for the couple. "As the Jewish people's living memorial to the Holocaust, Yad Vashem safeguards the memory of the past and imparts its meaning for future generations."[116] This is prefaced on their website with the following quote from Isaiah 56:5: "And to them will I give in my house and within my walls a memorial and a name (a "yad vashem") ... that shall not be cut off."[117]

Sylvia recounted it as probably the most powerful of all their travel experiences. "I just remember weeping at the enormity. There's a section where these big stones are, and it's a large area, and it's all the communities that no longer exist. Each stone had a region in Europe—Poland and Russia and Germany and France and Czechoslovakia—all of these places all over that no longer have any Jews in them. All of those communities are gone. It's staggering! And then you walk through the children's area, and there's like a million and a half children eighteen and under that they figure were lost."

A later trip to the Czech Republic and Hungary brought Sylvia to the realization that Fred was undergoing some deterioration in his mental abilities. This was in September of 1999. "I really knew there were some changes, subtle, but he just wasn't comfortable not knowing where we were going." Of course, it was possible that the stress of being back in his native land was responsible for this confusion. Following this trip, however, the couple chose well-planned cruises over self-planned land excursions.

Although Fred enjoyed traveling with Sylvia very much, he never got really excited about anything *per se*. While he was passionate about many things, Sylvia said that there was never anything that brought him overwhelming joy. "He never sort of got so happy that he wanted to do a 'happy dance' or anything."

For Fred, there was just something about getting the wind knocked out of his sails when he was young that made it immensely difficult to let loose and experience the pure joy of being. Sylvia remembers standing in the Skagit Valley tulip fields in Washington State:

> I think this was the first time we were down in Skagit County—in Mount Vernon, Washington—and I was so overcome by the staggering beauty. And then Mount Baker was just framed in the background. It was such a day. And I said, "Oh Fred, if I ever didn't believe there was a god ...

there's *only* a god who could have done this!" It was so overwhelming, the feelings. And I think he sort of had that sense, too, but I'm not sure if he would say it in such a manner.

Laughing, she added, "He would say, 'Yeah, it's pretty.'"

Fred was the one, however, who cried more easily. In fact, it took Sylvia a long time before she was able to let her emotions go in that way.

Fred could certainly have fun, nonetheless. He was as complex as his life. Sylvia tells of the four years when he played Santa Claus for a group of friends who lived in an old 1850s Pennsylvania farmhouse near the border of Delaware. Fred apparently didn't know any of the children involved and had that wonderful, thick European accent he never relinquished. This made him the perfect choice for Santa Claus. He did this for the children even though he felt really weird being Santa because, Sylvia recounts as she imitates Fred's heavily accented emphasis on rolling his Rs: "This is not my tradition!"

He was pretty swift in getting in and getting out of the farmhouse. "Hey, Santa's got five thousand more gifts to give!" According to Sylvia, it was quite hilarious, and she referred to her man as the "Yiddish Santa Klaus."

Fred always tried to accommodate Sylvia's every need. That is, as long as she didn't ask him to do any handiwork around the house. He never painted. He didn't change light bulbs. He wasn't a gardener and never was interested in a having a garden. But he almost always went along with anything Sylvia wanted as long as she didn't ask him to help.

In March 1989, they bought a condominium in Bellingham, Washington, and Sylvia lived there for several years after Fred's death. Because Fred was always concerned with Sylvia's needs, he said, "I'm going to pay off this house before I die." Fred had saved some money for his grandson, Ryan, to go to school. When Ryan demonstrated that was not his bent, Fred had the opportunity to pay off his mortgage in 2009. He was ninety-three years old and asked Sylvia to make all the arrangements with the bank. He signed the papers and got the money, and on February 20 [Friday] or February 21 [Saturday] he went down to the bank and paid it off, and they both celebrated.

"He kept his promise," said Sylvia.

He was so in touch with what he was. I never knew anyone who knew himself so well. I mean, most of us don't pay much attention to who we are. We sort of go through life, but he was very intentional. He really knew what he thought, and that's just part of how he was so unusual.

Fred always had pretty significant feelings right from the beginning about people. So it wasn't like he had to get to know anybody. He knew right away whether he liked them or he didn't like them and who was true and who wasn't true—who was honest and who wasn't. He knew immediately. He just had a sense about it. And I think that was one of the things that attracted him to me is that at my core I am honest, gentle, nurturing. He just saw that and somehow liked it, fortunately. And he just knew he wanted to be with me. He really had a keen sense about people and who he would tolerate and who he wouldn't.

Perhaps it was this accuracy about people that kept the Buchenwald SS officer from shooting him in response to Fred's question, "How can you handle Hitler?"[118] It was a question that was directed to someone with a reputation for shooting anyone calling his authority into question. Perhaps Fred was ready to die. Or perhaps he was brave enough to ask the truthful question, and it took the man aback.

And he was brave enough to have birthday cake with the officer whose quarters he was cleaning.

Sylvia thinks that Fred's encounters might have had the same flavor as a man talking to a prostitute. The officers could be authentic or spill their guts out to Fred because there was never going to be a relationship. He was, in their minds, of no consequence. She observed, "These people are so burdened if they have any kind of soul. I mean they've got to kill on the one hand, but on the other, do you want to have a birthday cake by yourself?"

Perhaps it was his timing. Sylvia was amazed that Fred always had a joke appropriate to the conversation. "That was an amazing talent that he had. It was something in the conversation and he'd pop out a story. And it was like perfect. I wish I had so many of those taped. He just had a knack."

Fred often told the story about the little girl who said he talked funny. His reply would be, "I know. I come from Indiana."[119]

Light and darkness. Darkness and light. Fred's life. Everyone's life, really.

His was marked by bravery, courage, and the will to keep going on. The sign of a great soul. He was a man willing to lay down his life for others in the woods of Czechoslovakia because it was the right thing to do, not the easy thing to do. How many can say the same?

Sylvia recounts a particularly memorable moment when Fred's dear friend returned from Europe with copies of Fred's papers from his Buchenwald incarceration. Ray Wolpow, a professor at Western Washington University, had gone looking for evidence of what had become of Fred's sisters.

A video[120] was taken to record Ray's effort on Fred's behalf at the ITS Archive at Bad Arolsen, Germany.[121] In a list generated five months before the liberation, Fred is shown as performing special work making tanks. He is on a list of 1,446 prisoners committed to this detail as of January 20, 1945, in the *Konzentrationslager*. According to Sylvia, "Ray brought back the copies of his papers. And we were all sitting together. Oh! It was just … that was another moment of just, wow!" Seeing these records was an overwhelming experience for the family. While Fred didn't cry when he found out that Ray found no evidence of his sisters, Sylvia did. And Ray had brought back pictures taken at Buchenwald, and they were overwhelming. Sylvia recounted the experience:

> It was horrible to see the pictures of these meat hooks they hung people from. And this and this and he began to remember those. It was like watching him do that. It was really difficult, and then to see his papers with his signature. This was just so amazing that a friend would search for him like that and take the time. I mean, that was such a powerful thing.

The videotape ends with Ray saying, "I am saddened that I cannot go home to him to tell him what happened to his sisters." The archive staff says, "We are sorry for this as well." Then the two women add, "It is disagreeable with us that we must state the death in the records." But they acknowledge that it is difficult whether the death is recorded or not because confirming brings pain, but it also brings closure with the sadness. To not be able to confirm information leaves a gap, but also leaves hope that may go unrequited.

Notes

110   Kay's story was captured on video in the later years of her life by the Holocaust Education Committee at Yale University. She tells of her life before the German occupation of Poland, the years leading up to her family's internment, the horrors of treatment under the Nazis, and life after her liberation. Although told in an almost deadpan style, her account is very moving. Kay Fragner, interview by Halina Wind Preston Holocaust Education Committee, a video taping project done in conjunction with Yale University and station WHYY television, April 2, 1989, http://www.lib.udel.edu/ud/spec/findaids/holocast.htm.

111   Anita Fragner (daughter of Fred and Kay Fragner) in discussion with the author, February 21, 2011. Unless otherwise noted, content contained in this chapter is from this interview.

112   Sylvia Fragner (second wife of Fred Fragner) in discussion with the author, June 11, 2011. Unless otherwise noted, all of Sylvia's quotes in this chapter are taken from this interview.

113   Fred Fragner, audio message to Sylvia Fragner, December 24, 1977.

114   A canopy under which a Jewish couple stand during their marriage ceremony. It symbolizes the home that the couple will build together. The word *huppah* (also spelled chuppa) originally appeared in the Hebrew Bible (Joel 2:16; Psalms 19:5). *Wikipedia*, s.v. "Chuppah," last modified May 11, 2015, accessed July 18, 2015, http://en.wikipedia.org/wiki/Chuppah.

115   As detailed on the Yad Vashem website, "The Central Database of Shoah Victims' Names is an ongoing endeavor to recover and memorialize the names and life stories of all the individual Holocaust victims. To date some 3.1 million Jews are commemorated in the database, which was uploaded to the Internet in November 2004. Yad Vashem is currently engaged in an urgent eleventh-hour campaign to recover the missing names and biographical information from the generation that witnessed the events." "The Central Database of Shoah Victims' Names" *Yad Vashem*, accessed March 1, 2015, http://db.yadvashem.org/names/search.html?language=en.

116   "About Yad Vashem" *Yad Vashem*, accessed July 18, 2015, http://www.yadvashem.org/yv/en/about/index.asp#!prettyPhoto.

117   Ibid.

118   During the interview with Sylvia, she recounted what Fred said about his terrifying encounter with this particular German soldier.

119   Fred Fragner. Presentation at Western Washington University, May 4, 2005, 1.

120   Ray Wolpow, videotaped trip to the ITS Archives at Bad Arolsen, May 18, 2007.

121   The International Tracing Service (ITS) archives comprise approximately thirty million documents about incarceration in concentration camps, ghettos, and Gestapo prisons, and about forced labor and displaced persons. *The International Tracing Service*, accessed March 1, 2015, http:///www.its-arolsen. org/en/archi.

Fred and Anita

DEVOTED FATHER:
THE LATER YEARS

To a father growing old nothing is dearer than a daughter.

~Euripides

THE RELATIONSHIP BETWEEN A CHILD AND PARENT is as complicated, perhaps, as any human relationship. It has the potential to be the richest of relationships—but also the most stressful at the same time. There is at once a psychological investment, because the child is an extension of the life of the parent.

For Fred and Anita, as well as for Anita and her mother, this investment was perhaps compounded by the reality that Anita was literally everything to them in terms of family. She was the only child of parents who had lost their parents, their siblings, and almost every single extended family member. For Fred especially, Anita was his only biological connection. All the proverbial eggs were indeed in one basket.

When she was interviewed for this book,[122] Anita was a few months shy of finding out that she was soon to be a grandmother, and she was also going through a tumultuous divorce. Anita has a deep, gravelly voice that is very distinctive and pleasant to the ear. She is petite and trim and has thick red hair, a trait that she shares with her son, Ryan, and with her father in his younger years.

I always knew about my parents being in the concentration camps—at least as far back as I can remember. It was always very painful for me to think about, and I felt a vague sense of guilt as well. I once told my father, "I hate what you had to go through, and I understand it intellectually, but I can never feel the feelings that you had because I didn't go through it." That must have made an impact on him, because when I was an adult and we were discussing the camps, he would mention that statement of mine. He totally understood what I meant.

I was always the center of my parents' lives because I was really their only family, except for my mom's cousins in Chicago. In a way, that gave me a kind of specialness, but it was also a huge responsibility. I didn't think about it when I was young, of course, but looking back, I can see it. The feelings are strong, yet subtle at the same time—that I am the only one they have and need to make up for everyone they lost. I think along with that comes a strong need to meet all of their expectations—the ones they really had, and the ones that I imagined or assumed that they had. They didn't really have excessive expectations and weren't rigid or even very strict at all. So I think most of it came from me. I know that they wanted me to be a caring person with integrity, and they wanted me to do my best in the things that I attempted. I know as far as schoolwork went, and I was an excellent student, my dad would say, "All I ask is that you do your best." I was brought up to know it's okay to make mistakes as long as I'm trying.

My parents were from very different backgrounds in one sense, and similar in another sense. Both came from wealthy families. My mother's father was a doctor, and she was very close to him. She was raised with servants and raised to think that life would always be wonderful for her. I have pictures of her family at a picnic, where they all were dressed up in their "dressy" clothing and had a blanket on the ground with china plates and platters. My mother was very bright as well, and she finished school at a very young age. She had her master's in business administration before being captured and also attended a music conservatory and played beautiful piano.

My father's father was in the diamond business, and my dad was really close to him. He would take him on business trips frequently. My dad also was raised with a governess. His father died, however, when he was about twelve years old. His father had put all their money into his business, and when he died, they lost everything. My dad said that his mother was very dependent on his father and loved him so much that when he died, she lost her will to live and went to the cemetery to his grave every day. She died a year after his father.

My father also had two older, married sisters, and after his parents died, he stayed with them off and on. Mostly though, he slept on the streets and in a cemetery and worked in a coal yard. He stayed in school, though, and almost had his PhD in psychology from the Charles University in Prague when the war broke out. He joined the underground and was in for three years when he was shot in the hip and knee, captured, and tortured by the Gestapo.

As difficult as his years on the streets must have been, he still had a sense of humor about some of it. He told me at one point he shared a room with another guy while they were both in school, and they couldn't both go on dates on the same evening because between the two of them they only had one nice pair of pants.

Of course, both parents had their share of damage from what they went through. It would be impossible to come through that without scars. I think, though, that my mother's damage was more visible—she talked about it, but also, I think she tried to live vicariously through me and wanted me to be the person she would have been had her life not been so drastically altered forever. Of course, I am not that person at all. I don't believe it was conscious on her part, and I think she would feel terrible if she realized that she was doing that, but I do think that in her mind she was still in upper-class Europe in many ways. I know my dad went to therapy after the war, but I think he also repressed a lot and just tried to move forward. He became very "Americanized" right away and didn't really talk about the war or the camps unless I would ask a question. He had nightmares about every six months, but I really think that as he moved into old age, his PTSD really became manifest.

I remember when my father came to my school and talked to one of my classes. I was in the ninth grade. I remember he didn't go into any gory details about the camps. But he said, "Just think if one minute you were living your life like you are now and the next minute it was all gone and you were alone, taken from your family and everything you know. Think what it would feel like to have absolutely no control over anything in your life." He went on from there to talk about the importance of respect for all people and treating each other with respect, but I have never forgotten that. When he was older and would occasionally get hospitalized for pneumonia, he really had panic attacks and insisted on leaving the hospital—usually before the doctor wanted him to. I think being in the hospital brought back those old feelings that he had in the camps—of being away from what he knew and having no control over what happened to him.

There are so many things I wish I could say to them and ask them. I think of them every day and miss them enormously. There are many, many questions I would ask my mother. And I always knew that I was loved by her no matter what. My dad and I had such a special bond, and I had such unconditional love from him. I'm so lucky to have had that, and even though he is not here physically—some people never have that experience in their lives at all—both of my parents will always be with me.

As an adult in her late fifties, Anita was just beginning to articulate the pressures associated with the subtle reality that "children are everything" to their parents. At the time of her interview, she was exploring the possibility of joining an international organization comprised of the children of Holocaust survivors. She talked a bit about "survivor guilt"— the guilt that many survivors of the Holocaust feel having survived when so many they loved had perished. While there is a joy in having survived and living to carry on for those who didn't make it, there's also a natural questioning, "Why me?"

For the children of survivors, the dilemma is different.

With my generation, it's more that you can't feel. You feel like you should be able to feel what your parents felt, and you can't. But it's hard because you want to. You know, it's like the worst thing you can possibly ever think of, and it's your parents, but you feel like you should feel worse, and you can't. You feel as bad as you can. I can't even read those things a lot of times or watch the movies, but it just gets me too internally upset. Yeah, it's a feeling of guilt that you can't feel as badly as you think you should be feeling.

Anita felt that she had finally arrived at a place in her life when she'd like to connect to others who have had similar experiences.

Anita truly was Fred's pride and joy, and she commanded an immense amount of attention. And in the normal course of a child growing up and breaking free from parental expectations, in the case of Anita, the expectations were perhaps overwhelming, and the task of breaking free and establishing her own life all the more difficult. For instance, Fred and Kay enrolled her in a prestigious college in Florida, but according to a friend, it didn't seem to suit her very well. She seemed much happier when she broke free and spent an educational year abroad.

Anita was particularly close to her father. They would talk on the phone every night, and she says that she misses him terribly now that he's gone.

His expectations for her seemed to center more on wanting her to have a fulfilling life than on a life filled with material abundance. She would eventually choose a career as a social worker, one that was very much aligned with her father's interests.

> I know he got me into volunteering when I was very young. I started at a day nursery when I was about thirteen maybe. I was a candy striper before that in a nursing home. I've always enjoyed doing volunteer work, so I suppose you could say I got it from him. Not that he set me down and told me to volunteer. He always did it too. My mom was like that too. I remember when I was a kid she translated things into Braille, and I used to help her with that. At one time, I knew the braille alphabet. But I was in elementary school then.

Anita had a great deal of respect for the lessons her father taught her, but she also respected how he reached out to other children. For instance, he spoke to students in classes she attended as well as other classes. Anita says that she has "a ton of letters from kids whose classes he spoke to" and that these letters are "just amazing." Anita created several scrapbooks from different periods in her father's life, and she said she still plans on doing one composed of these letters. She particularly remembered how grateful Bev—one of the girls from the Children's Home in St. Louis—was because Fred had gotten her money so that she could have a new dress for her senior prom.

In addition to her love for her father, Anita greatly admired Fred's humanity and caring for others.

Notes

122   Anita Fragner (daughter of Fred and Kay Fragner) in discussion with the author, February 21, 2011. Unless otherwise noted, Anita's comments in this chapter are taken from this interview.

FRIEND

Friendship marks a life even more deeply than love. Love risks degenerating into obsession, friendship is never anything but sharing.

~ Elie Wiesel

THE MARKELLS

Fred and Kay's relationship with Leni and Bill Markell and their family continued on after both families had left Denver and headed east. Although they visited from time to time, it wasn't until the Fragners relocated to Delaware that the two couples spent much time together. Leni felt that a key reason for Fred coming to Delaware was the fact that she and Bill were there. "We were like family to them."[123] And, of course, they had no extended family. Leni had heard that Fred was not happy in his work. She heard of an opening in the Division of Mental Health, and so she told him. He applied for the job and got it.

Although Fred developed many other friendships through his new position, the two families always celebrated holidays together—especially Passover and other big holidays, such as Thanksgiving.

> I think that because of what he had been through and because he survived, his attitude toward life was different than maybe it would have been if he hadn't been a survivor,

a victim of war. I don't use the word victim because he came out of it. But he was always planning. If he went on a trip, as soon as he came home he was planning for the next trip. If he bought a car, he was always planning the next car he would have. He was always thinking about the future in a way that many of us didn't usually do.

Leni felt that both Fred and Kay were a wonderful influence on the children they escorted to the United States, remarking that the children always seemed to keep in touch with them. "Maybe not everyone, but many of them did. And I think they were always very grateful, and I think that Fred and Kay, you know, gave them a new lease on life."

Fred and Kay were also very fond of the three Markell children. "We had two sons and a daughter, and our kids were very involved in sports and everything, and Fred was always interested in what they were doing and how they were doing, and would play ping-pong with them, and I played tennis with him."

One of the Markell sons went on to become governor of Delaware. Jack Markell described going to football games with his father, Fred, and his younger brother until he went away to college.[124]

We'd go to the university football games, and so I'd see him Saturdays during the fall and then when I was playing baseball. Fred would often come to my games to watch me play, and his wife Kay was a very good cook, and we would have dinner at their house sometimes, and she always made a special birthday cake.

Fred was always very outgoing. He asked a lot of questions, and he had a lot of energy. He was obviously a lot older than I was. He was even a lot older than my parents were, but he had a lot of energy and a lot of enthusiasm. I don't know that I ever saw him angry. I'm sure he could get angry, but I don't know that I ever saw that. He was good to me.

Jack didn't remember Fred talking about the Holocaust much, but he was very aware of Fred's background. "It was not something that was hidden, but it wasn't something that he wore on his sleeve either."

Leni agreed that Fred and Kay made a deep impression on their children without really sharing any of the traumatic details of their past. She emphasized to her children that they were very lucky to know the Fragners. "I stressed to the children what they had been through and that they were symbolic of what had happened to the Jews."

Jack was most impressed with how interested Fred was in the progress he was making. "I went years later when he was living in Washington State and stayed [with him]—probably around the early eighties, maybe 1984, something like that. I went to visit him. We went for a long drive. He took us to a really beautiful set of waterfalls. He was very excited about that area of the world. He called it 'God's country.'"

Jack said that Fred was important in his life because of the interest and support he showed him while growing up. "My parents had plenty of friends, but I don't remember anyone else ever coming to my baseball games, as an example. I just think that there's something to be said for that. I've never forgotten the interest that he showed in me. I just remember him very well and with a lot of fondness, with a lot of appreciation, and I think that probably says it all."

Leni had a deep appreciation for the fact that she could always speak freely with Fred. "You know, you have friends sometimes and you keep quiet about certain things that you don't approve of or what have you. But we didn't have that kind of relationship. I mean, if I didn't like something, I let him know, and he responded." It was implied in this statement that Fred's response was appropriate and kind.

However, there was one action Fred took that was very difficult for everyone involved. This was his divorce from Kay. "She was a good friend of mine, and their whole separation was a terrible trauma. For a long time it was terrible, but he just … he pursued us. It didn't matter that we were really mad at him!"

Although Leni worked with Sylvia in the same unit at work and knew her to be a fine person, it didn't really make Fred's choice to divorce Kay any easier.

Still, Fred and Leni remained close friends over the years.

When Fred learned that Jack had been elected Governor of Delaware in late 2008, he was very excited. Sadly, Fred died in March 2009, along with Leni's husband Bill, just two months after Jack took office. Leni said that the bond between her and Fred was probably stronger than that between Fred and Bill. She says that she doesn't know exactly why. "Perhaps because of the social work, or maybe," she said, laughing loudly, "because I was more willing to put up with his craziness!"[125]

Leni reiterated what other friends had also observed:

> He was the kind of guy who, once he got to know you, he didn't let you go. [*Laughs.*] And I mean that very seriously. There were things that happened in his life that we really did not approve of, but he hung in there, and he would come to the house, and he would talk. I mean he just—he did not let the friendship go. And I guess, you know, we recognized that. Both my husband and I recognized that, and so you couldn't help but feel that this is a person that was different from many other people and with whom you had a real connection. I think that was the thing—with Fred, you had a connection. You know, there are many people. We have many, many friends. My husband's in the academic community, and we had many, many friends. But with Fred, you had a connection, and he made sure that you knew you were connected.
>
> I think he was a very, very seductive person. I think he got along well with men, I mean, he was interested in sports and that kind of thing, but he was very seductive with women. And I don't think he even knew he was seductive. He was seductive with women. Not with me, I mean, we were buddies.
>
> He was a very special man. He aroused feelings in people. Either they loved him or they couldn't stand him. And there were people who couldn't stand him. But I didn't happen to be one of them. [*Laughs heartily.*]

ESTHER KLEARMAN[126]

Esther Klearman was one of the orphans who lived at the Children's Home in St. Louis, Missouri, where Fred took the position of director in 1953 and where he and Kay lived when Anita was born. Esther and several others made a point of staying in touch with Fred over the years.

Esther was fourteen about the time Fred arrived for his three-year term as director. She remembered Fred and Kay's darling little baby Anita, and she would sometimes babysit Anita.

> We all loved him. He was a very warm person, and he always tried to compliment [you] and always told you positive things about yourself. You're good, you're pretty, you're nice, you're smart. So, he was very positive.

> And then before I knew it, he was gone, and then later on over the years, I went to see him. He was living in Ohio— Cincinnati, Ohio. I think Mel[127] and I were just married, and I wanted to see him. So we did, but I never saw his wife, Kay, and I know he was very unhappy. Of course I was young. I was very disappointed that he was getting a divorce. I really liked his wife. I thought she was a very sharp lady—a very sharp lady. And it was very disappointing, but he said he was so unhappy with her and blah, blah. I said, "Hey, I guess you've got to do what you've got to do." I never did see her that day. And I never saw her after that.

Esther described the Children's Home as a place for children who had no parents or had a dysfunctional family. In 1951, Esther's mother died just five weeks after the family arrived in the United States with their four children. Although her father was alive, she said, "He couldn't take care of us." Her family had immigrated to the United States like Fred, but they were from Russia.

"I could connect with Fred a little because he lived through the terrible horrors of Europe, which I didn't. I was kind of saved as a one-year-old in Russia. We were running from Nazis anyway, but we didn't have the experience he did."

Esther had a little sister who was born on the trains. She remembered that they were always fleeing the Nazis. "I remember always moving, moving, moving. So anyway, Fred lived through a lot of hell. You know, nightmares he always had, but he made a life for himself. As far as making a living, he did great with his background in psychology."

Esther recalled that Kay Fragner had severe scarring on her upper legs from the fall she took while jumping trains in an attempt to avoid the Nazi camps. "I really felt for her. She was a darling lady. I really liked her."

She also remembered that Fred—at least in later years—found Kay to be very depressing for him. "Depressing is the word he used," said Esther, "She was hard for him. She probably was. Fred was such an upbeat person at all times, always upbeat. She wasn't. It wasn't her style. So it was a hard twosome. He didn't understand why she was so down. Well, everyone acts differently, right?"

When Esther was asked if she has any fond stories about Fred, she described the time he was an accomplice in her ruse to stay home from school.

> One time I tried to skip school, and he was there for a meeting in the dining room. I had put a bunch of Noxzema on my face to make my eyes look like I was crying. He looks at me and I say, "I've got a cold." And, you know he's not stupid, and he just let me stay home, and that was nice. It was probably one of those days when I didn't have my homework done, and I was afraid to go to school. I remember he didn't say a word. He just let me go. And over the years, he always called—always!

Esther described visiting Fred at his Washington State residence with Mel, and another girl who had lived at the Children's Home, Beverly Krause.

> She's no longer living. And a lot of the girls are gone. They have died. But we had a nice visit with him. Like I said, Fred was a very upbeat person—always thinking of the positive— which is wonderful. He always wanted to do things. He

loved cooking. He loved entertaining. He would complain about Kay, because if they had a dinner party, she would get so nervous. I said, "Gee, Fred. I can understand that." I used to get very nervous too. Everything had to be perfect.

Esther also pointed out that Fred liked to talk a lot about himself. "Fred liked himself, which is good," she said, laughing. Overall, she felt a bit more bonded with Kay than Fred. "I used to see her, and I'd study her face, her expressions. I know that I liked her a lot. I liked Fred too, but he could take over a little bit too much. She would listen to you more."

Although the Children's Home at 16630 Oakland Avenue went through many directors, Esther loved it there. "It was a good place. It was a nice place. I had my meals. I had my security. I had instant friends. Of course, you have loneliness. You still feel like you're alone sometimes, but it was a good place. I liked it."

Esther noted that Fred was the only director who came to a big reunion of alumni that happened in 1984. Even though Fred had vowed never to return to the humidity of St. Louis, he did return to see Esther, and Beverly, and his other now-grown charges. "He was very sweet. Everybody liked seeing him."

BEVERLY KRAUSE

Of all the Children's Home orphans, none was more special to Fred than Beverly Krause. Unfortunately, Beverly died before work on this book began. The following was written to the author by Alan Krause, Beverly's husband:[128]

Dear Susan,

I wish you the best with your biography regarding Fred Fragner. Quite a story, I'm sure you've discovered by now.

Bev met Fred sometime in 1953/1954 when she was fourteen or fifteen and when he became the director of the St. Louis Jewish Children's Home. She had often told me stories of her earlier years there, from the age of three; some not particularly pleasant, but she often recalled some good times as well, especially regarding her girlfriends and their escapades. Six or seven of [them] remained friendly well into their sixties, four having since died, including Bev, all of cancer.

I met Fred in 1984 at the Children's Home Reunion held here in St. Louis, which Bev and Hannah organized and which was an enormous, happy, tearful, meaningful experience for all who attended—and many, many did, perhaps 125 or so, maybe sixty to seventy-five who had lived at the "Home" at one time or another. (I recall WWII vets embracing who had not seen one another for some forty years, having gone straight from the Home into the military at seventeen to eighteen years of age.) Our group of "girls"—who met once a month or so—implored Fred to come, and he did. An exciting time. Bev and I visited Fred and Sylvia in Seattle, stayed in touch, even meeting them both a few years later in Sedona, Arizona, when our separate trips made that possible.

I wish I still had the pictures, memorabilia, etc., on display at that reunion for you now. We had kept it, and I placed it all out at Bev's memorial reception after her funeral, March 1, 2009.[129] I think I gave the material or certainly offered it to the others at that time; in any case, I no longer have it.

I best remember having being told that the changes Fred instituted at the Home made life there much more "humane" (an exaggeration, of course), but most importantly his insistence that the barracks-style sleeping arrangements—ten beds in a row, for example, shared space for a few hangers with clothes, etc.—were done away with, soon redesigned with walls, two to a "room," allowing them a sense of privacy for the first time. After all, they were girls in their midteens at that time.

Bev moved out sometime after her sixteenth birthday. I met her the month after her eighteenth, September 1958, and we were married four months after her nineteenth in December of 1959 ... narrowly missing our fiftieth wedding anniversary.

Thanks for your interest and good luck with your project.

Sincerely,

Alan Kraus

THE YOUNGER GENERATION: KATHIE ROON, ANN JESTER, AND NAN BUTTERWORTH

Kathie, Ann, and Nan all met Fred when they were attending college at the University of Delaware. Kathie's parents had sold their home in Newark and rented an apartment in Park Place Apartments where Fred, Kay, and Anita were also living. Kathie's parents—Walter and Kathleen McPherson—became very close friends with the Fragners, and eventually so did the girls.

One of Kathie's first memories of Fred and Kay was the wonderful brunch they put on every New Year's. Kay was a fabulous Old World baker, and so there were lots of wonderful pastries and baked goods. She also recalled that there were benches in front of the apartment where people would sit down and hang out during the summer.[130]

When Kathie's parents decided to live on their boat in Florida during the winter months, Ann and Kathie lived in her parent's apartment, and Nan lived upstairs in the same building. It was then that they all started to know Fred a little better. According to Kathie, "Fred always seemed to enjoy young people."

Fred was an avid tennis player, and Nan was also, so sometimes she and Fred would play tennis together and, according to Kathie, he would check up on the girls but not in an obnoxious or nosey way. It seemed he was just looking after them while Kathie's parents were away.

Kathie had a favorite story about Fred. Her parents' apartment was directly across the street from the Fragners. Nan and another friend, Kay, lived on the third floor above Kathie's apartment:

So there was a boy that really liked Kay. His name was John, and Nan and I and John and Kay had all gone to the same high school. So, John just was crazy about her, and she just sort of strung him along and really wasn't that interested in him. But I think she liked the attention that she received from him. [*Chuckles and pauses.*] One night, it was pouring rain outside, and the stairs in the apartment building were that old kind of linoleum. They weren't carpeted, so everything echoed. So, whenever anyone came or went, you would hear them going up or down the stairs. So, John was visiting Kay, and then we hear a door slam and then we hear running down the stairs, running down the next set of stairs and then the front door slamming shut and then somebody running outside. And a few minutes later we got a phone call and it was Fred. [*Laughs*]. And he said, "Is everything okay over there?"

And we say, "Yeah, why?"

And he goes, "Someone just came running out of your building and threw himself on the grass [*laughs again*] in the pouring rain" [*More laughter*].

So we look out the window and say, "Oh, it's fine. It's just John. He must have had a fight with Kay."

And Fred was like, "Okay, I'm just wondering." So, he was like the friendly older neighbor, interested in us, but in a nice way. He was much more outgoing than his wife.

Kathie explained that her parents and the Fragners were very good friends, but the strongest tie was probably between her mother and Fred. "My father at that point in time was in the Merchant Marines, so he would leave for long periods of time—months at a time—to go to work. And then in that period of time, it was wartime. The Vietnam War was going on, so they would take goods to Southeast Asia."

Kathie worked in Rehoboth Beach in Delaware over the summer, and this provided another opportunity for her and her girlfriends to get to know Fred better.

Many college students would go there and spend the summer. Girls would be waitresses, and the boys would be lifeguards or summer cops, and Ann and Nan also were down there. So several times in the summer, Fred and Kay and my mom would come down. And the University of Delaware had a program where every summer they would get teachers from Ireland to come and spend some time. It was some kind of education program. So these teachers would come every summer, and somehow there was a connection with my mom and this program. And I can remember Fred and my mother—I don't remember if Kay was there or not—bringing the teachers down to the beach. And the beach wasn't that far from Newark that you couldn't do it in a day. It was an hour and a half drive. You could go in the morning, spend the whole day, have dinner, and go home. So several times in the summers, either they would come or they would come with some of the Irish teachers to the beach. And then they would often use the apartment that I had rented as sort of a staging place.

But I know that my mom would say how much Fred loved being at the beach. Fred really loved being around people, and young people [in particular].

Just as with Aglasterhausen and the Children's Home, Fred always blossomed wherever young people were planted.

After college, Kathie moved to California. She heard that Fred and Kay had split up. "That was quite a scandal at the time. And some people were mad at him for a while. And I think it was hard for my mom. I think she initially sided with Kay just because Sylvia was so much younger. I mean Sylvia is my age," she said, laughing.

Kathie also laughingly recounted that her mom referred to Sylvia as "the chick—the chick who broke up Fred's marriage."

And then it was explained to me later that he felt that he'd given up so much of his life being in the concentration camps and the war and all of that. And as he was reaching retirement age, Kay really wasn't interested in doing anything. She didn't want to travel. And he really was a vibrant, high-energy person who loved people, and he just didn't want to sit in his apartment in Newark and live out his life. So that was the rift, really.

Kathie and Fred largely lost contact until Kathie and her husband, Tony, were married and moved to Everett, Washington. This is where Sylvia and Fred visited them on a retirement trip to the Pacific Northwest. It was after this trip that Fred and Sylvia decided to relocate to Federal Way in Seattle.

Kathie's marriage to Tony strengthened their bonds to the Fragners even more because Tony was Jewish. "And Fred liked Tony. Fred liked smart people. Fred liked professional people. So he and Tony got along, and he liked Tony."

After the birth of the Roons' first child, David, Fred and Sylvia attended his Bris.[131] And Kathie began to notice after the ceremony that Fred was becoming more observant of Jewish customs, ceremonies, etc. She knew that when they lived in Delaware Fred had a Jewish home, but neither he nor Kay had participated much in the Jewish community. "David became sort of the surrogate grandson, and Fred became the surrogate grandfather. And the link was through Judaism."

Fred would often visit to watch David play soccer, much in the same way he had taken an interest in Jack Markell's sporting events years earlier. "I think that David really was like a grandson to Fred. And that was really meaningful to him. And the relationship between Fred and my mother always stayed really strong."

When Kathleen finally met Sylvia, there was never a problem. People came around because Sylvia was such a lovely person. And it is likely that she never even knew that she was "the chick."

Fred and Sylvia maintained a close and loving relationship with Kathie, her family, and her girlfriends Nan and Ann throughout Fred's life—continuing it after his passing with Sylvia. "We would have Passover together. And then my mother would come out and visit me every summer, and she'd stay for three or four weeks, and so during that time she was here, she would always go up to Bellingham and spend several days with them."

The year Kathleen died, Fred and Sylvia attended the memorial service that Kathie's family held for her in Everett.

Fred also continued the relationship with the Roons by speaking about the Holocaust in the classrooms of Kathie's son David and daughter Lauren. He did this about five or six times—starting in elementary school and continuing into middle school.

> Well, the one thing he would always say when he spoke to the kids would be, "You don't have to agree with someone, but you have to respect them."
>
> Fred was living history. So to encounter someone who has gone through some really significant historical event—and then being married to someone Jewish and to have it be *that* particular event—is remarkable. And then I think about the way he moved forward afterward. It's certainly such a great role model. What worse could happen to a person? And then for him to be able to move forward and just through the strength of his personality and stubbornness. [*Laughs heartily.*] I'm sure you heard the word stubbornness in relation to Fred before.
>
> I'm sure it would help him survive all of that. And then he became like family. He loved my family. He loved the kids, and I have a really, really small family and no one out here. So just to have someone there who you've known for a long time, he really was very much like a family member to the children.
>
> David flew up for Fred's memorial service. That was something that was important for him to do. And then it was through Fred that we met Sylvia. That's been a wonderful thing. And I think, too, that that may be what helped with the relationship in that we had Fred, but here's Sylvia, and Sylvia is my age.

I guess that you meet people in your life, and there are some people who really impact your life, and I think of him as being one of those people.

Kathie's friend Ann Jester also stayed in touch with Fred over the years.[132] She became a high school English teacher and one year did a unit on the Holocaust. Her students generated a list of questions for Fred to answer, and Sylvia videotaped Fred's answers.[133]

For Fred, this was a huge change, because up until his later years, Ann knew that Fred preferred not to talk about what he had experienced during the war.

And so, as time went on, and as his life changed and everybody moved on to different directions, I was glad to hear that he had started eventually to talk about that. No matter how painful it was, he probably above everyone— being in the profession he was in—knew that it was a good thing to start talking about. And he really didn't go into details. Sometimes he'd give little glimpses. The horrific parts? I think he left a lot of that out. He wanted people to know. Yes, the Holocaust happened. I think he was concerned about revisionists saying it hadn't happened or downplaying it. So it was a very good thing.

Getting to know Fred really encouraged me to find out a whole lot more, particularly once I started teaching kids in high school and, of course, *The Diary of Ann Frank* was so much a part of the school curriculum. I started going to various conferences and finding out as much as I possibly could, and just trying to understand how that could have possibly happened.

Ann said that she would be forever grateful for having known Fred. It made a huge impression on her and on her students to know someone who had actually lived through this historic and terrible event. It gave them a better sense of the reality and the magnitude of what happened.

Nan Butterworth's friendship with Fred initially focused on playing tennis matches together. Also, Fred was helpful in getting Nan a part-time job as a drug counselor when she was in college. "[He was] just that kind of person, I think, you know, [who] watched out for other people." [134]

The friendship lasted in large part because of Fred's close relationship with Kathie's mom, with whom Nan was very close also. Nan didn't think Fred was too crazy about Kathie's father, but she said with a hearty laugh, "I think he liked Kathleen a lot. I figure some men just like women. And women love it—or they should."

She also described Fred as having a lot of curiosity and interest in others. Laughingly, she added that he also "had really quite an ego." He certainly liked an audience, "but that didn't take away from his charm."

"I think maybe what was interesting for me is that he was an adult, and yet I didn't feel that there was that huge divide between generations. You could be very, very open with him."

JOAN STORKMAN

Joan Storkman met Fred when Sylvia was working for Tacoma Pierce County Health Department in Washington. [135] Fred was volunteering at the alternative high school in Spanaway, and Joan was the social worker at the school. They became acquainted and teamed up to work with some of the students. "He would lecture and work individually with the kids." This was about 1987. He went to the school about every other week for about two to two and a half years. One very special event in Fred's volunteer life was the receipt of a plaque from the students he had worked with. The plaque said, "After forty years of liberation, you're still liberating us. We love you, Fred."

The Fragner and Storkman families began meeting socially, and eventually Joan worked Fred into speaking to students at the school. "I think he had an easier time talking with—he said this several times—talking with kids versus with adults. It's that level of trust and honesty that the kids have."

When asked what she remembered most about Fred, Joan replied that just that morning she, her daughter, and her son and his girlfriend were all talking about Fred:

> He was so honest and willing to take risks and talk about the pretty painful experiences he had when he was interned, and with the alternative high school kids, I saw that as well. It wasn't easy for him, and a lot of times it caused him a lot of pain to share those experiences. One time he was telling me how angry he was at an audience because they wanted to hear those stories, and he wanted to more intellectualize and just tell them about politics. [I said to him] "Fred, you know, one of the things people do want to hear is they want to hear what really did happen. I can't even imagine how hard that must be for you to share that. And you don't have to share that." But to get angry at the people for asking that? I think you just have to say, "I'm not willing to share that today or tonight or ever" and set that up.
>
> At that time he was just kind of going through a bit of an angry phase and, you know, he was such a man of contrasts. He had that anger of those terrible things that he went through.

Joan presented a picture of Fred sitting around the dinner table at her home with the Storkman family and another couple. She explained that this couple "just couldn't be with Fred. And a lot of people were that way. That anger just frightened them." But if someone could break through that, they would find "just this incredible kindness and loyalty to friends." And that's the part that made Joan feel so fortunate to have had Fred as a friend.

For instance, she shared an e-mail that Fred sent to her at her work on April 27, 1999:[136]

> Greetings! Your birth card and the previous e-mail were very appreciated. I want you to know that all of you mean a great deal to me. You are not friends but more like an extended family. We have just returned from visiting our

friends in Scottsdale, Arizona, where the temperatures were in the eighties. Enjoyed the sun and the dry heat. Hope that sometime during the next month [we] will have a chance to see you. Once again, I want to let you know how much you mean to me. Frankly, words don't do justice to the way I feel. Stay well and stay in touch. Love from all of us, Fred, Sylvia, and Yari.[137]

These types of notes showing Fred's abiding love for his friends were not infrequent. Joan also remembered Fred's response to one of her students when the student asked him if he was rich. She felt that the student probably made this assumption because of Fred's aura—the way he carried himself and spoke with such confidence. "He carried himself as a man of stature," said Joan. So, this was an accurate assumption on the part of the student.

Joan said Fred tackled his response to the question of one of her observant students by saying, "Well, I guess I am wealthy because I've got a wonderful wife, and I have enough money for food and clothing, and I have enough money to travel, and so, yes, I really am wealthy."

Joan added,

> I was just reading my notes about how I had forgotten that his parents were somewhat well-to-do, and then I remembered that he had been on the streets after he was orphaned. So that's why he wanted to volunteer at the alternative high school, because he wanted to talk to those kids who had similar circumstances. And they were extremely appreciative and looked to him as a model for how they could improve their lives and possibly be like him.
>
> Sylvia—I just admired and continue to admire her so much. She's just in her quiet way one of the strongest women I know and brought such joy to Fred. And I think she was a rock for him and helped him heal a lot. Just her joyfulness and her laughter. He just adored her. And, of course, she him.

Joan explains that she felt that Fred's life was really dedicated to kids. From the time he was at Aglasterhausen to his encouraging talks with her students, Fred was all about children and making their lives brighter and letting them know that they had the ability to move forward with courage and confidence.

Joan most enjoyed facilitating Fred's talks with the students and "getting to be there and hearing him talk—and Fred loved to talk—and he loved an audience," she said, laughing heartily. "So I felt like I wasn't taking advantage of that situation. I was hopefully honoring that. There was so much to learn from his strength."

Joan also felt that she could best honor Fred and what he had lived through by providing a steadfast friendship with her family.

> And I worked to keep that, and he certainly did more than his part to keep that going too.
>
> He just added a depth and a challenge to all of us. It was what he did. He challenged you to think and to be strong and to never, ever let our government ... never think that we can be lax on things that happen in politics. We have to be involved. So he worked so hard and tirelessly to make sure that we all heard that message to never let what happened in Germany happen again.
>
> You know, we just chuckled about how hardheaded he was, how opinionated he was, and laughed and loved him. And certainly Sylvia did that and continued to do that, and life was certainly enriched, and we were very blessed to have him in our [lives].

BUZ PEOPLES

Buz provided Fred's beautiful and moving eulogy at his memorial service.

Not wanting to do a formal interview, she did provide some additional information about her special friendship with Fred in an e-mail message[138]:

> I cannot, offhand, remember any stories about Fred. Those memories I could share hold a more personal meaning to me than what they might contribute to an overall understanding of the man himself. However, if others come to mind I will certainly share them with you.
>
> I do think his whole life reflected integrity, and a joyfulness (perhaps from surviving Buchenwald) in living and interacting with people, something which separated myself from him, as I am a solitary individual who seeks comfort within my own company and in nature.
>
> Fred and I shared a close relationship. I adored him. However, I never got to know his family. It was as if he and I, when together, had no connection to anything else within our own lives. Perhaps that is why I felt so close to him. I did not have to share him. I could be totally focused on what he was saying or doing, when we had time to see one another.
>
> After I moved to Colorado in 1974, having known Fred for only seven years, we kept in contact through letters. We rarely saw one another. Except for a few brief visits to Wilmington,[139] when I returned to visit my mother in Federal Way, after I moved to San Juan Island in 1984, an afternoon at Mount Rainier shortly after Mount St. Helens blew, and a couple visits at his place in Bellingham, we never saw one another again.
>
> Every once in a while, I will find one of those letters, tucked into a book or at the bottom of a box in storage. They are full of news of family, friends, and opportunities explored,

but they are always a cherished piece of Fred to hold in my heart.

I wish you the best, writing about someone you never knew, and may never come to know, as there are secrets each of us withhold from others, so as to treasure them as our very own.

Kindest regards, Buz

Ray Wolpow

As Buz so eloquently stated, not every story is meant to be told, and not every story told is complete. I would just like to use this space to acknowledge that Fred had a very, very dear friend named Ray Wolpow.[140] During many, many talks with those who knew and loved Fred, I heard, "Oh, have you spoken with Ray Wolpow yet?" and I would answer, "No."

I would just like to acknowledge that this book is lacking because of it, but perhaps it is enhanced, because it exemplifies that Fred's life still holds more treasures than are possible to fit within these finite pages.

Melenie Fleischer-Wilson
and Eric Wilson

While in classes in Vancouver, British Columbia, Fred and Sylvia met their forever friends Melenie Fleischer-Wilson and Eric Wilson.[141] Eric and Fred became very, very close. According to Sylvia, "They both shared passions and, you know, it's sort of nice to have a man-to-man relationship, and he didn't have that."[142] Although Fred had a very close relationship with his father, it had been cut short by his early death. Fred had been the treasured son who had been born a number of years after his sisters. He was the male heir, but when his father died, Fred's destiny was derailed.

All of Fred's life experience after that point hadn't afforded him the opportunity—the luxury—to have long-term friendships other than his university friendship with his roommate.

Then, there was the one "best friend" he talked about while at Buchenwald—and how that friend had been shot and killed. After that, perhaps he didn't have the will to connect with anyone in the camp. Why bother? Why risk more loss and heartache?

Anita thought that Fred did connect with her grandfather—Kay's father, Peretz Wilner—while in the camps. But again, this was during a transitory period for Fred and, therefore, the relationship was brief. Peretz died just days before the liberation.

Also, as confirmed by many of those who knew him, Fred was very attractive to women and generally spent more time in deep conversations with women than with men. So his relationship with Eric, a cellist by profession and a very thoughtful individual, was rich and very meaningful for him. His relationship with Eric's wife Melenie—a painter—was no less meaningful.

They first met at Temple Shalom in Vancouver, British Columbia. Eric and Melenie were going to conversion class in 1989, and so were Fred and Sylvia. These classes took almost an entire year, and both partners in a marriage were required to attend together. While it was Sylvia who was interested in converting to Judaism, Fred was also interested in learning more about it. Eric explained that in this process, it's really as though both people are being converted.

Melenie and Eric were much younger than Fred, closer to Sylvia's age. Later in their relationship, Melenie had a genuine sense that Fred had chosen a relationship with a younger couple because he was always planning ahead and somehow knew that Sylvia would need them when he was gone. "Fred was always thoughtful in that way and so very protective of Sylvia. He didn't just think of himself." Sylvia agreed that it was different with Melenie and Eric because many of her and Fred's friends were closer to Fred's age than to her own.[143]

The specialness of the relationship was not just because of the difference in their ages:

Stories are stories, but it's all of what Fred gave me, and that was the unconditional love, unconditional acceptance. He wanted to listen, wanted to know "How do you feel?" "What are you thinking?" I think the focus on him would be that he himself was given tremendous gratification from the connection, the interaction, the dialogue. I think it was so self-fulfilling to him.

Eric added that early in Fred's life, the opportunity to be free, including the ability to speak out, was taken from him.

I guess I have a certain sense he thought about human beings as having this tremendous capacity for dialogue and for having relationships, but you had to get to it. So you had to get to it in your relationships with people and your friendships. So, and I think on that sort of level he felt there was a meeting of minds. It's almost like a sense of purpose, a sense of truthfulness the way we talk to each other. There was a layer there that was consistent. I think he was always trying to reach for that in his friends and also in himself. He assumed you could really talk about things. Like a tuning fork you can sort of balance it. And I think the root of it was always this tremendous acceptance he had for people, for our natures and the way we think about things.

This included acceptance for human foibles.

He would say, "Sometimes I'm angry. Sometimes I'm sad. Sometimes I'm loving," you know, he said, "I'm a human being." He was very much an adult in that way. So he lived life in a very gigantic, meaningful way.

Eric thought this had something to do with Fred coming face-to-face with death and having survived.

Melenie noted:

He was so loving and caring, and he wanted to give everyone the gifts that he himself learned, and wanted people to enjoy life because he realized the essence of that. So he was always saying, "What are you willing to sacrifice? What are you willing to give up so that you can enjoy your life?" He'd always say that to you.

Eric said:

> He would address large groups of people about things that they were thinking. So one of the themes that he would use was this idea of, well, if you have a lot of things to do and you're not able to do them, maybe you should think about giving something up. He was very concerned about how much people would work. You know, he'd always ask me, "How hard are you working?" and "What are you doing?" and so I'd always have a lot of things that I'd be doing all the time. So he'd say, "Well, you have to take time off" and "You have to do this for yourself." So I think that had a very big effect on us in terms of what we were thinking, what [our] obligations [were] to life.

Laughing, Melenie added, "He was also very concerned about America, about democracy, and about how people perceive what democracy is—what the responsibility of it is. He was very big on being responsible. And he was tenacious, making sure that we *got* it like he wanted us to."

"We would always look forward to seeing Fred," said Eric, "because we would always have these amazing conversations."

Eric described how Fred became involved in Eric's summer music program at the University of British Columbia. This was called "The Young Artist's Experience." Fred and Sylvia came up and spoke to the students. "He talked a lot about what it's like being a teenager and all the pressures of parents and teachers and all these things, and how important it was to be centered and what that meant."

Melenie said, "He could relate to them."

Eric added:

> Yeah. Instantly you could see that whatever he was saying was having a really positive effect on them. And one young

lady in particular was very affected by this conversation. I think it really might have been a turning point for her. I think she felt that, "Oh gee, here's an adult who's saying it's okay if you have a conversation with yourself," "What would *you* like?" that sort of thing. That's a big empowerment.

"He also talked about the Holocaust," Melenie said. "And for some of these children to meet a survivor was their first and maybe the only opportunity that [they'd] have in their lifetime. So that, in itself, was extremely profound."

Rena Ziegler

Fred and Rena initially met at Whatcom Counseling and Psychiatric Clinic shortly after Fred and Sylvia moved to Bellingham.[144] Fred volunteered at the community mental health center where Rena was the clinical director from the late seventies until she left in 1998. Later, after Fred left the clinic, a strong bond developed between them, and an abiding friendship emerged.

"We were just drawn to each other. He was a brilliant man and also very gentle and very interested in the world around him. It just felt as if I'd known him forever."

Rena recalls having a client who had relocated from New York. One day, the client inquired about "the gentleman who is wearing a tie and looks very trim" and perhaps added the word "elegant" to the description. She wanted to know who he was and added, "That's the way therapists *look* in New York! Not scruffy like in Bellingham!" Rena laughed at the recollection, one of her many fond memories of Fred.

"Fred always came dressed very carefully, but he didn't come across as uptight at all. He had a wonderful sense of humor." Rena then added that Fred's accent was pretty amazing as well.

There was a time—one particular lunch we had that always stands out in my mind. Fred used to talk to me about the fact that he thought I was working too hard and that my job was too stressful. And I assured him that I loved what I did, loved the people I worked with and so forth. But gradually, he could see and I could see that I was starting to get kind of worn down by some of the problems, and he said to me, "Rrrrena, when are you going to rrrretire?"

During our interview, we both laughed at her emphasis on Fred's amazing accent that he never surrendered. She continued to describe the conversation:

"But Fred, I don't know what I would do if I retire."

And he said, "You don't know what you are going to do because you are *not* there yet!"

And it had me in stitches. I mean, he was *so* right. And I had the opportunity many times later to let him know how right he was, because whole worlds opened up for me.

Rena knew the trauma of his Holocaust experience followed Fred until the end of his life. What impressed her was how he handled his experience and grew from it:

First of all, he emphasized the importance of learning how to eliminate hatred from the world, or at least from one's life. That hating people for whatever they are was part of what produced the horror of it all. When he would give talks about the Holocaust, that was really a lot of what he told me he emphasized—and along with that, a message of hope. Fred was a realist; there was not a shred of Pollyanna about Fred. But he had hope for a better world.

He also talked about situations that he had faced in his life doing community mental health administration. He was involved in facing legislative panels and fighting for mental health issues.

When Rena asked Fred if he got nervous in these situations, he said, "After what I went through? You know I faced worse. So a bunch of legislators was going to frighten me?"

She laughed heartily in recalling his response, adding, "Oh god, I miss him!"

In the last three years of his life, the pair got together every week for lunch at the now closed International House of Pancakes on Samish Way in Bellingham.

> We always sat at approximately the same table, and both ordered exactly the same thing—Swedish pancakes with lingonberries. That's good stuff and we enjoyed it!

> He would talk in a very almost matter-of-fact way about anticipating his death. I knew that he suffered a lot of physical pain. He hardly mentioned that but spoke often of wanting to make sure that Sylvia was well taken care of and that everything that he could pay for was paid and that she wouldn't have worries.

> When I would come to pick Fred up, he would be sitting in a chair facing the door waiting for me, and his little dog would be sitting right in his lap. Fred was very independent, right up to the end. As we would be going out the door, I would ask him if he wanted a hand, and I always kind of stood near him. He had a cane and he'd say, "I'm doing fine." He was a very active, physical man.

When asked why Fred was so important in her life, Rena paused for a long while. Then she said:

> He was a dear friend. I think that in addition to the things I've said about how incredibly sharp he was—picking up on very subtle cues from me and other people—he was very affectionate. He expressed his caring very straightforwardly.

> I told him that I loved him, and he told me that he loved me and what our friendship meant to him. And we would hug each other before and after every meal, every gathering or get-together. He was so no-nonsense, you know? He was able to cut through bullshit wherever it was found. He knew

when to keep quiet with others, but when he decided to speak, one was never in doubt about what Fred thought about something.

The other thing is, Fred is the only person who survived the Holocaust to whom I've been that close. And that affected my life. I've always had a very intense feeling about the Holocaust, but being so close to Fred made it very, very real to me. And I feel like just being around Fred tended to lend one courage.

It's a bittersweet thing to remember someone you loved and miss so deeply.

Rena ended our interview with the following statement: "I don't know if you know the expression. There's a Hebrew expression, *Yishar Koach*, which means 'forward[145] with strength.' In English, it would be 'way to go.' And that's what I want to say to you." When she spoke these words, I felt chills. She was speaking words of encouragement that my book-writing enterprise would bear fruit. What she spoke to my heart was that this was to be the title of this book, because if ever there was a person who took the words "forward with strength" to heart and lived his life accordingly, it was Fred.

NOTES

123   Leni Markell (very good friend of Fred Fragner), in discussion with the author, February 5, 2012. All subsequent comments from Leni are taken from this interview.

124   Jack Markell took office in January 2009. Jack Markell (Governor of Delaware), in discussion with the author, February 29, 2012. All subsequent comments from Jack are taken from this interview.

125   During the interview with Leni, she asked me if I'd ever read the biography of Harper Lee by Charles J. Shields. I replied that I had not. She said that, as in the case of my writing about Fred, Shields had never interviewed his subject for whatever reason, and Harper Lee allegedly told people not to read Shields' work. It was encouraging to hear the parallel, and that a biography can be successful without a first-person interview with the subject. It also reminded me of what Sylvia told me—that at least three individuals had attempted to write about Fred. One had lost interest when he moved away from Washington, and Fred didn't like the writing of the other two. I told Sylvia, "Well, he can't have that problem with me."

126   Esther Klearman (friend of Fred Fragner), in discussion with the author, July 6, 2011. All subsequent comments from Esther are taken from this interview.

127   Esther's husband.

128   Alan Krause (husband of Beverly Krause), in an e-mail to the author, July 19, 2011.

129   Fred passed just six days later on March 7, 2009.

130   Kathie Roon (family friend of Fred Fragner), in discussion with the author, February 3, 2012. All subsequent comments from Kathie are taken from this interview.

131   The Brit Milah (Bris) means "covenant of circumcision" and is performed by a rabbi eight days after a baby boy is born.

132   Ann Jester (friend of Fred Fragner), in discussion with the author, January 28, 2012. All subsequent comments from Ann are taken from this interview.

133   A transcript of this interview can be found in the "Spokesperson and Teacher" chapter.

134   Nan Butterworth (friend of Fred Fragner), in discussion with the author, March 16, 2012. All subsequent comments from Nan are taken from this interview.

135   I interviewed Joan in March and later sent her the word-for-word interview transcript for her to review and edit. She e-mailed me back on March 10 to make sure that when I wrote about Fred the word "painful" would be reflected in the final manuscript. "I feel Fred carried so much pain from his

experience that this is an important word to be sure is used, if you would please." Joan Storkman (friend of Fred Fragner), in discussion with the author, March 3, 2012. All subsequent comments from Joan are taken from this interview.

136   Taken from Fred's e-mail to Joan.

137   Yari was Fred and Sylvia's dog.

138   Buz Peoples (friend of Fred Fragner), in an e-mail message to the author, April 1, 2012.

139   Delaware.

140   As of this writing, Ray is Professor of Secondary Education and Director of the Northwest Center for Holocaust, Genocide, and Ethnocide Education at the Woodring College of Education, Western Washington University, Bellingham, Washington. The reader can read Ray's account of Fred and his Aglasterhausen experience in his 2009 journal article "Through the Dead of Night: Lesson in Trauma and Resiliency from Child Survivors of the Shoah," *Prism: An Interdisciplinary Journal for Holocaust Educators* 1, no. 1 (2009): 89–95.

141   Melenie Fleischer-Wilson and Eric Wilson (friends of Fred Fragner), in discussion with the author, January 11, 2013. All subsequent comments from Melenie or Eric are taken from this interview.

142   Sylvia Fragner in discussion with the author, June 11, 2011. All subsequent quotes from Sylvia in this section are taken from this interview.

143   Sylvia made this comment during the interview with Melenie and Eric, as she was listening in from the kitchen while preparing dinner.

144   Rena Ziegler (friend of Fred Fragner), in discussion with the author, May 15, 2012. All subsequent comments from Rena are taken from this interview.

145   *Yishar Koach (Hebrew)*, or *Yasher Koach (Yiddish)* means congratulations. Yishar koach might be said when congratulating someone on performing a mitzvah or other worthy task. Literally, the words can be translated "May your strength be firm." Rena and I have taken a bit of poetic license with the book title of Forward with Strength but by doing so are congratulating Fred for performing such a great mitzvah by remaining strong and continuing on through the most dire circumstances.

MENTOR

Ancient as ashes, I reason
And as integral as olive trees.
~Betty Scott

BETTY SCOTT

BETTY SCOTT IS A MENTAL HEALTH ADVOCATE and poet.[146] She and
Fred met through meetings of the National Alliance on Mental Illness
(NAMI) chapter of Whatcom County, and Betty looked to Fred as her
friend, colleague, and mentor.

Betty noted, "There are experiences we open ourselves up to when
we connect to an organization like NAMI because we gather together
around the common connection of chronic mental illnesses, which includes behavioral disorders that can be confounding. That world is so
complex, and often our society doesn't meet the challenge."

They first met around March 1999 when Fred was president of the
Whatcom chapter. At that time, they both worked on a state children's
conference for NAMI. They brought nationally recognized speakers
to St. Luke's Community Health Education Center in Bellingham,
Washington, where they both lived. For a while, Betty was vice president

under Fred. Then in 2000, the notice of his resignation appeared in the local NAMI bulletin:

> President Fred Fragner Resigns: Fred Fragner resigned as president of NAMI of Whatcom County in March 2000. "It is with great regret that I resign," he said, "because I believe in and support all the goals and objectives of NAMI and will continue to do so in any way I can." He added, "I had to make this difficult decision because I felt I was overinvolved, and since I want to continue to be active in NAMI, I need to take on a role other than president."

The bulletin also indicated that Fred wanted to work specifically on mental illness in the elderly and to chair a committee that would educate and support the elderly "who are too often neglected." The article concluded by saying, "The NAMI executive board wishes to thank Fred for his leadership throughout 1999. During his tenure, NAMI set up a central office and expanded many of our services to the community."

After he resigned, Betty became president:

> I remember Fred telling me, "Betty, I have sat on these board meetings, you know, the county-level boards." He said, "Don't do that. You do what you've been doing, which is supporting and administering family-to-family classes and support groups and being a support person—all of that stuff you do. Don't sit on those boards. I don't think you can accomplish anything by sitting on boards. They are a big waste of time."

> I took his advice. We were better off providing our own education to the public and providing support services to people, and we didn't have to define ourselves by being included in mental health advisory boards when sitting on those boards meant being the token—the token consumer, the token family member—where we didn't have much say. I spent fewer hours in community meetings on boards than most presidents, because I believed Fred's advice and because

he was a hard act to follow. Fred's gift was serving on boards and speaking out; that's what he would do, and that's what he would give. But he didn't necessarily believe in it. There's a certain authority that men have, and he had an impressive bio. He had extraordinary life experiences that began in his childhood and were impacted by the brutality of war.

While Fred didn't go into the details of his daily life in the camps, he talked with Betty about having survived the Holocaust just as someone would talk about having a child with a mental illness. Fred was important to Betty for many reasons. "He was a creative mentor. Whenever someone in his or her eighties has had significant life experiences that could have created a bitterness in him or her, and they decide instead to help others, to spend their time making other lives better—this speaks to the best in us."

Fred made contributions to others throughout his life. When he played tennis, he'd bet his friends. If Fred won, the proceeds would go to The Rainbow Center—a drop-in facility in Bellingham where those with behavioral disorders could go for food, camaraderie, and connections to services. Said Betty:

> His actions were lessons for us younger NAMI advocates. And because I grew up in a Jewish family, his being a Holocaust survivor had a great impact on me. As a child in a community with few Jewish people, I learned to avoid ridicule by hiding my religious origins. I'm not even sure if Fred knew I was Jewish. However, I believe he knew we shared similar cultural gifts and beliefs—a love of learning, a sense of humor, a focus on giving to others and to the community, and an ongoing care of loved ones.

> Fred also understood the power of hope. He encouraged all he met to find their creative passion and pursue it. He believed if people were creatively active, they would be less inclined toward hate and war. And he made sure younger people realized that they were good enough to succeed in their passions.

When you go through something that is so hopeless and you survive, or you find your inner strength, you redefine who you are. We often talk about that in NAMI. For many years, I cofacilitated the suicide survivors' group for those who lose loved ones to suicide. Their life changes the day they get that devastating news. They often ask, "Who am I now, now that I know my life includes such grief?" Over time, people recover with the right support; they may find joy, creativity, love, all the things that we want in our lives, though they continue to struggle through waves of loss, sometimes daily, sometimes at anniversaries. Community support is vital. Fred integrated his tragedies really well through community service, didn't he?

The following is a poem that Betty wrote in Fred's memory:

Poem for Fred Fragner, 1915 to 2009, with homage to Daddy-Long-Legs author Jean Webster, 1876 to 1916

When Germany invaded Czechoslovakia,

You joined freedom fighters saying:

Every man and woman must stand up

For what they believe. Shot, captured.

Interrogated and tortured, you maintained:

Every man and woman must stand up

For what they believe. Five years

Later you were freed. Beyond Buchenwald.

Starved and sick, you crossed the ocean in 1946

To bring sixty orphans to the US

Along the way, you taught the children

To stand up for what they believe.

Years later, you reported: *those kids saved me.*
Through your 70s and 80s, you served the elderly,
Fought for those with mental disease,
Urged our region to stand for peoples' needs.

Now, I think of you with immortals
Beside the writer Jean Webster, debating the tyranny
Of pain brought on by behaviors no generation escapes:
Hate, betrayal, greed—embedded in our anatomy.

While time, cultures, and class kept you two apart,
I imagine your souls now woven, singing
For creativity, for those in poverty,
For people quieted with disabilities.

Singing for women, children, the elderly,
For acceptance of love in sexuality;
An army of souls linked in spirit
Singing their heavenly songs:

For the rights of immigrants to get along,
Singing for health care for every one,
Singing for our water, air, and trees
Singing for our community's rights and needs.

Thank you, dear friend. To survive, you found
What you believed, and ever after stood for humanity,
Urging humane boundaries—your cragged
Voice and face staked to that sacred, loving place.

Betty explained that she took her poem from what she read in Fred's obituary, from an article in the *Bellingham Herald,* and from her own experience of his death. At his memorial, she read a version of the poem.

She mentioned Jean Webster, author of *Daddy-Long-Legs,* a childhood book that made an impression on Betty. Webster was the niece of Mark Twain. The story was about an orphan who was sent off to college by an unknown benefactor. Fred, too, was an orphan. Betty reread this book just before Fred died. Jean Webster was of the ilk, fashionable at that time, who believed that one way to improve social conditions was through eugenics—sterilizing women to control crimes against society. That meant sterilizing lower-class women with "bad genes." That was also the theory behind Nazi Germany. The idea of the orphan is important. Some in society go through life being orphans—actual or in other ways—like Fred, who was not only an orphan, but also part of the "orphaned religion of Judaism" during the holocaust. "I could easily imagine Fred and Jean Webster having lively debates in heaven," Betty said.

There were about ninety to a hundred people at Fred's memorial service, which Betty said was "extraordinary for someone of that age":

> What an incredible person he was. He was able to cross generations; his accomplishments were relevant to many. He wasn't an easy man. He was cranky, challenging, and he loved to debate and win. At the same time, he championed your creativity and your passion, and he was going to hold you to high standards. You spent time listening when Fred was in the room, and I say, "Thank goodness."

This is an early version of a poem Betty wrote about Fred just after his passing:

AFTER WORDS

Seven months before you died
You were shopping at Trader Joe's.
92-years frail, in a neck brace.
Yet once again you walked in stony triumph.
This time surviving pneumonia and a broken neck.

We spotted each other between the meat and dairy displays.
Our last moments together, you held onto a grocery cart.
In those golden minutes, by cartons of milk,
It was easy to renew our kinship.

Before we spoke of our work as compatriots,
In human history a mere decade earlier,
I confessed gratitude ever awkwardly
For your integrity and strength.

Then patterns repeating, dear mentor,
I made an emotional request.
Give me a sign when you pass on
And you, ever ready with an opinion
Followed back, "I don't believe in an afterlife."

Yet still, with me you eagerly planned possibilities.

Seven months later on the day you died—a blink in astral time—
I was again at Trader Joe's.
I received the sign.
I thought I was after a bargain of what at home I call "liquid gold."
I stood before row after row of green, brown, and amber bottles of olive oil.
And then, a stranger beside me said,
"It's my 55-year-old friend's beauty secret to ward off wrinkles.
She looks barely 30."

Dear Fred,

I trust you'd understand why I am now intrigued by olives,
oil, and trees.

How remarkable that the day you died

This stranger who gave me beauty tips

Beside bottles of oil

Repeated the sum and subtotal of troubling words said to
me earlier in the week.

For after we laughed about olive oil

As a hedge against aging

She said, "I see things in black and white.

I work with numbers. Numbers don't lie."

Impulsively I replied, "Yeah, but people use numbers to
prove anything they want."

"That's my point," she said,

Affably unaware of her impact.

"People lie. Numbers are right or wrong, black or white.

I like numbers. I don't like people."

Since then, I've learned that olive trees

millions of years old are sacred pillars of ancient societies,

Hallowed drops of oil seeped into the bones of dead saints
and martyrs

Through holes in their tombs.

Dear Fred,

Since repression and silence haunted you

I trust you'd understand my nightly ritual

a few drops of olive oil on my face and hands.

This golden mark of time defends against decay

and shadows in the wake of white and black.

Still, as I pay homage to you and afterlives

I wonder

Where are you, dear friend?

Ancient as ashes, I reason

and as integral as olive trees.

CHARLES ALBERTSON

Charles is a gentleman who lives in Bellingham, Washington. He was a mentee and friend of Fred's from the Rainbow Center.[147] Our interview took place at the Unitarian Church in downtown Bellingham and Charles arrived early. He was waiting in a small room at the church and seemed very much ready to go. He requested that I not ask my interview questions immediately. He had certain things that he wanted to say and wanted to present what these were without questions or interruptions. I agreed, and Charles began:[148]

CHARLES. Fred didn't talk about the Holocaust a whole lot except as it related to decisions and choices and freedom. That in the Holocaust no one could take away his ability to make his own decisions. They might have given him bad decisions, but he was still able to make decisions. And it didn't matter what they did. They couldn't take away choices. So he always had choices and he always valued choices. And he was very responsible about his choices, and he encouraged everybody to be responsible about the choices [they] make. To do what's best for ourselves, but just as much as what's best for the people we love, and I think … I don't know what the Jewish people think about sacrifice, but I got the sense that he was a sacrificial friend and a sacrificial father and husband and believed in sacrifice to that extent. And he believed that all of our choices are something that we are individually responsible for. We all had a role in choosing our destiny no matter how bleak or dismal it might seem. And certainly, when I would bring current issues about a girlfriend or something, he would *never* [*with great emphasis*] tell me what to do. He would make a point of never giving advice. But he was always ready to listen, and to reflect the listening that he heard, and the understanding, and he certainly was willing to be opinionated and have opinions. But he never gave advice. He never urged this or that decision. He always left the decisions to me because he was my friend and saw himself as supporting me as much as I saw my role as supporting him.

And I had a hard time understanding how I supported him. He always told me that wasn't important. He always told me I was a very supportive friend, and he didn't feel a need to elucidate anymore about why or how I was supportive. I know I was concerned when he got ill. I wanted him to take care of himself and get the care he needed. And he always assured me that if the hospital couldn't take care of him, Sylvia always could at home.

SUSAN.   [*I check the microphone to make sure it is operating properly "because we're going pretty fast." Charles agrees, and I laugh.*]

CHARLES.   We're going pretty fast, really, because I half lay there in bed and thought about it for quite some time …

SUSAN.   That's good.

CHARLES.   … about what I wanted to say.

SUSAN.   Stream of consciousness is good.

CHARLES   So, he really relied on his family, and his family really relied on him, and he relied on his friends, and his friends relied on him. Our friendship was always in the here and now. We didn't talk too much about the Holocaust. I think I said that right off the bat. And when we did talk about it, it was just to say that he enjoyed getting to groups of people and talking about the Holocaust. But he just felt anathema to the questions people would ask about what they did to him or suffering he had to go through. He never wanted to talk about what he had to face. He wanted to keep that in the past. What he wanted to say about the Holocaust was that it was a terribly confining experience, and he didn't have parents at the time. They were separated if they weren't already dead. I think they were already dead.

SUSAN.   Uh huh.

CHARLES.   And he was alone, except for the friends he made there. And they were good friends, but he was just a teenager, I think.[149] He had no interest in talking about suffering. He had no interest in rehashing the suffering and remembering the suffering. I had an inkling about what some of the suffering was, but I wouldn't say what it was in this interview because he wouldn't have wanted me to [laughs nervously for the first time]. So I think that if Sylvia wants to share that book with you she will, and it might be there or it might not. I don't know what Fred would have written down for posterity, but [more nervous laughter].

SUSAN.   And I do have some of his interviews and things that he's written—mostly video and audiotapes.

CHARLES.   Uh huh. So, I would just say that he was really helpful to me when I was making a decision to break off with my girlfriend before it got serious, and he didn't encourage me. He commented that she was a pleasant woman, that she had a lot of fine qualities. He always tried to remain neutral, and yet when it was dissatisfying to me, and I thought that

I preferred to be alone, he always supported my decision. He never questioned that. He always supported the right of the individual to make [his or her] own decisions and *live* with them because we all have to live with our decisions.

SUSAN.   Right.

CHARLES.   So, of course, you don't interfere with that process. So he just had that as a hard and fast rule with his friends. I think it kept a lot of friends, because people don't want people taking too much interest in your business. You want somebody who is going to be supportive, understanding, hear you when you're agonizing over a decision, and being part of the agony, but you don't want them to tell you what to do. And he kept good boundaries with that, absolutely good boundaries with that. And taught me to keep good boundaries with that.

I find it difficult now sometimes with friends from the Rainbow Center. The ones that are trained in case management would like to take over my case and tell me that I can't do this or I can't do that because it's not good for me. I don't appreciate that [*a bit of laughter, and then his laughter grows*]. I try not to tell people what they should do or what they shouldn't do. Although I have to admit when I see a friend of mine do his artwork, I really badly want to see him make something of a name for himself—for his art. And not that he should sell it and get rid of it and lose an attachment to it, but even just to make prints of it so he could sell the prints and maintain attachment to the original. But I think he should get his name out there. I *want* ... and yet this friend just doesn't seem interested in doing that. I don't know what he's afraid of, but he's schizophrenic and a little bit paranoid and probably afraid that something bad might happen. I can't see that it would. But that's his decision, right? [*More laughter.*] Yeah. So I have to accept that and, if Fred were here, he would be saying that. "If you want to lose a friend, just push him too hard." So ...

That's about all I could say about Fred except that really we did try to keep our friendship always in the present. He would have a bad ankle or a bum knee, wasn't always able to play handball or tennis or whatever it was. And that was always a disturbing thing for him when he couldn't get his exercise. That made coping harder. So I would hope when you do the writing that you would understand that he did need to vent occasionally. That's an important point to make. And don't get too bogged down in detail about it. He needed somebody who understood mental illness because he saw himself as somewhat mentally ill. And he didn't always have the answers—none of us does for mental illness. And that was frustrating for him, because Fred was someone who liked everything to fit. If it didn't fit it was always frustrating. But he managed to accept it and to control things that he needed to control for his own safety and for the safety of the family. But it wasn't always a pleasant task, and he was glad to have a friend around when those times came.

SUSAN.   And that was a lot of the basis for your friendship?

CHARLES.   Well, I think it was. I think it was. That was the only thing I can think of—that he would really have appreciated about me having a mental illness. I understood what it was like. Yeah. I think that was [a perspective] that he valued—having a friend with something like that.

We didn't talk about the future too much. He said that he didn't know when his time would come, but he didn't think it would be soon. He always didn't think it would be soon. Never thought it would be soon, but you never knew what "soon" was in his mind.

Other people came and passed. Lyle Stork passed away. Lyle Stork always said he thought he wouldn't live to be as old as Fred. I think Lyle meant to say, also, that he didn't think that he would outlive Fred, and it turned out he was right. But then there was…

SUSAN.   May I ask who Lyle Stork was?

CHARLES. He was the director of Rainbow Center. And there was Tom Richardson and the Howes, and they were all on the advisory board of Rainbow Center. And we would get together once in a while for a party. I remember one particular party, they talked about "Is there life after death?" and most of them weren't really in on the answer to that. They didn't necessarily have a belief of life after death or any knowledge of life after death and didn't really believe anyone had come back to say so. And they made an entire—I think it was Thanksgiving—discussion about "If you knew when you were going to die, how would it affect the way you would live your life?" Those kinds of things. It was about life before death and life after death. It was a time in their lives when all of them were keenly aware of their mortality, whereas the younger members of the party stood off to the side and watched [*rousing burst of laughter*].

SUSAN.   Can you share anything Fred might have said about what his belief was?

CHARLES. I don't think Fred had a solid belief in the afterlife. He certainly didn't want to discourage anyone else from believing in an afterlife. He very well may have believed in some sort of an existence that was peaceful, but he certainly didn't have a clear idea of what it might be. But I got the sense that he wasn't afraid of death, or that he needed to accomplish this, that, and the other thing before he died. So, that tells me that he must have known it was going to be peaceful; it wasn't going to be a bad thing. He wasn't afraid of it. Certainly, there were a lot of things in life that were worth being afraid of, but death wasn't one of them.

Before I quit talking, I want to talk about his relationships with his employees at different mental health facilities or children's homes, the places where he worked as a boss, as the CEO. He talked about employees not always acting with compassion and empathy for the people that they served. And this drove him into a complete frenzy! He would fire people over it. He would lash out and give people tongue-lashings over it! You had to be a responsible caregiver, and he would not stand for anything less. When he was an ombudsman for the elderly homes, he had very definite ideas about what the residents wanted and supported the residents in their request[s] about where a mirror should be placed, so that you couldn't see their bed when you walked by the door—things like that, which were important to the residents. They wanted privacy. And the home itself thought that it was convenient to [put] the mirrors in positions where they could keep an eye on everybody. And he insisted that couldn't be what ruled the place with the mirrors. It had to be what the residents wanted. They had rights to privacy, and they were not to be violated.

And that was just one example of something like that. But also, in the other places—in the children's homes—he said that he didn't care if none of his employees liked him. He didn't care if they all thought he was a jerk. He didn't care what they thought of him. It didn't matter. What mattered was that he did his job and that his job was compassion and serving the people he served. And they had to do it, too. He was their boss, and they had to do it, and that was all there was to it. So, he did talk about that [in] that way and encouraged me in my dealing[s] with people at Rainbow Center to be a good advocate for the rights of the mentally ill.

And let *them* say what their rights were! If they wanted to be treated differently than they were being treated, [then] listen to them and don't just say, "Well, you don't know anything, because you're mentally ill," "We're not here to give you everything you want," or "You don't need to feel entitled"; those were all poor excuses. So, he wanted people at the Rainbow Center, or anywhere else they were serving mentally ill people, to understand what the mentally ill people were feeling, what they were needing, and recognize that their needs were different from the rest of the people, and that they were no less than anybody else just because they were mentally ill. He was very, very dogmatic about that, that everybody is different and has different needs. But just because you don't understand their needs doesn't mean they're not valid. So he was very, very outspoken about that—about being compassionate.

SUSAN. So, do you want me to ask questions? Are you ready for that?

CHARLES. Why don't you see if the recorder is working?

SUSAN. Let's do that, because that's pretty important. Yep! Looks like it's doing fine. So, I'm going to ask you some questions. Some of it fits into what you've said and I might also go back and ask you some questions based on the things that you've said. What you've already said really rings true with what I've already heard and understand about Fred, but it really adds a different dimension to it, which is really nice. So, one of the things I wanted to know is how did you come to know Fred? Do you remember when you first met him and the circumstances?

CHARLES. I don't remember the first meeting, but I remember that he was on the advisory board and I was on the advisory board, and it wasn't long after I was on the advisory board for the Rainbow Center. I was the chair of the advisory board. And I remember Lyle wanting to have a clubhouse and NAMI wanting to make the Rainbow Center into a clubhouse, which is just something they do in New York City and have duplicated all over the world.

SUSAN. NAMI wanted to do that?

CHARLES. NAMI wanted to do that, and they wanted to duplicate [the] program in New York City here in Bellingham, and a couple of us members were like, "We like what we've got. We don't want them doing anything different."

SUSAN. What would a clubhouse be?

CHARLES. Well, that's another ball of wax. I don't know if you want to go into all of that. It would be a place where people would come to socialize and get vocationally ready to go to work. They might do work of some sort, such as working in the kitchen making sandwiches or putting out meals for people during the day when they are there and needing to eat. And they might do other things. They might go out and work a job with one of the staff alongside, so if they weren't able to be there every day of the week, the staff member could at least take over, and the job wouldn't be lost on that account. It's really strong on employment, getting paid employment, I should say, not just employment.

SUSAN. Was Fred around then?

CHARLES. Fred was around then.

SUSAN. Did he have an opinion?

CHARLES. He did have an opinion. He said this is working so well, and he said time after time [in] his years of mental health treatment that we just get something that works and everybody's happy with it, and somebody comes along and says we have to do it a new way—or an old way, whatever. We have to do it differently because we have to try something out. He said it is ridiculous. Something that is working as well as Rainbow Center—the members love it and speak highly of it—then why should we change it? So, he became a champion for us.

Fred's dissenting voice was enough to stop anything from happening for a while. He was on the county advisory board as well as the Rainbow advisory board. Fred was well-known in mental health at the time and had a large influence in policies of the county, especially, and the Rainbow Center was part of that. He had an influence in NAMI, too. NAMI had some money that they helped Rainbow Center with that was private money.

The very last appreciation dinner we had was in the basement of the United Methodist Church, and Fred was retired from the advisory board. We wanted to show appreciation for Fred, and we gave him a special award called the Luminarian Award because we saw him as a beacon of light. That was the title of the award, and it was a special bronze plaque. But he got that special award because he was on the side of the members.

Like I said earlier, that was just the way he was. He didn't always stick with everybody else. He didn't always stick with his peers. He didn't always side with his peers. He sided with what he thought was right.

And I don't think most of the members of Rainbow Center understood why he got that award.

SUSAN.   Really?

CHARLES.   Yeah. I don't think they followed that. I don't really think the members understood what his significance was. They thought he was an old man on the advisory board, and he was a big shot, and that's all they thought.

SUSAN.   What you're saying is almost what I would expect from him, that he would answer to his own vision of things.

CHARLES.   Uh huh.

SUSAN.   He's going to do what he sees as the right thing.

CHARLES.   Yeah. He was a visionary person.

I was concerned that he wasn't going to keep living through bout after bout of pneumonia. When he did die of it, it surprised me because he'd had it so much and it was summer!

SUSAN.   So why was Fred important in your life?

CHARLES.   He was just a good friend who I could count on. If we needed to get together, we would get together and see each other. We'd just call each other on the phone and arrange to meet and we'd meet. It wasn't a standing appointment. Maybe every couple of weeks we would stand an appointment. Mainly, it was whenever I wanted to get together we'd get together. Anything I wanted to talk about we could.

And I would get discouraged. I remember at that particular time of my life I was getting discouraged pretty easily. He kept saying, "Never give up, it's not worth giving up on. It's always worth seeing it on through to the end. Never give up."

Especially don't give up on yourself, you know. But any project I was doing—always—if it was worth doing it was worth seeing it through. Don't give up on anything.

SUSAN.   You said you were kind of discouraged fairly easily back then. Do you think that your life is different because Fred was in it?

CHARLES.   Yeah, I think so. I think I'm stronger. I think that he nurtured some strength that wasn't there before.

Sylvia doesn't believe it when Betty and I talk about him still being alive with the memories we carry of him, that the memories stay with us. Like the question that you just asked. We are different people because we knew him, and he changed us. And the fact that he's not here on the planet anymore doesn't change the fact that we're different because of him. We do carry him on.

SUSAN.   It's hard.

CHARLES.   Yeah. I remember I wanted to go to his house and meet his dog and see his home. And he never came to my home and I never went to his. We always went out to meet each other.

An excuse that he used was that his dog wasn't friendly. [*Very loud laughter.*] His dog was trained to ward off anti-Semitics [*more laughter*].

SUSAN.   He said that?

CHARLES.   Yeah, pretty much. We both exchanged a lot of laughs over it.

Notes

146   Betty Scott (friend of Fred Fragner), in discussion with the author, October 15, 2010. All subsequent quotes from Betty are taken from this interview. Poems are Betty's original works.

147   Located in downtown Bellingham at 209 W. Holly Street, the Rainbow Recovery Center is a recovery program designed to help mentally ill adults recover from the effects of their illnesses and reintegrate into the larger community. "Our Services: Rainbow Recovery Center." Compass Health. Accessed July 26, 2015. http://www.compasshealth.org/services/rainbow-recovery-center/.

148   Charles Albertson (friend of Fred Fragner), in discussion with the author, January 25, 2011. All quotes from Charles are from this interview.

149   Fred was a teenager when his parents died but during the Holocaust he was in his early 20's.

OMBUDSMAN

Yet, while he was himself beginning to feel his own mortality, he was helping and counseling people who were struggling with that very same challenge.

~ Becky Beach

FRED PLAYED MANY PARTS DURING HIS LIFETIME, with a common theme being roles that were focused on helping others. The United States government requires that ombudsmen[150] are available to every long-term care program. Federal money flows to the states, and then Washington State also contributes a bit more, so there is one federally funded ombudsman at the state level and one for each region of the state, including the northwest region, which includes Whatcom County. Serving under the paid ombudsman for the northwest region are volunteers, such as Fred was in the late 1990s.

To understand Fred's role as an ombudsman at St. Francis of Bellingham,[151] I interviewed Tonja Myers,[152] the executive director there for almost seventeen years, and Becky Beach,[153] a now-retired St. Francis social worker. They both considered Fred to be a friend as well as a colleague.

Strangely enough, Tonja's ex-husband had undertaken to write a screenplay on Fred's life, but after extensive interviews, Fred had decided he didn't want anything published. I had met Tonja because my twenty-eight-year-old son, Joseph, had a progressive neurological condition and had lived full time at St. Francis since 2010.[154] So, this web of circumstances led me to the discovery of Fred's role as ombudsman.

The first ombudsmen were said to have flourished during the Qin Dynasty in China around 221 BC and in Korea during the Joseon Dynasty. Wikipedia describes the term ombudsman[155] as an indigenous Scandinavian term etymologically rooted in an Old Norse word essentially meaning "representative." In government realms, an ombudsman is an official appointed to check on government activity in the interests of the citizen. In the case of St. Francis, Fred was responsible for understanding the unfilled needs or problems of residents and interfacing between the resident and institution to bring resolution—preferably in the form of enhancing the resident's life within the institution. Success depends largely on the talents of the individual ombudsman and the goodwill of the institution. Regarding the latter, it is fortuitous that St. Francis' mission—posted throughout the institution and practiced with enthusiasm as well—is "to enhance the life of every person we serve." Regarding the former, they found in Fred a man of rich life experience and acumen.

Tonja was a new administrator for St. Francis when she first met Fred. She thought he was the institution's first ombudsman, but Becky remembered two before Fred and two after he left. Tonja also served with Fred on the Ombudsman Advisory Group, which demonstrated how involved the institution was in the ombudsman program back then.

Fred's role was to drop in unannounced at least two times per month and just talk to people. He visited to advocate for residents and to be a sounding board for their concerns. According to Becky, "If we had issues that we needed help resolving, or needed help getting the family and the resident to agree, I would call him and he would come in and help us. He had an appreciation for life that not very many people have because of what his situation was—being a survivor of the Holocaust."

Tonja said that when Fred dropped in, he would "walk around and talk to people, and he always talked to me. We just hit it off." She noted that Fred's fairly thick accent was problematic for some. Becky agreed that those who generally did not hear very well sometimes had difficulty understanding what Fred was saying. "He tended to share his stories, which was helpful for people if they could hear him."

So, Tonja would often offer to interpret for him during meetings:

> I've always had a good relationship with the ombudsmen we've had in the building. I think it's a fabulous program. I believe they're advocates for the patients, and sometimes what's happening in a person's life is really hard to accept. Having somebody from the outside to be able to talk to is really important. If I know a resident is struggling with something, I'll actually call the ombudsman on their behalf and say, "Can you just come in and talk to this person?, because this is really a hard time for them." Not that [an ombudsman is a] counselor, but someone who understands things. And Fred was always funny to me because he had a very different perspective than a lot of people. Most of the people in my life have been born and raised in this country—have not had the kind of history that Fred had. And so he brought a unique perspective.

Tonja said that Fred's role as principal at Aglasterhausen gave him a real understanding of what it was like to manage a social services agency. He understood what it was to manage with a lack of resources and what it was like for a lot of people to live and work in a confined space.

> And I've never had another ombudsman do this, but he used to come in and just check on *me*! He probably saw more tears from me than most people because I'd be like, "Oh, thank you" [*imitates crying and then ends with laughter*]. For me it was just refreshing, and he was just such a support to me personally, as well as to the residents here. His job as ombudsman was to support the residents, but I always appreciated the fact that he would just come and check on me too. And I imagine that he did that with other people too, other staff members.

Becky confirmed that this was the case, saying that Fred would always stop in to chat with her and get a hug.

According to Tonja:

> And then he was funny. We have dicey situations where roommates weren't getting along and just kind of people being people things. And he was always so kind [and] understanding and down-to-earth about that. Fred was always, "Well how can you have two hundred people working and living in a space this size and not expect that there's going to be conflict?" It's so refreshing because [of] how often I had heard stories of ombudsmen and other people with expectations [of] "Well, you'd better fix this." And sometimes he'd come in and go, "Well, I guess those guys just better learn to get along, or one of them is just going to have to leave."

Fred was both a skilled advocate and a realist. "Yes, *very realistic*! He was very realistic and very blunt, actually," added Tonja. "And I just appreciated it. I did."

Becky also stated that when there were family council meetings to resolve an issue, Fred was usually the most outspoken one there. "It was just part of his personality—to be the speaker. He was a very loving person."

Tonja described one particular incident where Fred's skills really impressed her:

> There's one incident that comes to mind that I don't know if there was real resolution, but I think he was incredibly important in the journey toward acceptance for this individual. This was a man who was younger than a lot of our residents—not really young but like probably in his fifties—who had a progressive disease, and I honestly can't remember, it was probably MS, but I can't at this point remember. I don't remember all of the details, but this man was angry. He had been here awhile. But he was just angry. And he had every reason in the world to be angry. But we couldn't reach him. He was lashing out at us and his family. His wife was very, very supportive but also unable to really get him to accept some of the changes that were happening

for him. One of them that we had to orchestrate—which was just painful for all of us—[was in connection with his] electric wheelchair. The progression of his disease got to a point where he couldn't safely maneuver that electric wheelchair, and we had to take it away eventually for his safety, as well as the safety of others. We had children, and we had other residents, and he was literally running into people. Well, this man had had this electric wheelchair for a number of years, and then having to give it up, he was already angry. Again, understandably. And I didn't know what to do for him, but I couldn't have him continue putting other people at risk, or himself. And I called Fred and I said, "I need your help. I don't know how to help him. He's not allowing us to help him. And I don't have a choice. I have to take the chair away, and this is just killing all of us." It was just hard.

And Fred met with him a number of times over a period of time, and [they were] private meeting[s]—I don't know what was said. I think Fred's counseling background probably came in really, really handy. It wasn't like it ever became a joyful thing, but he did eventually accept the transition.

And, you know, we all put the peace that he eventually found with that—we all directed that, in our minds at least, to Fred, to the intervention that he was able to do—whatever that was. And he invested significant time and energy into that. It wasn't like a one-time meeting. And he met with us as a group around this very table, the whole team with this man and his wife and Fred, in trying to explain it. I think that happened a couple of times. And Fred also spent a lot of time just one-on-one with him, and I think that was critical in that transition for him.

And we still sometimes refer to that, and we go, "Do you remember how hard that was and how grateful we all were to Fred for helping this gentleman through that?"

Something else that Tonja really remembered about Fred is something he said that was very endearing to her.

> It's come back to me actually in recent months. I would ask him, "So, how's Sylvia doing?" And he'd always say—he'd say something like, "She's fine," or "She's well," and then he'd get a little sparkle in his eye and he'd say, "I'm going to see her tonight." Always like that. Every time. At first it was kind of like, that's sweet, whatever Fred. But what's interesting is that it's come back around in my life where I don't always get to see my own partner because he travels a lot, and that's a significant thing for me right now. And now it's like there are times when I'm not even sure when I'm going to see him again. And I think about that now, and it wasn't just a throwaway line for Fred, and that it wasn't just a cute thing to say. I think that having been through what he went through, I think that it was important. I think that was actually a telling thing for him. I think he genuinely was happy and excited about the fact that he was going to see her [that] night.

One of Becky's memories of Fred was how proud he was of his daughter, Anita, a social worker like her. She also remembered that Fred was very sensitive about the decline of his well-being. "He struggled with that." Being such an athletic person, it was difficult for him to experience a physical decline that prevented him from playing tennis and the things he loved doing. Yet, while he was himself beginning to feel his own mortality, he was helping and counseling people who were struggling with that very same challenge.

Tonja also mentioned that Fred could be pretty overwhelming sometimes when he just dropped in on her. That was actually what he was supposed to do as ombudsman—drop in unannounced. But sometimes it would come at an inconvenient time when her attention was focused elsewhere.

> And he was always so gracious about it. He was always just ... he wouldn't go, "Oh, I'm bothering you at a bad

time. I'll come back." No, it wasn't like that! But he was always kind of ignoring my sigh or roll of the eyes or however I responded initially. He would just kind of like gloss it over like, "How are you?" And you know, most of the time—without putting on rose-colored glasses—I think probably almost all the time, by the end of even a brief conversation with Fred, I felt better. Even though it may have been an inconvenience or whatever, it was almost as if he would just stay with you, stay with the conversation until it got comfortable. And so I felt, I guess, a mixture of that sometimes, [but] more often I felt really quite honored that he sought me out as a human—not just because I'm the administrator here, but he actually wanted to get to know me.

As the interview drew to its end, Tonja described how absolutely important Fred was to her life "in myriad little ways." She also switched to talking about Fred in the past tense. She described how important it was to her to have known someone who had been through what Fred had experienced and had the attitude he did. She had heard people speaking about the Holocaust and focusing on the positive aspects of having gone through such an experience.

I so appreciate and admire that. But the fact is that Fred was not like that. He was just really honest that the experience was terrible. It was terrible, and he was angry about it. And it shouldn't have happened. It was a real wake-up call for me. And when I went to the Holocaust Museum in Washington, DC, it was a far more personal experience for me because of knowing Fred.

How close we live to that edge. And that's part of what Fred brought to me. It may have come to me in a different way given different circumstances, but for me, talking to him was an opportunity to look in that mirror, look through that thin veil that separates us from being pretty monstrous to each other. How easy it is or would be to cross over that.

He was a force to be reckoned with. He just had such strength of spirit and tenacity. And that didn't always come across as sweetness. I think that he had to probably be pretty darn stubborn and forceful just to survive. And not only just Buchenwald, his life on the streets and all of that. I think he was one tough kid.

But he didn't let what he had been through stop him from finding joy in life and being useful and making a significant impact—a positive impact on people's lives. He made those choices to do that.

NOTES

150   *Washington State Long-Term Care Ombudsman Program*, accessed March 7, 2015, http://www.waombudsman.org/.

151   St. Francis of Bellingham is a residential care facility for both long-term care and rehabilitation. It is part of the Avamere family of companies. http://stfrancisofbellingham.com/.

152   Tonja Myers (Executive Director of St. Francis of Bellingham), in discussion with the author, February 20, 2014. All quotes from Tonja are taken from this interview.

153   Becky Beach (retired social worker), in discussion with the author, approximately March 7, 2014. All quotes from Becky are taken from this interview.

154   My beloved son, Joseph Byron Sloan, passed into the next world on Friday, February 28, 2014, two years before this book was completed. The day of his death, I finished reading Michael Perry's wonderful book *Truck: A Love Story* to him. My next reading project was to share this manuscript with him, but it wasn't meant to be. While Joseph was in hospice care during the last six months of his stay at St. Francis in Bellingham, Sylvia Fragner was his hospice volunteer and read to him faithfully each week. It is surely a small, interconnected world.

155   *Wikipedia*, s.v. "Ombudsman," accessed July 26, 2015, last modified May 17, 2015, https://en.wikipedia.org/wiki/Ombudsman.

Fred's grandson, Ryan, and Fred's great grandchildren, Caleb & Samantha

GRANDFATHER & GREAT-GRANDFATHER

*From the lips of children and infants you have ordained praise
because of your enemies, to silence the foe and the avenger.*

~ Psalms 8:2

THREE YEARS, FIVE MONTHS, AND TWENTY-FOUR DAYS after Fred's death,
his great-grandson Caleb was born on August 30, 2012, establishing the
third post-Shoah generation of Fred's family. And his second grandchild,
Samantha, arrived July 2, 2014.

Caleb's father, Ryan Cornell, spoke affectionately about his grandfather's great sense of humor, saying, "A lot of his humor was dry, and yet
a lot of it wasn't at the same time." He also described their relationship as
being a bit difficult because it was always somewhat long-distance.

He remembers a trip they took to Cannon Beach to see fireworks on
the Fourth of July when Ryan was eight. "This was my first time to see
fireworks." He also remembers his grandfather speaking to his fifth grade
class about the elder's experience in the war. "The kids weren't engaged at
first, but the questions came rapid-fire in the end."

Generally, though, Ryan always felt that the topic of his grandfather's
World War II experiences was a bit off limits because of the trauma. "I
didn't really understand how it impacted him until recently. Just having
family there was important and knowing that, no matter what happened,

they would be there. The distance, though, was tough." Ryan had always been appreciative of how he was raised and the fact that his grandfather made it through everything he confronted in World War II. "I've thought a lot about the fact that if he hadn't made it, I would never be here."

PHOTO COURTESY OF THE FRED FRAGNER ESTATE

Young Ryan and Fred.

Dear Mr. Fragner,

First off I want to thank you for your visit to our school. It was the <u>most</u> inspirational speech I have ever heared. Your words made so much sence to me. Everything you said sank deep into my mind and will stay there forever. The Holocaust was something to me that was very sad. Lots of hatred was put into those years. There are many things that I don't understand about it. I still don't know how one could conduct such a horrible thing. It's hard to imagine what it was like. It's almost imposible. You gave me a better idea of what it felt like. The other things you said that branched out from your original topic were very true. You said things about how we are the future, which we are. And how we take things for granted, especially family. Your Right, there is so much hate and greed and all kinds of bad things that have intensified over the year. Everyone is so mean to eachother, the world doesn't get along like it used to. Your words will stick with me.

THANK YOU SO MUCH FOR YOUR TIME,

One of many student letters that Fred received.

SPOKESPERSON
AND TEACHER

The mark of solitude is silence, as speech is the mark of community.
Silence and speech have the same inner correspondence and difference
as do solitude and community. One does not exist without the other.
Right speech comes out of silence, and right silence comes out of speech.

~Dietrick Bonhoeffer

THE TALK FRED DID FOR HIS GRANDSON'S FIFTH GRADE CLASS was during a time in Fred's life when he was becoming open to discussing his war experiences. For many years after the war, Fred had refused to talk about his five years in Buchenwald. But while it was possible for him to suppress the terrors of the war by day, they resurfaced frequently at night throughout his life. The night terrors defied his attempts at a final liberation.

When he finally made the decision to open up, it was only when he realized that neo-Nazis had begun to challenge the veracity of what he had lived through. He acquiesced reluctantly that it was time to speak up to memorialize his experience in the same way that Spielberg[156] and other documentary filmmakers were attempting to create a permanent record in film that would survive the last survivor.

With his love of children and passion for preventing a recurrence of the horrors of his own youth, Fred was a passionate and knowledgeable teacher. Not only did he have life lessons to bestow generously on the Aglasterhausen children, his wards at the Children's Home in St. Louis, and his friend's children, he also enjoyed speaking to students of all ages to answer their searching questions about the Holocaust.

The following are the questions and answers contained in the video-taped interview that Fred did in 1995 for Ann Jester's high school students at Caesar Rodney High School in Camden, Delaware.[157] This is followed by a sampling of student letters of gratitude presented to Fred following public school presentations he gave in 1996 and 1997. Finally, documentation of an audio interview done by two Western Washington University students is presented.

Q&A WITH TENTH GRADE ENGLISH STUDENTS

This DVD was sent to Sylvia by Ann Jester on November 14, 2011 with the following note.[158]

> Dear Sylvia,
>
> I hope this finds you well. Kathie tells me you are happy and I'm very happy for you.
>
> Please share this DVD with Anita and her son. Hopefully they will take some joy and inspiration from it.
>
> Happy holidays, Ann Jester
>
> PS You were a great cameraperson!

In the video, Fred is seated in a chair facing the camera. Blinds are pulled down behind him over two floor-to-ceiling windows. In the background to Fred's left is a stereo system. Fred is holding notes in his left hand as the video opens.

Hello. This is Fred Fragner and I'm addressing all you nice people from the English class who have sent me all the questions regarding my incarceration in Buchenwald concentration camp.[159]

Let me tell you a little bit about myself. As you know, I have an accent, and there's not very much I can do about it.[160] I was born and raised in Czechoslovakia. I went to graduate school at Charles University in Prague, receiving a graduate degree in clinical psychology.

In 1938, Czechoslovakia was invaded by German troops, and shortly afterward, I joined the Czech underground. In 1940, I was wounded and captured and spent my next five years in Buchenwald concentration camps.

Presently, I'm retired after having spent forty years in the field of mental health doing almost everything, working with people with deep emotional problems, sixteen years of which was in the state of Delaware, where I was the director of the Community Mental Health Center in Newcastle County. I was in charge of all outpatient clinics in the state, and I retired in 1982, leaving Delaware for the West.

I've been in the West since 1982. I reside in the State of Washington. Washington is a very picturesque state, and the city of Bellingham in which I reside has a population of fifty thousand to fifty-five thousand in a county of roughly about one hundred–plus thousand.[161] We are close to the Cascade Mountains on the east side and the Pacific Ocean on the west side, and are twenty minutes from the Canadian border.

I consider Washington to be a god's country—especially the area in which we are living. Being close to the mountains, we can do a lot of skiing. And being close to the water, we can do a lot of boating and fishing.

Since I retired, I've done a lot of volunteer work. Presently, I am chairman of a five-county board of mental health. I'm working as an ombudsman, and I travel quite a bit. In addition to this, I belong to the tennis club and play tennis three to four times a week.

Well, so much for my background. I hope that you will get a greater sense for who I am and what I am all about.

[*Fred raises his glasses that were in his right hand and puts them low on his nose. He looks down at the papers in his left hand. These are evidently the questions he received from Ann's class. He takes off his glasses with his right hand and looks into the camera again.*]

How can one explain in a relatively short time the Holocaust—six million Jews dead, including one and a half million children?[162]

My daughter, who lives in Spokane, has once during our conversation about the Holocaust made this comment to me: "Dad, I'm sorry. It had to be terrible, but I cannot understand. I wasn't there." And she was right. One needs experience in order to understand. And in my practice, I have never told any of the people I have worked with "I know how you feel," because I don't.

I would like to take this opportunity to share with you some of my experiences and some of my feelings.

[*Fred reads again from the notes he has in his hand.*]

How can one understand the loss of a family, including uncles, aunts, cousins, etc.? How can one explain the sense of [powerlessness] and hopelessness and anger and frustration? How can one convey the brutality and the daily violence to the human spirit and dignity? How can one convey the sense of emotional and spiritual integration living only with a biological urge to survive?

Well, in the five years in Buchenwald Concentration Camp, I have seen a lot, and I have experienced a lot. I have seen Jews being forced to dig their graves and then being shot. And I have seen a sixteen-year-old boy who was forced to hang his parents. This boy, who is now an old man, and I understand lives in the US some place, and I do wonder quite often what is his state of mind.

And now, in trying to answer your questions, I have decided to deal directly with each question and address myself directly to you. There may be some overlap and duplication, but I would really hate to skip any of the questions and [leave] some of the questions unanswered.

[*Fred now reads the questions off one of the papers that he holds, gripped tightly between both his right and left hands.*]

The first question is by Anthony, who says, "I don't think that I—nor any of my classmates—have the vaguest idea of what happened during the Holocaust. Would you try to explain what it was like to be Jewish and live during this time period?"

Well, it would take more than a short period of time to explain what was the Holocaust. There are many good books to explain how the Holocaust has happened. One has to understand what happened in Germany. One has to understand Hitler's rise to power. One has to understand Hitler's obsession with exterminating Jews. And one has to understand the whole issue of his war against Jews and what led to what he called "The Final Solution."

[*Fred looks up when he starts talking about the loss of his family.*]

I believe that one experience—the loss of families I said before—I know that I have no one left for a family. I lost my parents, I lost my sisters, I lost my brother-in-laws [*sic*], I lost aunts, cousins, uncles, etc. All I'm asking you is to try and put yourself in my place and try for a second to think how would you feel and what would happen to you if you would suddenly find yourself all alone and knowing that all of your family was killed, and that their ashes or their bodies may be some place in unknown places.

The second question is by Kristine, who said, "When Hitler came into power, did your gentile friends turn against you and your family?"

Well, when Hitler came to power in Germany, we in Czechoslovakia didn't feel the impact at first. Czechoslovakia was always a very democratic country, and there was no such thing as anti-Semitism in Czechoslovakia, and our gentile friends, who are truly friends—I cannot say this for other countries where some of the gentiles have turned against Jews ... and this again is another story.

The next question is by Quintin, and he is curious as to what my life was like prior to the Holocaust.

Well, as I said, prior to the Holocaust, prior to my imprisonment, I was a student at Charles University getting my degree, and my life was as normal as the life of a student can be.

The next question is by James, who said: "Do you think about the Holocaust often?"

[*Fred looks up and sighs.*]

Well, this is something one just cannot forget. I have gone to therapy. When I came to the United States, I would wake up every night screaming, and I went to a therapy with a psychiatrist who specialized in working with combat fatigue cases. He used hypnotherapy and was able to help me to remember and to deal with a picture of my best friend being killed by Nazis. I also went later to three years of therapy, and I still have nightmares about once every six months, where I am being killed all over again.

[*Looking up, he sighs once again.*]

Susan asks if this experience scarred me.

Well, I think that probably my answer to a previous question is partly an answer to your question. I'm sure that I have deep emotional scars. I still feel a lot of anger in me. Anger because of my sense of helplessness and frustration with the past five years that I spent in the concentration camp, and I'm afraid that the scars will be with me forever. It's interesting that children who are survivors of concentration camps are scarred, too, and I'm sure as my daughter has a few emotional problems like the other children of concentration camp survivors.

[*The next question is asked by Jessie, and Fred takes it quite literally, as if the student were suggesting that he wanted to go to Buchenwald.*]

"How did you manage to get into the concentration camp?"

I didn't manage to get in concentration camp. I didn't try to get in concentration camp. As I said, I was shot in an encounter with the German Army, and I was captured and was sent to Buchenwald Concentration Camp.

Michael also asks, "How many people tried to escape and [how] many really did?"

Well, Buchenwald was a big concentration camp with about forty thousand inmates at any given time, and there were people from all over the world. There were Germans, there were British flyers who were shot down, there were French, there were Czech, there were Poles, there were Russian soldiers, almost just everybody. And the camp was surrounded by electrified wire, and outside the camp, there were very deep ditches filled with water, and outside of the perimeter of the camp, there were German guards with trained dogs. So it was impossible to escape from there, and I don't think that anyone escaped from our particular camp.

Melissa says, "Were there many people in your camp? Were the sexes segregated? Were there many children?"

In our particular camp, in Buchenwald, we were segregated by the sexes. Almost all inmates were men and, as I said, at any given time there were about forty thousand people.

Haley asks, "What was it like during the Holocaust as a prisoner?"

[*Fred looks up again from his notes.*]

Well, as I tried to say before, it is impossible to explain what it is to be a prisoner in a concentration camp. You have to realize what it means to be deprived of freedom. You have to realize what it means to be consciously aware of the fact that today may be your last day. You have to realize that you are witnessing unbelievable brutality and ... [*long pause*]. And well, it is kind of a sense that you eventually, as I said before, you stop feeling, and you stop thinking, and your body is trying to survive, but your mind no longer works.

Jason has a question: "How old were you when Hitler came into power? And do remember how you felt [during the] time when he was in power?"

Again, I would highly recommend to all of you to read books, maybe because I am a buff on history, maybe because reading those books is going to help you to understand what exactly did happen: how that Hitler came to power, how that the German industry helped him to become as [powerful] as he was, how the German military hoping to use him were used by him. It's a fascinating story. It was, I think, an exceptional time in world history, and I think that you all really should make an effort to talk to your teacher, to talk to your librarian, to get some books—good books—not novels but good, sound, historical books which are going to help you to understand.

When I came to the United States, I went to the University of Chicago, where I got my graduate degree, and our chancellor would say, "How can you understand the present or plan for the future if you don't understand, if you don't know your past?" So I feel it would be very important for you to understand how something like this could happen in a nation which was the most cultured nation, and how it is important to understand some of the forces—which are even in this country, operating now—which try to deprive people of their human rights.

Rose asks me, "Which camp were you in, and how long were you there?"

As I said before, I was in Buchenwald, and I was there five years.

And Shannon asks, "What was it like to live in a concentration camp? What did you do there?"

Well, I worked there at first in a stone quarry, about twelve to fourteen hours a day, dressed in very inadequate clothing, very hungry and being cold most of the time.

"How long were you there?"

As I stated, I was there five years.

"What was the very worst thing that happened to you or others at the camp?"

[*Periodically, Fred looks up when answering this question, and it appears to be a particularly difficult question for him to answer. He pauses.*] I cannot say what was the worst thing because there was a continuity of bad things. One day was as bad as another day.

Paul said, "During the Holocaust, what kinds of areas were you kept in, and what kind of food did you eat?"

Okay. Well, we were sleeping in barracks. Barracks had kind of wooden layers of ... I cannot call these beds, more like shelves with some straw on it, and we were closely packed like sardines, and it was very primitive, as primitive as anybody can think of.

As far as food is concerned, most of the time we were—especially toward the end of the war—we were given some coffee, which I'm not sure what it was made from—we suspect it was made out of beets—and we were given a chunk of bread, which was dark, and it tasted like [it was] made out of clay. For the big meal, we were getting a bowl of what they used to call cabbage soup, and we were very fortunate if we found a leaf of cabbage floating in the soup. And this basically was the food we were given.

Danielle asks, "What was the concentration camp like?"

[*Fred stares at the paper with the question on it.*]

Well, how can one answer this really? Again, the concentration camp was a line of barracks. There was a so-called hospital where the Germans conducted … the German doctors conducted all kinds of experiments on inmates. Some of the experiments killed people, or other experiments that left them crippled for the rest of their lives were very inhumane experiments. And, of course, there were crematoriums where human bodies were burned after they were shot, and there were gas chambers.

The next person is Donnie, who asks, "Did you ever see anyone killed by Hitler's people or troops?"

I hate to admit that I've seen a lot of people who were killed by the SS, the Gestapo. Most of the time, they were shot by a big shot in the back of the neck. Many people were hanged. As a matter of fact, every day we had to congregate in a so-called parade grounds—all forty thousand of us. And no matter if it was rain or snow, we had to stand there for a long time, and we also had to watch executions for activity that the Germans called infractions.

As an interesting note, you may want to know that the wife of the camp commandant, Mrs. Elsa Koch, who specialized in nice lampshades, would periodically parade in front of the inmates at the parade grounds, and we had to strip from the waist up. And if she found somebody with a nice tattoo on the chest, this person would be executed, and the tattooed skin was used for lampshades for Mrs. Koch.

Alexis said, "During the Holocaust, what were your feelings when you saw people dying, especially when you knew some of the people were killed for no reason other than their race or religion?"

Well, as I said, at first you feel angry—very angry. You feel helpless because there's nothing you can do about it. And a sense of frustration. You eventually start to deteriorate mentally and to stop thinking, and I guess that's the worst thing that can happen to a human being.

Matt Knight asks me, "What was a normal day for you?"

And as I said before, they would wake us up at five in the morning, we would have to soak our breakfast,[163] then we'd stay on the parade grounds, and then we'd be marched off to work. For the last year and a half, I worked in a V-1 factory—these are the rockets that are used to bomb England.

Laurel said, "Were you ever moved from one camp to another? If so, what was the transportation like?"

Yes, I was moved sometimes to smaller camps on what they called a "special commando," where in the smaller camps we would perform a certain function. I was sent to one camp, where I was assigned to an apartment where a high SS officer was living, and I was supposed to keep his place clean, shine his shoes, also working in the canteen for the SS officers. I remember that one day, one evening, I was told to come to the canteen. All of the SS officers were drunk and they gave me ... they told me to stand against the wall. They gave me a bottle of vodka, and I had to drink the whole vodka, otherwise they would shoot me. And I, of course, drank the whole bottle, and that's the last that I remember what happened. I don't know what's happened afterward, because I passed out. So, this just illustrates to you this continuous sense of terror and frustration.

Jacob asked me, "At what age were you when you were sent to the camp?"

When I was captured, I was about twenty-three years old.

Valerie asked me, "How is it that you survived six years in a concentration camp without being killed?"

Well, this is a very interesting question. Wish I could answer it. I think that I was a tough kid, raised in tough conditions, and maybe this gave me some physical strength to survive. I spoke fluent German, and this helps. I guess I was very lucky. I'm very determined and very stubborn, and this helped too. But only God knows, you know, why I survived and how I survived.

Aileen said, "Did you ever give up hope?"

[*Fred throws his head back here and grimaces for a fraction of a second.*]

One never believes that one is going to die, no matter what, but it doesn't mean that one has hope. I don't think that I had hope. I just had nothing, and I felt nothing.

Signing her question, "your friend," Shawn said, "What was your worst experience, and how long were you in the camp?"

I appreciate you having me for a friend, and maybe someday we can meet, and I can tell you more about it face-to-face and answer a lot of the questions in a more adequate way. [*This was likely Fred's way of not going into the more traumatic details of his camp experience.*]

Polly said, "In the concentration camp, did you see a lot of your friends die?"

Well, I saw a lot of people die, and some of these people were also my friends. I know that when I was finally liberated, I was very lonely and all alone.

Jeff said, "How did you entertain yourself when you were in the concentration camp?"

Well, we did not entertain ourselves. We just were existing. We went to work. We ate whatever little food we got. And then we went to sleep. And yes, our greatest entertainment was to delouse ourselves once a week, which means to try to get rid of lice, which were leading many of us to be sick with typhoid fever.

Joseph said, "What happened to your family? How did you manage to stay alive?"

Well, as I said before, my family no longer exists. I don't know where their ashes or bodies were buried. I don't know if they were killed. I don't know if they were gassed in crematoriums. I just don't know. And I don't know how I stayed alive.

Jessie said, "What was it like to be separated from your family? Did you ever find them when it was over?"

I made every effort when the war was over to find my family, but it was a total failure.

Jules said, "What were your plans after you got out of the concentration camp?"

Well, it's a very interesting question, and I'll try to develop on it as much as possible. Let me tell you a little bit about my liberation. It was the end of 1944 when the Russian troops started to move into Germany and the American troops started to move. And Germans, the SS, started to move people from other camps into Buchenwald. It got really very bad because there was no food, and I was fortunate enough to be shipped to a smaller camp in a small town in Germany. But when the Russian troops came very close, and the American troops came very close, they started to march us. We marched from southern Germany up to northern Germany I would say twenty-five kilometers per day, and we were marching in very thin striped suits—prisoner suits—and wooden shoes. And since there was not much food, probably the only thing we ate was about two pounds of potatoes. We'd baked them on a fire.

It was in May, about 2 or 3 … May 2 when we came to a little village, and they put us into barns, and I was, at this point, so sick—I was swollen up from the waist down—from hunger and exhaustion, and I was running a high fever, and I have decided that when they started to march us the next morning, I wouldn't go anyplace, knowing very well that this means that I'm going to be killed. But at this point, I just couldn't [go any farther].

Then, a miracle happened. Because about one hour later, they called us out of the barns, and Swedish Red Cross trucks came and gave us Red Cross packages. This was a miracle. We had never seen anything like this before. We ate everything in the packages, and the next morning, I woke up and had a new energy, and we were marching.

Then, we came to another German village, and we stopped there and bathed in a stream and just did nothing until a crowd came with German officers and [told] us to move on because the front was close by. Then, as we were marching through the woods, the American artillery was shelling the woods. Fortunately, nobody got killed or wounded.

Then on May 4, after a whole day of [marching] we came to some woods, and there were [plenty] of German soldiers who were lost and German civilians who were running from Russia, and finally we were allowed to make some fire—which was exceptional, because during the war they wouldn't allow us to make fire during the evening because of the airplanes.

Next morning, when I woke up … when we woke up, we noticed that our German guards were gone. Well, we didn't know what to do, and everybody [started] to walk in different direction[s], and I was sick like a dog. Really sick, feverish and swollen, and I started to walk on this road, and I walked maybe two hundred feet, and there were German soldiers on both sides of the road, and suddenly a German sergeant on a bicycle came running and called to the German soldiers, "You'd better run, because the Russians are just a couple of kilometers behind."

Well, when I heard this, I turned around and started to walk back. I didn't care at this point who or what, but maybe I walked a hundred feet, and a Jeep came with two American GIs, and suddenly I was free. And I think this was the most dramatic point in my life. Here I was, sick, in a strange country, in the middle of nowhere, free, and not knowing what to do.

I don't believe you can understand how it feels to be in this position. Suddenly, after all those years, you have your freedom, and you don't know what to do.

I remember, I stood on this road, and I was crying. I didn't know what to do. Anyway, to make the story short, I walked, and the first night of freedom, I spent in an open field. It was a rainy night—I got soaked—and later the American troops took us and built a tent city, and they gave us some food, which we shouldn't have eaten because it was very rich. I developed diarrhea and almost died from diarrhea.

Then, a few months later, I was approached by the United Nations, and I got the job as the director of a United Nations children's center for two hundred seventy war orphans of all ages. The kids were from six different nationalities, spoke six different languages, and this was, I think, the highlight of my postwar education. I think it was the kids who brought me back to life. They were anxious to learn. They were getting along great with each other in spite of the fact that they came from different nationalities; they came from four different religions.

So, I stayed there until I came to the United States when I brought the first group of sixty kids to the United States. It was a fantastic experience, and I wrote it up, and if some of you are interested in it, I would be glad to share this written-up story with your teacher, who then would be able to share it with you.

So, basically I came first to Chicago, and I got a job as a childcare worker in a children's institution, and I went to graduate school at the University of Chicago. And, from after graduation, in 1951, I spent my first fifteen years of working with kids who had emotional problems, and then I was in all kinds of teaching positions and administrative positions and therapeutic positions, and my life was very rich and very full. And if I could do it all over again, I would do *exactly* what I have done in those forty years of my professional life.

Nate said, "Do you still to this day resent the Germans for what they did during the Holocaust? Why or why not?"

Ah, well, the Holocaust was a long time ago. As a matter of fact, May 5 of this year will be fifty years of my liberation. Many Germans who were Nazis and who—most Germans were Nazis—are dying out. Like many survivors, including myself, are dying out.

I don't believe that the new generation of Germans should be held responsible for the sins of their fathers. I travel all over Europe since the end of the war, since I came to the United States, and I continue to travel. I never went back to Germany, to Austria, because somehow I feel that whenever I would see an old German I would fear he was another Nazi. But, as I said, I've no grief with the young generation of Germans who understand about democracy—with the exception of neo-Nazis.

Ted asks, "Is it a painful subject to talk about?"

Well, I don't talk about it too often. I talk about it probably to a group of people on the anniversary of the Holocaust, which is called in Hebrew Yom Hashoah [Day of Remembrance], which comes at the end of April. Last year, I talked to about one hundred twenty people at St. Paul's Episcopal Church. This year, I have about four speaking engagements.

I think that it is my responsibility to share with people—not my experience, but what did happen—and warn people that it might happen just anyplace if we are not constantly on our guard against groups who try to superimpose their way of life, their way of thinking, their way of doing things, and who basically are in the hate business. So this I feel is my responsibility as a kind of educational process.

"Do you live in fear still, even though the Holocaust is over?"

[*Fred looks up from his notes and again grimaces.*] My only fear is that something like this may happen again. There is too much hatred in this world today. There's too much hatred in the United States today. It's just frightening. It's terrifying to me to see so much hatred toward each other.

I just, you know, my experience with children from different nationalities, from different regions, impressed me by the fact that people can get along with each other in spite of differences. There's no reason to hate each other. We have to respect each other's right to be different, to think differently, to feel different, to respect differences.

And so, I'm having a lot of problems, a lot of fear with all this hatred that we see daily all over the world.

Andrew asks, "What did you learn from your World War II experience?"

I think what I have learned is how precious life is, how precious freedom is, and how dangerous hate is. And how it is important for us to respect each other, to live in peace with each other.

Caleb says, "Do you think that anything else in this world could be worse than what you had to go through?"

I don't know. I would like to say what is worse and what is not worse, but to me this was the ultimate horror, and for the six million Jews who were killed and for the one and a half million children who were killed, this was the ultimate horror too.

And there are a few others things that I would like to share with you. There is a man called Elie Wiesel who is a survivor of a concentration camp and who won the Nobel Peace Prize. And when he received the Nobel Prize, he had a few things to say, and I would like to share excerpts of what he said with you. And this is what he said:

> I remember, it happened yesterday or eternities ago. A young Jewish boy discovered the kingdom of night. I remember his bewilderment; I remember his anguish. It all happened so fast. The ghetto. The deportation. The sealed cattle car. The fiery altar upon which the history of our people and the future of mankind were meant to be sacrificed. I remember, he asked his father: "Can this be true? This is the twentieth century, not the Middle Ages. Who would allow such crimes to be committed? How could the world remain silent?" And then I explained to him how naïve we were, that the world did know and remained silent. And that is why I swore never to be silent whenever and wherever human beings endure suffering and humiliation. We must always take sides. Neutrality helps the oppressor, never the victim. Silence

encourages the tormentor, never the tormented. Sometimes we must interfere. When human lives are endangered, when human dignity is in jeopardy, national borders and sensitivities become irrelevant. Wherever men or women are persecuted because of their race, religion, or political views, that place must—at that moment—become the center of the universe. [164]

I would also like to share with you something that a German pastor, Martin Niemöller said. He said:

In Germany they first came for the Communists, and I didn't speak up because I wasn't a Communist. Then they came for trade unionists, and I didn't speak up because I wasn't a trade unionist. Then they came for the Jews, and I didn't speak up because I wasn't a Jew. Then they came for the Catholics, and I didn't speak up because I wasn't a Catholic. I was a Protestant. Then they came for me, and by this time no one was left to speak up. [165]

I hope that I was able to answer most of your questions and that you have some kind of a feeling of my experience and a sense of my many comrades who perished, who experienced concentration camp. I strongly urge you to go to the library and get some good history book[s] and to get a good understanding of what did happen during the Second World War. Because of all this hatred around us, I am very frightened, and I think you need to pay attention to what is taking place today in the whole world and in the United States.

Thank you for letting me address you.

STUDENT THANK-YOU LETTERS TO FRED[166]

Dear Mr. Fragner,

I would really like to thank you for coming to the junior high on Thursday to talk to us about your life. What you said really impacted me. I'm thinking about how lucky I am to have a family that loves me and to have a home, and to be able to eat three healthy meals a day. I have realized that I have been taking all of these things for granted. Sometimes I really don't like being around my parents and especially my brother because they are all *so annoying*! I'm tolerating them better, and appreciating them more.

PS If you would like to write me, I would love to hear from you.

Dear Mr. Fragner,

Though I have been researching the Holocaust for months, it only now just made sense to me. Before your visit, the Holocaust had always seemed so distant, so long ago. The people mentioned in my research books were just names on a piece of paper, they didn't have a face nor did they have feelings. Your visit opened up a whole new world, a side of the Holocaust that I had left uncovered. Your visit was like living the experience, and that held more value than any textbook. Thank you.

The memory that stuck with me the most was when you described what it felt like to lose everyone important to you, and the feeling of loneliness. I could never understand what that must feel like but it was powerful, nonetheless.

Also, I felt that when you pointed to us and said that "our future is up to you" really made an impact. It made me realize that we are the ones who can make a difference and can change things, from being the way things have always been to the ways we want them to be.

If I were to come away with one lesson, it would be to always respect people. You don't have to like them yet they deserve the respect that everyone is entitled to.

Thanks again for speaking to our class. That short ninety minutes made a difference.

Dear Mr. Fragner,

I am writing this letter to tell you that your story was the best-explained story of the Holocaust I have ever heard. I also want to tell you that you inspired me to try not to fight over minor problems like when someone calls you a name or something. Because you went through the worst possible thing that could ever happen to anyone. Thank you so very much for taking time out of your life to come such a far distance just to tell us about what happened. Thanks a lot!

Dear Mr. Fragner,

Mr. Fragner what you had to say changes my life in a way that is hard to explain. When you started to talk about hate and why people hate one another it got me to thinking that people don't think of hate being as bad a thing as you see it. See they see it as a way to tell someone they don't like them or they disagree with something about their lifestyle. And then you see it as a thing that starts wars and killing. Really they are continuing an era of madness, hate, and killing. So I am glad you talked with us because every time you talk you might change three or four lives. It's not a lot but it's a start.

Thank you.

Dear Fred,

Thank you very much for coming to our classroom. I know from you coming to my class you have change[d] my life. I greatly appreciate you coming. I have realized there is a lot of hate all around us. You had a wonderful message for us. I have never met a Holocaust survivor, or maybe I have but they just did not tell me, but you are the first to talk to me about this stuff, this horrible stuff. I love myself and I'm proud of who I am. Again, thank you very much.

PS I will do all that I can to not have this happen again.

Dear Fred

Thank you for coming and talking to us. I will do my best to not have this ever happen again. The message you were trying to get to us was clear and informative. I think you are a wonderful man. I wish you good health and a happy life. Thank you again for talking to us. It is good to be proud of who you are. I am half Korean.

Dear Mr. Fred Fragner,

I'm writing you to tell you how much you educated me on the Holocaust. I never thought it was as bad as the movies or books, it really made me think. Also, I wanted to tell you what a strong and brave man you are. I know if it was me in the camps I would probably kill myself. That was very brave of you. You made people realize that the choices we make are the future. Maybe if the Holocaust never happened, then it would happen now. So in a way you put your life on the line for us. You also made me realize how thankful I am for a lot of things. Once again you are a strong and brave man, thank you for coming.

Dear Fred,

Thank you for coming. I had fun talking to you. You really taught us a valuable lesson. I really like your accent. You are a really nice person. I hope I meet you again sometime. I think things are going to change because you talked to us.

[*This letter ended with several smiley faces and hearts drawn by the young author.*]

Dear Mr. Fragner,

I really enjoyed your speech on Thursday. I have seen you, and listened to you for three years in a row, and yet it has been just as touching as the first time. I think that you should write a book about the Holocaust, and what your feelings are about it. You are a very dedicated man and I thank you for your time in letting us know and helping us to realize how important our families and friends really are. Good job!

Thank you for your time! *Have a nice day!*

Dear Mr. Fragner,

I really enjoyed listening to you on Thursday. It gave me something to think about. I remember all the times I've been treated wrongly and the times I treated others wrongly. I think in everyday life most people say things that are cruel and don't realize it until it has already left their mouth, but I'm going to make it a point not to do this, especially to my brothers. What you said Thursday really affected my decision.

STUDENT AUDIO INTERVIEW[167]

DAVE.   So Fred, what is the best life lesson you have ever learned?

FRED.   You start tough [*laughter*].

DAVE.   Or, one of the best life lessons you've ever learned.

FRED.   I think be considerate to others is probably the best life lesson I have learned. I live a long life so I have many stories—so I'm going to throw something at you and see if you think this is a big story or not. But I think it [tells] my life philosophy. Someday when I die, I want to feel that I made a difference to somebody. So along this line about two or three years ago when I was still driving, I drove my car and came to the intersection, and I stopped, of course. And as I stopped, I saw a gentleman in his late forties probably, on crutches, crossing the street. And so of course I was waiting, and he almost completed, but as he was stepping on the other sidewalk he slipped and fell. So I stopped to help him and, of course, the cars behind me got very impatient with me because they were in a hurry. So they started to honk, but that was not important. What is important is that when I came to him, I asked him if he could get up, and I wondered if he was okay and asked him if there is anything I can do. He said, "No. Thank you very much. I'm fine." And so he went on, and I drove forward. What I'm trying to say is that what I have done, there is nothing special about it, you know, what I have done. Just somebody in trouble and you reach out. He took it as, it's okay. But when I got home, I realized that it is important to reach out to someone who is in trouble. It sometimes is more important to the person who reaches out than it is to the person who is in need.

JAMIE.   This one's kind of really general, but if you could change one thing about the world, what would it be?

FRED.   You mean start from scratch? [*The female student laughs at Fred's question.*]

JAMIE.   Yeah, if you could fix one problem, or kinda like what you think is the biggest problem in our world, and maybe how you would change it if you could?

FRED.   Well, it's a very complex problem, very complex problem because of the nature of human beings. We are dealing with billions of people, different cultures and different lifestyles and different beliefs, different everything, and we haven't learned yet how to accept each other and accept each other's right to have their own lives and beliefs and etc., etc. And this is the result of a lack of acceptance. And the result of it is to try to be hateful to each other. Instead of reaching out and trying to work together, we are so preoccupied with anger and hatred and our own wrong beliefs that we are right and everybody is wrong, and what we believe is the only thing that should be believed. As a result, this leads to hatreds, wars, etc. It's a simple answer, but that's the best I can do.

DAVE.   It's a very complex question, that's for sure.

FRED.   But life is very complex.

DAVE.   Yes, absolutely. Especially that we'll be teachers, a very important question. What is the most important thing that you think that young people, kids, should learn about the Holocaust?

FRED.   I think that the most important thing that young people should learn about the Holocaust is to research and if possible gain a thorough understanding of the forces that led to Holocaust because there have been other holocausts, too, and that same thing. There are still holocausts now in Africa and other places, and in order to try to cope with the holocausts, we have to understand what are the forces which pushes us to holocaust. There [are] all kinds of reasons—psychosocial and all kinds of hatreds—but the most important thing [to do] is to do research, as objective as possible, to study the historical background. You really need to know something of the history of the world and see what led other people to this kind of hatred of each other.

DAVE.   Really tied into that question also, have you seen in your recent experience, maybe going out to schools, have you seen anything that can be changed about the way teachers teach about the Holocaust? What would you like to see that teachers could do specifically to teach about the Holocaust better?

FRED.   Well it takes two parties, the students and the teachers. The teacher has to have some knowledge and some conviction that what he or she is teaching is important enough and meaningful enough that it should be taught. The students hopefully should be motivated or should become motivated to do their own research or their own study [as part of a group]. When I was teaching at a college with small classes, I had forty-five students, and you could divide the class into four or five groups, and they could do their own research.

JAMIE.   How do you think the state of schools in America [is] today? And, do you have any advice to school principals or teachers?

FRED.   That's funny. It's sad. It's sad. This is not a fair question to ask of me, because I really go primarily by the European [model], and it raises other questions. I don't think that schools in the United States understand their mission. So, you have to start a question with a question: What is your mission? What is the mission of teaching? I think the whole process of growing up is a gradual process of learning. We learn from parents, we learn from teachers—hopefully. And learn different things. We should try to observe as much information about different cultures, different political issues, social issues, and this information should be processed in high school, possibly even before. If possible, I would like to see a situation where a smaller group of students would have the opportunity to digest—like we are talking right now. What do you think? And see what ideas we come up with. Nobody has all of the answers. I wouldn't be the president for anything. Anyone who wants to be the president is crazy. [*Both Dave and Jamie laugh.*]

This is a great question. And I don't know if the solution can be found in big or small groups or what, but there should be some people who represent the wide range of views, and those people should sit down together and see a total picture.

DAVE. So, if President Obama—President-elect Obama—called you on the phone today and asked you?

FRED. Mr. President, just be Obama. [*Jamie and Dave laugh again.*] What I read about him and what I studied about him, he's a very sound man for the job. I originally was for Mrs. Clinton because she is more experienced, but after listening to both sides, I became a fan of Obama. He's fantastic. I hope I'm not disappointed, but if he continues to be the way he is, and he is high quality. He's patient, to be concerned with the welfare of the world, and not to look for easy answers, because there are none.

DAVE. I really like his willingness to be surrounded by people who share different opinions and different perspectives. I think that's really important.

FRED. Yes and no. I think that in principle, he should surround himself with people who pretty much share a certain philosophy of life, certain philosophy of the government's responsibilities toward people. But this doesn't exclude people who have different ideas of how to do it— republicans, democrats, independents who may have different ideas. From my experience when I was Director of Outpatient Clinics, I always had open discussions. I would stay a good listener because I was just one of many. And there's something about it. It's a very interesting experience that I had when I was asked by the governor to open substance abuse clinics in the state. I said I was willing to do it for only six months. He said okay, and I appointed a colleague of mine. He was a great guy. During the six months, I came to visit him, and I said, "Ben how are you doing?"

And he said, "A funny thing happened. When I was one of Jeff Barnes' staff, I was one of many. Here I'm all alone, and whenever you talk to a person who is [in] charge, it's a very lonely position, because there is no one to complain to." So this is a lesson one learns in a life—[one of] many lessons.

[*Dave and Jamie pause for some time, perhaps reflecting on what Fred has said and/or deciding where to go with the interview.*]

JAMIE.   So, from the perspective of a survivor of the Holocaust, why do you think there is so much hate in the world? This one's kind of two parts, [hate] either directed toward Jews, or directed toward others?

FRED.   That's a hundred thousand dollar question. The question is, why is there so much hatred? Period. Somehow, we manage to find someone we can hate. I know people would consider that I'm way out, but this is what I've learned in my life— the whole world is mentally ill. Why do people have to hate? Why do people have to hate somebody? It's a highly pathological thing. War, it's a manifestation if you hate Jews, if you hate Catholics. You can always find someone to hate if you want to, if you need to. There is so much hatred because people haven't yet learned how to respect each other, how to love each other sometimes in spite of each other, to respect our rights, to respect our differences and respect and find ways of resolving troubles in talking with each other. All the answers our president has. [*Fred laughs.*]

JAMIE.   The second half of that question is, could what happened in Eastern Europe happen in the United States?

FRED.   Could it happen here?

JAMIE.   Uh huh.

FRED.   That's the question?

JAMIE.   Do you think it could happen here?

FRED.   When I came here, I got the same question from somebody.
            I said, "Absolutely. I've seen it." One of the things that I
            saw in the papers was that in the sixties in Indiana and
            Iowa, the farmers had a lot of problems, and suddenly they
            turned against the Jews. There was no connection between
            one and the other, but it seems you always have to hate
            somebody. Before the revolution [in Russia], most of the
            land was owned by the rich, and people didn't own anything.
            When people started to get upset, what they did in Russia
            was easy. They had pogroms where they killed Jews. Going
            back to Christians, when Christianity started it became a
            voice, a threat. It at least was seen as a threat, and what did
            they do? Just a different kind of pogrom. They killed the
            Christians in the circuses. So, different methods. All of this
            doesn't sound very good. Unfortunately, it reflects in a kind
            of sad way how we deal with us and how inhumane we
            are. We do many inhumane acts depriving people of their
            rights, including rights to be alive.

JAMIE.   Did you ever wonder why it took the US so long to enter
            the war, and did you wonder where the US was during the
            war?

FRED.   Again, like the other questions, there are not simple
            questions. It depends to whom you talk, what kind of
            excuses they have and what kind of interpretations they
            have. I take all interpretations with a grain of salt. I
            know as a fact that during the ghettos in Europe, when
            thousands of Jews—including my whole family that was
            sent to extermination—there was a Polish Army captain

in the underground army and he was shipped, smuggled out of Poland and out of this concentration camp and to England. He met with Churchill; he met with Roosevelt with proof about what was going on. Nothing happened. Well, you question why not.

One of the questions, for example, people in Buchenwald, why didn't we help ourselves? We had B-2 factories to bomb England. It was trades that brought people to concentration camps. The last camp I was in, which was in a place called Staßfurt, was [in] a small town. There was a British munitions factory in it. We didn't find out later until after the war, and we were this concentration camp of about two thousand people who were supposed to fix German tanks, which we never did. But that fact, you see, we wondered how come they bombed the town but they never touched the factory. We found out that it was a factory owned by British interests.

You look at a map of the world. Who are our quote "friends," and who are our quote "enemies?" What kind of criteria do we use to declare who is our enemy and who is our friend? Are we going strictly on who has oil or who has uranium or other resources? Before the Civil War, who provided free slaves? What I'm trying to say is really that our way of thinking is somewhat corrupt. We don't think that what we're doing in international relationships may be a question of international economy based on who is going to provide a group of very important people in any given government the greatest profits and benefits. England almost owned the whole world at one point as the British Empire. Look at Germany and France. The whole Middle East was owned by Germany, France, and England. Why? Why do these countries do it?

I would like to think in more positive terms. Get your paper, not just one paper. I read. Reading is not just about the present, but the past. Here's a question. In one of the discussion groups I'm in, a question came up that nobody has an answer to. Why was Abraham willing to kill his son? All kind of answers. All kinds of rationalization for all kinds of things.

NOTES

156   *Schindler's List* is a 1993 award-winning film directed and coproduced by Steven Spielberg and scripted by Steven Zaillian. The film earned $321.2 million worldwide on a $22 million budget. It won seven Academy Awards out of twelve nominations. *Wikipedia*, s.v. "Schindler's List", last updated July 23rd, 2016. Accessed July 26, 2016. http://en.wikipedia.org/wiki/schindler%27s_List. A list of additional holocaust films by date can be found here: http://en.wikipedia.org/wiki/List_of_Holocaust_films.

157   Fred Fragner, interview by Ann Jester's tenth-grade English class, February 1995, DVD, Caesar Rodney High School, Camden, Delaware.

158   On the front of the notecard is the oil on canvas painting by Claude Monet (1840-1926) *A Pathway in Monet's Garden*, Giverny, 1902.

159   The names of the students are provided in the video, but the names have been changed in this transcription.

160   This was a common shtick that Fred used to lighten his Holocaust presentations. According to Wikipedia, A shtick (Yiddish) or schtick is a comic theme or gimmick. *Wikipedia*, s.v. "Shtick," last updated June 27, 2015, accessed July 26, 2015, https://en.wikipedia.org/wiki/Shtick.

161   The population of Whatcom County just topped two hundred thousand based on the 2010 US Census. "State and County Quick Facts: Whatcom County, Washington," *US Census Bureau*, accessed July 26, 2015. http://quickfacts.census.gov/qfd/states/53/53073.html.

162   It is estimated that the Germans and their collaborators killed some 1.5 million children, including over one million Jewish children—approximately 99 percent of all Jewish children in Europe at the time of World War II. "Children During the Holocaust," The United States Holocaust Memorial

Museum, accessed March 15, 2015, http://www.ushmm.org/wlc/en/article.php?ModuleId=10005142.

163   The bread that prisoners were given was so hard it had to be soaked to be edible.

164   Elie Wiesel died at the age of 87 on July 2, 2016. Read, watch, or listen to Elie Wiesel's entire acceptance speech on the occasion of the award of the Nobel Peace Prize in Oslo, December 10, 1986. "Elie Wiesel Acceptance Speech," *Nobel Prize.org*, accessed March 14, 2015, http://www.nobelprize.org/nobel_prizes/peace/laureates/1986/wiesel-acceptance.html.

165   According to the Martin Niemöller Foundation, the text is as follows: "First they came for the communists, and I didn't speak up because I wasn't a communist. Then they came for the socialists, and I didn't speak out because I wasn't a socialist. Then they came for the trade unionists, and I didn't speak out because I wasn't a trade unionist. Then they came for me, and there was no one left to speak for me." However, Niemöller created numerous variations of the speech, including versions with references to incurable patients, Jews or Jehovah's Witnesses, and civilians in Nazi-occupied countries. According to Wikipedia, "Niemöller was a national conservative and initially supported Hitler. But when Hitler insisted on the supremacy of the state over religion, Niemöller became disillusioned. He became the leader of a group of German clergymen opposed to Hitler. In 1937, he was arrested and eventually confined in Sachsenhausen and Dachau. Niemöller was released in 1945 by the Allies. He continued his career in Germany as a clergyman and as a leading voice of penance and reconciliation for the German people after World War II. His statement, sometimes presented as a poem, is well-known, frequently quoted, and is a popular model for describing the dangers of political apathy." *Wikipedia*, s.v. "Martin Niemöller," modified on August 11, 2015, accessed August 23, 2015, http://en.wikipedia.org/wiki/Martin_Niem%C3%B6ller.

166   Letters from students to Fred Fragner, 1967–1968, Anita Fragner's Family Papers.

167   This interview was transcribed verbatim by the author from a CD supplied by Sylvia Fragner. The CD was dated November 28, 2008. The WWU graduate assistants' interview summary can also be found on WWU's Woodring College of Education website, https://wce.wwu.edu/nwchgee/fred-fragner. Fred Fragner, interview by Jamie Daniels and Dave Morrin, November 28, 2008, Western Washington University, Bellingham, WA.

MORTAL,
IN THE HANDS OF EL RACHUM
—THE GOD OF COMPASSION

*For the Lord your God is a compassionate God; He will not fail
you nor destroy you nor forget the covenant with your fathers
He swore to them.*

~ Deuteronomy 4:31

IN THE END, WE ARE ASSURED OF THE PREDICTABILITY OF DEATH. We
may hide from it. We may run from it. We may become obsessed with
it and make it our constant companion. But in the end, is our end. We
return to God, to the universe, to the pool of atoms that comprise the
universe, and we no longer have a name that is separate. We become one,
and the God of compassion escorts us on our way.

Neither the believer nor unbeliever is immune to God's compassion.
God loves each one.

This is Sylvia's account of Fred's last weeks and parting from this
world.

It was a Sunday. That day, Fred had visited with Denise Fisher and her
husband, who is also named Fred. We met them through other Jewish
couples. He's not Jewish, but he's a former medic and just a nice fellow.

My Fred was just sitting in the chair after having a nice lunch. It was pretty typical that he would doze in the chair.

So he just had a nap, and then about six thirty, I said, "Fred, do you want to get up and watch *60 Minutes* or whatever? Do you want a little tea or something?" And he woke up, but he said, "No." So I said, "Okay, I'll just let you stay napping." But by eight o'clock, I thought, "Oh. Hm."

He was awake, but he wasn't interested in moving. I said, "Well, maybe you just want to stay all night in the chair? I'll just bring down blankets and a pillow." And he just seemed to indicate, yeah, that's what he wanted: "I'm not going to move. I'll just stay right here."

He was getting pretty frail at this point in his life. You know how older men tend to sort of be bent over and shuffling? And he was always proud of the fact that, boy, he was not shuffling. And he had started to shuffle. And he'd fall when he went to the mailbox. And so I think he was very aware of his failing condition.

That was a big deal. He had always been so athletic—very, very athletic. And then, there was the loss of not driving, giving up his car a little after ninety. He just knew he was failing. And when he gave up his car, he also gave up going to play tennis. So all of those things fell away like dominoes one after the other.

I think he just knew that he wasn't well enough to do that anymore. And he wasn't capable of being safe driving, so those were really good choices. He was stepping into disability. It doesn't happen all at once.

So that night, he slept in the chair.

Of course, I slept on the sofa. I brought everything down and slept on the sofa. And he slept. But at six o'clock in the morning, I *knew* something was just not right. He was not normal. He just looked groggy, and I thought, "Oh, my gosh." This was totally not normal that he would stay all night in the chair. And then he was less responsive, and so I called. I knew that Peace Health was open about eight o'clock. [I was] just going to do our plan.

We had a plan. No ER. No bringing the medics in. I just knew that this was probably near the end. I was just going to call his doctor and say, "I need hospice." So, I did. At eight o'clock, I called. I knew that he wanted to be home. I wasn't going to put him in the hospital, because

I knew it would be out of my hands. And they'd do things that I didn't want, and he didn't want that.

And just the Friday before he got sick, he went to the bank and paid off the house. He told me *always*, "I'm going to pay off this house before I die." So that was probably the last day he could have done that. Saturday he probably couldn't have gone in and done that. Friday was the last business day. And he got the check a few days before, and we went to the bank, and Fred paid off the house. And we both did a happy dance!

And then, just two days later, he had this event. And so I called the doctor at eight o'clock, and he wasn't in, and the nurse said, "Well, you have to call the medics and have him taken to the ER."

And I said, "I want the doctor to call me back. I want you to pull his record and you look it up. I am going to fulfill his wishes. He wants to stay at home and have hospice. He wanted comfort care only."

So, the nurse called me back at ten o'clock, and she said, "Did you take him to the ER?"

I said, "What did I tell you at eight o'clock this morning? I want to talk to the doctor and I'm keeping him at home, and I want to talk to the doctor because I'm asking for hospice care."

At ten thirty, the nurse called back and said, "The doctor's ordered hospice."

So, hospice came at noon. And Fred was awake enough at noon to be able to answer the hospice nurse. She asked the question, "Do you want us to do anything other than comfort?" And he said emphatically, "No!"

And he knew this was hospice, and we couldn't get the bed and everything until the next day, so we're going to keep him comfortable at home downstairs. And that afternoon, four ladies from the synagogue came over, and it's like they were just there like bees. And the ladies were there in shifts and helped me. These were ladies from the church—the care committee. Yeah, so they just came, and then they came in the next morning with a bed, and we got him in bed.

And then he got pneumonia. So he was pretty much unconscious from Wednesday through Friday. And, oh boy, did he have pneumonia. Wow! I mean listening to his lungs, he sounded just like a motor. He had emphysema, so any time he wasn't moving and not swallowing and moving around, that just gunked up. And the next morning, he was just very congested.

And so, I turned him every two hours and gave him baths and just sat with him.

And he had visitors starting on Monday when he regained consciousness and could talk a bit. Ray, Ray was there. Tony and Kathy came up from Marysville. Rena came. The only person who didn't come was Rick, Rick Adelstein. And Rick was in Hawaii.

And the rabbi called from Jerusalem and a couple of other rabbis from Seattle who he had known well. They called and all he could really say was, "Eh." But he recognized who they were and that they were reaching out to him.

So people were visiting him. Melenie and Eric came down from British Columbia. They came for Shabbat[168] that Friday night. So we turned his bed so that he could face the dining room and the candles, even though he wasn't real conscious. But we sang the Shema.[169] He was definitely facing us and involved in our prayers and conversation, etc. He wasn't very conscious.

And Ray came on Saturday, and that's when Fred was sort of aware, and he was really trying to have a conversation. So, he woke up!

And he coughed. He had terrible pneumonia, but he coughed it out. He was basically nonstop coughing for three days. And how he did that, I don't know. I mean it was very distressing, because he coughed and coughed and coughed and coughed. But, I mean, I listened to his lungs.

Saturday he was awake enough, and Ray was there for an hour, and he talked back and forth. I mean, he didn't say much to Ray, but he was aware of Ray and could sort of participate in the conversation.

But there was someone else in the room—an unseen person in the room whom only Fred saw—and Fred was introducing Ray to somebody "over there." There was definitely a presence in the room, and Fred said—he was looking up there at the flowerpot—and he said, "This is my friend, Ray. He's a professor at Western."

And I said, "What am I over here—chopped liver?"

He never told us who the person was, and I didn't ask. That's the problem, I didn't ask. I feel guilty sometimes. It wasn't until I'd been through hospice training recently that I understood. It's like this stuff really is, really is, and I should have asked. I was just assuming he was hallucinating.

There was somebody. These are the people who come or are present according to hospice. It is generally someone precious or very much loved who comes to be with them. Yes, so somebody was there.

So, this was on Sunday. Fred's daughter Anita left because she needed to go someplace for a day or so, but she was going to come back.

And he lived for another week. This was the middle of the two-week timeframe from when he had the brain event until when he died. So he coughed out the pneumonia from Friday through Sunday. He was coughing, and he still continued to cough a lot, but he was present with Ray and this unseen person. And he knew that Tony and Kathy were there. But he dozed a lot.

On Sunday I had an hour between when Anita left and my sister and her daughter were coming for the night. So, I thought, I've got to get this conversation in. And I just wanted some quiet time alone with Fred. I'd been reading some Native American materials and was just sort of reflecting lots while I sat with him. And I thought, this is my time to tell Fred how much I love him, what he's meant to me.

This was a full week before he passed.

I was talking to him and he was *very much with me.* He was alert. *I knew* he was very present for me because I could tell in his eyes he was with me, he never said a word, but he was very much tracking.

This was Sunday afternoon, and I said, "Fred, do you need me to help you now? This is a time where we know that you're not going to go to the hospital. You're going to be home. I'm going to take care of you no matter what. But is this a time when you need help?" And he never answered me. But he reached out his hand and he put it on my head, and there was very much a powerful connection, but there was no answer. It was like he was saying, "You're going to know what to do. You will just know what to do."

When he put his hand on my head, it felt like a blessing. Unspoken. A very powerful connection. He was saying how much he loved me, and it was very, very special. In Jewish traditions, they often bless with the laying on of hands and say a blessing. And, of course, he couldn't do that, but this was the closest he could get. I mean, I didn't ask. There were no words. It was just so powerful. I know his passion for living was so intense.

And then, he rested after that, and my sister came and, you know, he would sit up on the bed. We'd sit him up on the edge of the bed. And then he wanted to get up, and we sat him on the edge of the bed and I said, "Let's get you up and sit you in the chair." And he was, "No!" I mean he was really firm. "No." He didn't want to get up. I said, "Fred, this is not a safe place at the edge of the bed." But he sort of batted me away. He got a little combative. I said, "Well, I've got to go upstairs, and I've got to do laundry and …" And he was really firm and I said, "Okay. You want to sit here, okay." Well, about fifteen minutes later, *boom*! I heard the sound of Fred falling off the bed. He was on the floor. Okay, so we called my sister, and I called in the reserves and Joseph, my sister's son, came over—a great big strapping six-foot, eight-inch guy—and he just hoisted him up and put him in bed.

And so, Monday he'd gotten even more alert. He was just really amazing. The care committee people came, and then some of my friends would come by from work, and people just sort of dropped in.

I thought, "Wow, Fred wants to get going here." Because after the Sunday conversation I thought, well, maybe he's gonna just decide he's going forward, and he might recover. This guy is really working hard here.

So, I thought, "Okay, we're going to increase your food intake, we're going to get you some pudding," or thicker pudding—we didn't go to solid food yet—pudding and egg and stuff, you know. So, Tuesday morning he sat up at the table in the wheelchair and we were just on the downstairs floor. We went out and sat by the TV, and he couldn't tell me what channel he wanted to see. He always had favorite channels, CNBC, and I said, okay. I wrote out all of the favorite channels and he couldn't tell me, but I said, "Why don't you point which number?" Well, he couldn't do that. So I went, "Oh, well he's definitely had a stroke." And so he couldn't process stuff, but we shaved him, and hospice came in, and they gave him a bath and kept him clean.

And that's the day the hospice minister came, and Fred really liked her. They had a real connection, and so she came a couple times. She and Fred had met before. He had been in hospice the year before when he broke his neck. They made a really strong connection.

A year before he had fallen out of bed and snapped his C3 [vertebrae]. It was a miracle that he wasn't paralyzed. He could have been a quadriplegic. The break was like a millimeter before it snapped his spinal cord. I took him in, so it was the June before, and he said, "You know, my neck is still hurting. I'd better go in." I said, "Okay. Let's go to the doctor." And they did an x-ray or something, and the doctor comes back at five o'clock white as a sheet. And in his hand he's got this massive neck brace. The doctor says, "You're going to go to the ER right now. We're putting this on, and you're seeing a neurologist. They're coming in immediately once you get there."

The bone healed, but he was on hospice for two weeks then, because they didn't know whether he'd get pneumonia. So anyway, he got to know the minister then, and they just really made a good connection. She came back then when he was on hospice the second time. Also, he knew Nancy, who was the same nurse—same hospice nurse. So that was nice.

He was doing better Monday. And Monday night I hired someone to help, because I realized that after a week of being 24–7 on duty and not sleeping a lot that I needed help. So I hired a gal who was terrific! Man, did she know how to take care of Fred. And bathed him and turned him and boy, he looked more comfy than anything I'd ever done.

I thought, oh my, I need to go back to nursing school to learn this. He was so comfortable looking. This was so wonderful, well worth every cent to have those nine hours of nighttime when I could go to sleep and Fred was cared for so beautifully.

So then Tuesday he was up. He went to the bathroom on the commode, and I gave him some pudding, and he was looking like he was doing better. And then Anita and I tried to get him back on the bed after we'd cleaned him up. And we put him on the bed, but something happened that we couldn't get him *in* the bed. I mean, he couldn't help us. And we could not … I mean, something happened that he couldn't push, he couldn't do anything.

We had to lay him on the bed where he was because we couldn't twist him and move him up. And so I propped him up, got the chairs and the pillows, and I called Joe, my nephew. And I said, "Joe, you've got to come over here right now. I need help." And so he was there like in seven minutes and pulled him up in bed.

But that process started Fred having seizures. That's when everything went bad. I gave him the oral narcotics but it didn't stop it. And nothing's working, and I called Nancy an hour later. He was actually having a seizure then. He'd twist and stiffen and he looked like he was in horrible pain. And he was crying out. It was terrible, and this went on and on. I was just a wreck.

His breathing was about seventy breaths a minute. He'd breath seventy breaths a minute and then he'd calm down a little bit, but he'd have the seizure and this would be, maybe every twenty minutes he'd have a seizure. The medicine wasn't working.

Nancy came twenty minutes after I called her. I just knew something was really wrong. Nancy said, "Give him another dose." So we gave him another dose of both medicines, and nothing.

And then she looked at the medicine and she said, "Sylvia, I think this should be pink, and it's yellow." And this was the same medicine we'd had when he was on hospice less than a year ago. We'd never used it—what would I use morphine for? We just kept it. It had just changed color. It was supposed to be pink, and it was yellow.

So we realized that the morphine was out of date. Something happened to it—to the effectiveness. And this is what I'd been giving him all week. You know, whenever I needed to give him a little something to relax I'd give him two drops or whatever.

So Nancy called the prescription into the pharmacy, and I ran down and got the right medicine, and even then it took at least two more hours before it gave him relief.

And she said, "You know, I've got to put in these little intravenous lines." So she called the doctor and got permission to put in just the subcutaneous lines in order to stop the seizures. So it goes under the skin versus in the mouth.

He needed more relief than he was getting. This was Tuesday somewhere late afternoon about five o'clock. And half an hour after the first dose, it all went away. But he was essentially gone. You know, I mean this put him out, and so he never really woke up from that—except when Rick came.

Rick came Thursday evening. He came back from Hawaii, and the first place they came was to see Fred. And, of course, Rick comes in and says, "Hiya Fred!" in his big voice, and Fred is making noises, really trying to wake up and be present for Rick. Because he heard him—Rick's booming voice. Oh, he heard him! He wanted to converse, but, of course, with the meds and everything, he couldn't do that. But he knew and he definitely heard him. He was the only person Fred hadn't seen to say good-bye to.

Basically from then on he just didn't respond anymore. He was very calm. Yes. And he had pneumonia again. I mean, you could hear it in his lungs, but this time we knew he would not recover, and so it was just keeping him comfortable. And then he was weaned off the medicine a bit. He didn't need to have as much—like instead of every three hours it was like three times a day.

But the first time Nancy put in the little intravenous lines, she said, "Sylvia, you need to give this." Oh, I just wept. She put it in and she said, "I want you to give this."

I knew he wasn't coming back, and I just wept. Even though he tried really hard, but it would have been an awful existence for him. It would have been an awful existence because he couldn't communicate. And you know Fred. If he couldn't communicate—he wouldn't have wanted that.

So he died. I was right there. Melenie and Eric on either side. I was at his head, and we called Anita, and said, "Come quick." And she came down, and we were all right there, saying our good-byes. It was four of us at one thirty on Sunday.

He just took his last couple of breaths, and we just told him how much he was loved. We just know he was surrounded by people who loved him so much. That's the last thing, you know.

Fred didn't believe that there was anything beyond this life. The end is the end. What mattered to him was making a difference to the people who mattered here on earth, and he likely rested assured that his name is forever inscribed in the book of life.

NOTES

168   "Shabbat (Hebrew: שַׁבָּת, "rest" or "cessation") or Shabbos (Yiddish: שׁabbes) is the Jewish day of rest and seventh day of the week, on which religious Jews remember the Biblical creation of the heavens and the earth in six days and the Exodus of the Hebrews, and look forward to a future Messianic Age. Shabbat observance entails refraining from work activities, often with great rigor, and engaging in restful activities to honor the day. The traditional Jewish position is that unbroken seventh-day Shabbat originated among the Jewish people, as their first and most sacred institution, though some suggest other origins. Variations upon Shabbat are widespread in Judaism and, with adaptations, throughout the Abrahamic and many other religions. According to halakha, Shabbat is observed from a few minutes before sunset on Friday evening until the appearance of three stars in the sky on Saturday night. Shabbat is ushered in by lighting candles and reciting a blessing. Traditionally, three festive meals are eaten: in the evening, in the morning, and late in the afternoon. The evening dinner typically begins with kiddush and another blessing recited over two loaves of challah. Shabbat is closed the following evening with a Havdalah. Shabbat is a festive day when Jews exercise their freedom from the regular labors of everyday life. It offers an opportunity to contemplate the spiritual aspects of life and to spend time with family." Wikipedia, s.v. "Shabbat," accessed March 14, 2015, http://en.wikipedia.org/wiki/Shabbat.

169   Shema Yisrael (or Sh'ma Yisrael; Hebrew: שְׁמַע יִשְׂרָאֵל; "Hear, [O] Israel") are the first two words of a section of the Torah, and is the title (sometimes shortened to simply Shema) of a prayer that serves as a centerpiece of the morning and evening Jewish prayer services. Wikipedia, s.v. "Shema Yisrael," accessed March 14, 2015, http://en.wikipedia.org/wiki/Shema_Yisrael.

HAVING THE LAST WORD

One person of integrity can make a difference.

~ Elie Wiesel

IN 1995, FRED SECRETLY RECORDED AN AUDIOTAPE and then gave it to Sylvia, telling her that she shouldn't listen to it until after his death. The following is what he said.

I am dictating this tape while looking at three pictures of us: one in London, one in Acapulco, and the third one in Israel. The reason for dictating this tape is twofold: personally, I need to have the last word, and secondly, because I want to leave a message for you.

There is not much I can say about the first one. But there is a lot I can say about the second. You have given me the most beautiful gift a person can give to another one, namely, love and companionship. I have always felt deeply loved by you, and there was never any question about it in my mind—about your caring and commitment. It was like a warm, penetrating sunshine, which baths my body and my soul—every day and every night.

As you know, my life was not necessarily a bed of roses. But you have made all the difference. [*The clock ticks loudly in the background.*]

You have provided me with the incentive for loving and enjoying life, which I have never experienced before. Every day and every night became an unending source of pleasure and feeling of well-being for me. Every outing, every trip, and every vacation became an exciting event because you have shared your excitement with me, and because you allowed me to share my joy with you.

You have indeed given me the gift of life, and there is no way I can thank you for it. Sylvia, you are a warm and loving human being. You are caring for people. You're honest and brave. You deserve to be respected because you are so human. You deserve to be totally loved because you are so totally loving.

Believe in yourself as I have believed in you.

Never allow people to do things to you, because there's no reason for it.

You have given me so much, and I am grateful for it. You have changed my life and have made it meaningful. I have felt love, your love, every minute of the day and night. And there is no way that I can thank you enough.

As you know, I was not always the easiest person to live with. I can appreciate your tolerance and your patience for my many moods and, at times, irrational behavior.

I hope that you won't be too saddened by my departure, knowing that I really don't want to leave you, and that I have always appreciated the good life I've had with you. But death is a part of life, and I hope that you will always remember me, my love for you, and my compassion for you.

I hope that you will always remember the good times we had—to laugh, and enjoy and the companionship we shared. I hope that you will fondly remember London, Paris, Florence, Rome, Switzerland, and

Israel—and all the other places we have visited, and all the other vacations we have enjoyed so much sharing with each other.

There is not much more that I can say to you at this time. Stay as you are. Remember me as I was. Try to be a friend to Anita, and try to be grateful for the good times we had, realizing that I had a full and rich life. And make the best of it, as I made it in my own way, and that you have helped me to enjoy my life.

There is a little poem I found some time ago and I remember well, but which expresses my feeling at this time better than anything I have said [*the noise of Fred unfolding a piece of paper can be heard*]. The poem says:[170]

> If I should ever leave you whom I love
>
> To go along the Silent Way, grieve not,
>
> Nor speak of me with tears,
>
> but laugh and talk
>
> Of me as if I were beside you there.
>
> (I would come ... I would come, could I but find a way!
>
> But would not tears and grief be barriers?)
>
> And when you hear a song or see a bird
>
> I loved, please do not let the thought of me be sad ...
>
> For I am loving you just as I always have ...
>
> You were so good to me!
>
> There are so many things I wanted to do with you ...
>
> So many things I wanted to say to you ...
>
> Remember that I did not fear ...
>
> It was just leaving you that was so hard to face ...
>
> We cannot see Beyond ... But this I know:
>
> I love you so ...
>
> It was heaven here with you!
>
> By Isla Paschal Richardson

[*Fred took long pauses during the last few lines of the poem, especially at the line, "It was just leaving you that was so hard to face." You can then hear a sniffle when he gets to, "It was heaven here with you!" In the background, the clock can be heard ticking loudly.*]

Good luck, Sylvia, and good-bye.

Fred had cheated death in his youth and had moved forward with courage and strength. And while death called his name at ninety-three, his was a life redeemed and made joyful by his caring and regard for others—and their caring and regard for him. He was truly a person of integrity. Good night, dear Fred. Your memory lingers in our hearts and minds. We are so much richer for having known you—whether in story or in fact.

Notes

170   Fred's version of this poem is not the predominant version.

This is the author's favorite picture of Fred. "To me, it captures his nobility and his scars, his courage and the wisdom he gathered and so liberally blessed others with along the way."

ABOUT THE AUTHOR

SUSAN LYNN SLOAN is an author who lives with her husband in Maple Falls, Washington. She was born in Chicago, graduated from California State University, Chico, and worked as an evaluator and public health professional for many years. Her interests focus on her family, gardening, snorkeling, books, and film. Her biography of Holocaust survivor, Fred Fragner, is her first published book.

CPSIA information can be obtained
at www.ICGtesting.com
Printed in the USA
FSOW02n0046271016
26607FS